Industrial Systems

Spatial Analysis, Industry and the Industrial Environment

Progress in Research and Applications

Volume I

Industrial Systems

Edited by

F. E. Ian Hamilton

Lecturer in Social Studies,
London School of Economics and Political Science
and School of Slavonic and East European Studies,
University of London

and

G. J. R. Linge

Professorial Fellow, Department of Human Geography,
Research School of Pacific Studies,
The Australian National University, Canberra, Australia

JOHN WILEY & SONS

Chichester · New York · Brisbane · Toronto

Library of Congress Cataloging in Publication Data:
Main entry under title:

Spatial analysis, industry and the industrial environment
    progress in research and applications.

   Bibliography: v. 1, p.
   Includes index.
   CONTENTS: v. 1.   Industrial systems.
   1.   Industries, Location of—Addresses, essays,
lectures.   2.   Manufactures—Addresses, essays, lectures.
I.   Hamilton, F. E. Ian.   II. Linge, G. J. R.
HD58.S674   338.6′042   78-10298
ISBN 0 471 99738 2 (v. 1)
Photosetting by Thomson Press (India) Limited, New Delhi
and printed in Great Britain by The Pitman Press, Bath.

Acknowledgements

F. E. Ian Hamilton and G. J. R. Linge wish to acknowledge both the helpful suggestions made by Dr. D. J. Walmsley (University of New England, Armidale, New South Wales) and Dr. P. A. Robins (Australian National University) on an earlier draft of Chapter 1 and the stimulating discussion of the first version by the participants in the conference of the I.G.U. Commission on Industrial Systems held in Kraków, Poland, in August 1977.

Dr. A. P. Gorkin, Dr. L. V. Smirnyagin, and the editors express their grateful thanks to Elena E. Yarantseva for her assistance in translating Chapter 2 from the original Russian into English.

David Smith acknowledges, with gratitude, the permission to reproduce the following figures in Chapter 3: the editor of *Area* for Figure 3.1, the editor of *Economic Geography* for Figure 3.2, the editor of the *New Zealand Geographer* for Figure 3.3, and Edward Arnold, Publishers, for Figures 3.4, 3.5, and 3.6.

Peggy Lentz and H. Wade VanLandingham express their great appreciation of the patience and help of the Urban Studies staff at the University of New Orleans and particularly of Jane S. Brooks and Ellen M. McKinnon.

Lars Håkanson wishes to convey his thanks to Docent Leif Ahnström, Professor Gunnar Alexandersson, Professor Claes-Fredrik Claeson, and Dr. Thomas Falk for helpful comments on earlier versions of Chapter 7.

Carl Fredricksson and Leif Lindmark are deeply indebted to Dr. Gunnar Persson and Dr. Ian Layton for invaluable help with translation, comments on drafts and suggestions regarding the restructuring of Chapter 9.

David Wadley wishes to acknowledge the Department of Human Geography, Australian National University for supporting the original research upon which Chapter 10 is based and for clerical and cartographic assistance.

Neil Dorward would like to express his deepest gratitude to Professor M. J. Wise and Dr. J. E. Martin of The Department of Geography, London School of Economics and Political Science for their substantial advice and encouragement on his research for Chapter 11.

Editors' Acknowledgement

The editors extend their cordial thanks to: Janet Baker of the Drawing Office, London School of Economics and Political Science and to Theo Baumann of the Department of Human Geography, Australian National University for their drawing or redrawing many of the illustrations; Pauline Falconer of A.N.U. and Pat Farnsworth at L.S.E. for their extensive typing assistance; and to Grace Richardson, Research Assistant, Department of Human Geography, A.N.U., for her meticulous checking of references.

Contributors

Neil M. M. Dorward, B.Sc. (Econ.), Ph.D. (London) is currently Principal Lecturer in Business Studies at the Polytechnic of North London following ten years at the City of London Polytechnic, England.

Carl G. Fredriksson, M.B.A., Ph.D. (Umeå) is working now for the Swedish Ministry of Industry in Stockholm after teaching in Business Administration at the University of Umea, Sweden.

Aleksandr P. Gorkin, B.A., candidate of geographic science (Moscow) is a Senior Research Worker in the Institute of Geography, Soviet Academy of Sciences, Moscow.

Lars Hakånson, B.Sc. (Econ.) is Lecturer in Geography, Stockholm School of Economics and also a consultant to The National Swedish Industrial Board.

F. E. Ian Hamilton, B.Sc. (Econ.), Ph.D. (London) is a Lecturer in Social Studies in the University of London and Chairman of the International Geographical Union Commission on Industrial Systems.

Peggy A. Lentz, B.A. (Syracuse), M.A., Ph.D. (Clark) is Associate Professor of Urban and Regional Planning, Urban Studies Institute, University of New Orleans and currently a vising Scholar, Office of Policy Development and Research, United States Department of Housing and Urban Development.

William F. Lever, M.A., D.Phil. (Oxon) is Senior Lecturer in Urban Studies in the Departments of Social and Economic Research and Architecture at Glasgow University, Scotland.

Leif G. Lindmark, M.B.A., Ph.D. (Umeå) is Assistant Professor in Business Administration at the University of Umeå, Sweden.

Godfrey J. R. Linge, B.Sc. (Econ.) London, Ph.D. (New Zealand) is Professorial Fellow, Department of Human Geography, Research School of Pacific Studies, The Australian National University, Canberra, Australia.

Doreen Massey, B.A. (Oxon), Ph.D. (University of Pennsylvania) is at present Principal Scientific Officer with the Centre for Environmental Studies, London.

Jan-Evert Nilsson, M.B.A., Ph.D. (Umeå) is currently Research Associate at the

Resource Policy Group, Oslo, Norway and formerly Lecturer in Business Administration in the University of Umeå, Sweden.

Leonid V. Smirnyagin, B.A., candidate of geographic science (Moscow) is a Senior Lecturer of the Geography Faculty of the M.V. Lomonosov Moscow State University, U.S.S.R.

David M. Smith, B.A., Ph.D. (Nottingham) is Professor of Geography at Queen Mary College, University of London.

H. Wade VanLandingham, B.A. (Florida), M.U.R.P. (New Orleans) is Research Associate in the Urban Studies Institute, University of New Orleans, U.S.A.

David A. Wadley, B.A. (Sydney), Ph.D. (A.N.U.), formerly teaching in the University of Melbourne is now Lecturer in Economic Geography, University of Queensland, Brisbane, Australia.

Contents

Editors' Preface

This is the first volume in a new series which sets out to debate and to disseminate progress in research and applications in a broad field entitled 'spatial analysis, industry, and the industrial environment'. Some papers will, of course, be concerned with location theory and practice, techniques of analysis and measurement, industrial production systems and linkages, and will present case studies of specific industries, organizations, and regions. But others will go beyond the 'traditional' preserve of industrial geography and will investigate the patterns, processes, and impacts of evolution, changes in industry and industrial organization, and the complexities of the multifaceted relationships with the broad environment within which industry operates. Manufacturing is treated as a pivotal object of study and applications, as a major recipient of 'inputs' or 'influences' from the environment and as a key source of 'outputs' to or 'effects' on the environment. Whether it be economic, commercial, governmental, political, or social, or local, urban, regional, or national, environment has itself a spatial structure shaping and, in turn, being shaped by world manufacturing. Thus papers in these volumes will expound theories, concepts, methods, techniques, and case studies regarding the spatial structure of industry, industry-related activities and their environments: they will not only be concerned to synthesize and re-evaluate past and present frontiers but to suggest fruitful avenues for future research and policy applications.

An important object of this series will be to encourage contributions from people working on 'industry-space' problems in countries having differing political philosophies and being at various stages of 'development'. It is not unfair to suggest that in the English-speaking world much of the evolving body of location theory has been narrowly conceived in terms of managerially and technologically sophisticated firms operating in capitalist or mixed economies. But the reality is that by no means all manufacturing activities in the world take place under these conditions. Moreover, the rapid industrialization of the developing countries (see Chapter 1) provides new challenges for those concerned with location theory and practice but as yet these have hardly been recognized, much less accepted. Editorially, then, every effort will be made to draw on work from a wide range of sources, to disseminate research and policy results from diversified experience and to facilitate cross-cultural comparison.

This volume, *Industrial Systems*, also indicates another intention of the editors. Rather than publishing disparate research papers in the spirit of most scientific journals or of volumes reviewing progress in a certain well-defined field, each book will contain a group of contributions focusing on a particular theme or problem. Depending on the subject, it may sometimes be appropriate (as in this present book) to have a fairly wide-ranging set of contributions to illustrate the diversity of approaches; on other occasions it may be more appropriate to explore a problem by means of a tightly structured group of papers. However, this approach does not preclude the publication in each book of other high-quality papers on any topics relevant to the series: indeed the editors welcome offers of such contributions.

Through several of its chapters, therefore, *Industrial Systems* sets out to initiate a 'new look' at the industrial sphere by examining its structure and some of its components from a systems viewpoint. Overall, the chapters are ordered from the more conceptual to the more empirical, but broadly the idea of an industrial system and its subsystems operating in an environment threads them together. Clearly no part of the system and its environment can be treated in isolation: all parts interact with all other parts.

The editors in Chapter 1 set out to define the salient features of the world industrial system, illustrating their argument by reference to similarities and differences between the capitalist and socialist industrial systems, a theme which is also taken up, from a Soviet viewpoint, by Gorkin and Smirnyagin in Chapter 2. However, Hamilton and Linge also refer to the increasing scales and complexities of interdependence both within and between industrial places in advanced capitalist and developed socialist economies and also between them and the developing economies. In Chapter 3, Smith builds upon the fairly extensive re-examination of location theory that has been accomplished in recent years to cast the spatial modelling of industrial systems into a broader conceptual framework which incorporates welfare criteria. Massey lends further support in Chapter 4 to a structural approach to the understanding of spatial patterns of industry under capitalism in her critical review of the 'state of the art'.

The middle chapters of the book examine distinctive aspects of the interaction between industry and its environment. Lentz and VanLandingham discuss in Chapter 5 aspects of the interrelationships between energy supply, industrialization, and regional economic growth by reference to Louisiana in the American 'Sun Belt'. In Chapter 6, Lever outlines the spatial pattern of labour markets in Great Britain and examines, in particular, industrial influence on the environment in the form of the domination of local labour markets by certain industries and industrial organizations.

Then follows a group of Chapters (7–9) which contain other common links. Written by Scandinavians, drawing largely on the experience of their own part of the developed world, they all adopt something of an historical perspective, examining the evolution of industrial organization, structure, and space economy. Each points to important, yet changing, regional, interregional, or international interdependencies in that evolution, so emphasizing the significance of links between evolving industrial systems and various levels of the spatial hierarchy. In Chapter 7 Håkanson conceptualizes the spatial pattern and process of corporate growth from a modest one-plant firm to a large transnational organization. Nilsson in Chapter 8 uses Swedish Norrland as a laboratory in which to investigate changes in industrial structure, location, regional development, and the consequent interregional linkages. Chapter 9, by Fredriksson and Lindmark, elaborates on the progression of interregional interdependencies that result as firms evolve into systems of firms.

The last two chapters focus upon examples of particular engineering industries in two contrasting national economic environments to illustrate a neglected field of analysis: the interaction of the marketing of industrial products and the spatial pattern of production itself. In Chapter 10 Wadley examines the role of wholesaling by reference to the Australian farm machinery industry and emphasizes the importance of analysing industrial activity under conditions of diminishing, not growing, market opportunities. Finally, in Chapter 11, Dorward studies the impact of marketing strategy and product differentiation upon growth and spatial change in the truck industry in the German Federal Republic.

All references have been amalgamated into a single list at the end of the book. Not only is this convenient for users, but it is believed that such an arrangement will, during the course of this series, make the bibliography itself a useful and continuing source of information about the literature available in this general field.

F. E. Ian Hamilton,
London, England.

G. J. R. Linge,
Canberra, Australia.

Chapter 1
Industrial Systems

F. E. IAN HAMILTON AND G. J. R. LINGE

Exposure to quantification, computer logic, and the techniques of the natural sciences has led geographers in recent years to seek more rigorous intellectual frameworks in which to develop general models of spatial behavior. Although there are some notable exceptions, it is perhaps not unfair to suggest that much of the research in industrial geography has been concerned with individual and unrelated case studies which—though admirable in themselves—yield both low order descriptive and classificatory propositions about the real world and somewhat vague generalizations with poor predictive powers. To try to improve this situation, the view that a systems approach has much to offer social scientists gained impetus during the 1960s (Haggett, 1965; Harvey, 1969). Yet only now is this attracting the attention of industrial and economic geographers who, increasingly, are appreciating that changes taking place to the organization of industry in one particular area have repercussions for the other areas with which it has direct and indirect linkages. Formal recognition of the appropriateness of this approach came from the International Geographical Union in 1976 when it established a Commission on Industrial Systems with the task of advancing the conceptual and theoretical understanding of the spatial distribution and interdependence of industrial activities. From such a stimulus, this chapter reviews some aspects of the nature and functioning of industrial systems and attempts to provide some elements of a framework for future research in this field. In particular it draws attention to the similarities and differences between the operations of industrial systems in capitalist and socialist economies and the ways in which these relate to each other and to the global system of which they are part.

DEFINITIONS

At the outset it is important to clarify the meanings attached here to the words 'industrial organization', 'industry', and 'system'.

Industrial Organization

The term 'industrial organization' describes any administrative-managerial structure responsible for planning, policy-making, administering and operating one or more industrial units. It thus embraces a variety of situations:

(a) a capitalist firm of any size or form which is independent;

1

(b) a capitalist corporation controlling subsidiary firms (e.g. Nestlé Alimentana S.A. of Switzerland which has 198 factories of which only 4 are in its home market);

(c) a state-owned nationalized industrial board or agency (such as the British Steel Corporation or British Shipbuilders in the United Kingdom) in a 'mixed economy' (a term denoting direct state intervention to ameliorate, but not to replace, a capitalist economic system);

(d) a central government ministry or agency in a socialist country with responsibility for running an entire industry (e.g. the Ministry of the Automobile Industry of the Soviet Union—*Ministerstvo Automobil'noy Promyshlennosti SSSR*);

(e) a republic or regional industry ministry or directorate such as the Ministry of the Food Industries of the Russian Soviet Federated Socialist Republic (*Ministerstvo Pishchevoy Promyshlennosti RSFSR*), or a regional association of industrial enterprises in a socialist country, such as the Kharkov Industrial Equipment Union, called *Soyuztekhnosnastka.*

In many industrial organizations sections of the administrative-managerial structure are spatially separated. For example, the head office of a typical transnational corporation based in the United States concentrates on devising and supervising world-wide strategy, and delegates some of its authority through a hierarchy of regional, national, and operating unit managements located in perhaps 50 or 60 countries.

Industry

In many languages the equivalent word to 'industry' is used unambiguously to mean factory activity in which materials are processed or transformed by mechanical or chemical means into more valuable products. In English-speaking countries, however, the word *industry* is used more loosely in such phrases as 'the dairy industry' to mean simply dairy farming, or 'the tourist industry' to embrace the wide array of activities concerned with the organization, transport, accommodation, and entertainment of tourists. Ironically, this less precise usage (or abusage) has led many social scientists to avoid the word industry unless modified as in 'manufacturing industry' or to turn instead to the word 'manufacturing' (as in 'manufacturing sector'). The irony arises because the word 'manufacture'—stemming from Latin and French roots—literally means 'to make by hand' which is, of course, the reverse of the meaning now intended.

But even if the words 'industry' and 'manufacturing' are both understood to include activities carried on in operating units—such as factories and plants— other definitional problems remain. One of these is the extent to which small-scale 'workshop' activities should be included in analyses of industrial systems in advanced and developing societies (Hamilton, 1978a). In Australia, for instance,

27 per cent of all factories (excluding places simply engaged in repair work) have fewer than 4 workers but these occupy less than 2 per cent of the manufacturing labour force and contribute less than 1 per cent to the value added by the manufacturing sector. In developed societies small establishments tend to be numerically more important in certain kinds of activities (such as printing and instrument-making) but in all industries they make up an important part of the complex production chain or network through which inputs are transformed into more valuable outputs. Moreover, small industrial organizations form part of the life cycle of manufacturing enterprise, some of the world's largest corporations having emerged from very modest origins (Edwards and Townsend, 1961; Jewkes *et al.*, 1961). In developing societies, small-scale workshops are important culturally and socially. Thus in Melanesia they enable completely new skills (such as welding) to be diffused into remote areas; in South-East Asian countries, family workshops provide employment opportunities for elderly and handicapped relatives who might otherwise have no means of support. In various ways, then, small-scale establishments form an integral part of the evolution and operation of industrial systems so that distinctions between 'manufacturing industry' and 'workshop industry'—perhaps using measures like floorspace per worker, energy consumption, or fixed tangible assets—would be both artificial and arbitrary. In practice, however, such distinctions are often taken out of the hands of social scientists who for the most part have to rely on data collected by official agencies.

Another major definitional problem arises because of uncertainty about what activities should be treated as part of the industry sector on the one hand, or as part of the general environment in which industry operates on the other. It is convenient to divide such activities into those that take place *prior* to the manufacturing stage and those that occur *during* and *after* this stage.

(a) *Activities preceding manufacturing* The industry sector—directly or indirectly—depends on supplies of raw materials from fishing, farming, grazing, mining, and forestry operations. The relationship may be very close (both spatially and entrepreneurially) as is often the case, for example, in sugar milling, fruit canning, forest sawmilling, and brickmaking when the crops, trees, and minerals are produced and processed in an integrated operation. Then there are instances where the production of the raw materials is spatially separate from the processing operation even though both are controlled by the same management: this is true of aluminium smelting plants in Europe which draw on alumina produced in refineries operating elsewhere in the world as part of the same transnational corporation. Finally there are industrial organizations that have no spatial or entrepreneurial connection with the firms supplying them with raw materials. No one completely satisfactory line can be drawn but basically the production of raw materials that pass into the manufacturing sector should probably be regarded as industry-related activities rather than as industrial activities in themselves. Again, in reality, the social scientist sometimes has little choice but to accept the inter-sectoral divisions used in official statistical publications which, increasingly, are adopting recommendations of international bodies such as those associated with the United Nations. For example, in several countries the extraction of a raw material is included within the definition of industry only if it forms an integral part of the operations of a manufacturing establishment at a single physical location and if the gross value of the extractive operation does not exceed a fairly modest specified value.

(b) *Activities during manufacturing*   There is little need to debate the view that people engaged in managerial and administrative functions associated with an industrial unit (including those in a separately located head office) should be regarded as part of the manufacturing workforce. The 'white collar' personnel of a factory enterprise in a capitalist society or in the private (capitalist) sector of a mixed economy are, clearly, part of the industry. To be consistent, the officials administering state-owned industries or industrial units in a mixed economy and the staff of the ministerial-level organizations responsible for the various branches of manufacturing activity in a socialist economy should also be regarded as part of industry. A clear distinction must be drawn, however, between bureaucrats *directly* involved in industry decision-making and those that influence the behaviour of industrial organizations—whether these be capitalist, socialist, or government-owned—through their management of such matters as prices, tariffs and taxes, or of planning, all of which form part of the general environment in which industry (and other activity) must operate.

(c) *Activities following manufacturing*   There are problems, too, about whether some activities that follow the actual processing/production stage should be included within industry. For example, some industrial organizations, such as those operating petroleum refineries, run large-scale, multimodal transport operations, and almost every operating unit has at least some investment in delivery vans and trucks. As a further instance, some industrial organizations are closely related to marketing enterprises that act as their wholesale or retail distributors and provide after-sales servicing of their products. Some of these are directly owned and managed by capitalist industrial firms or form part of socialist enterprises administered by a ministerial-level organization or a self-management board. As a case in point, a chain of shops selling men's suits in the United Kingdom has used the slogan 'from weaver to wearer' to publicize the close association between its production and retailing operations. Others are separately owned, financed and managed firms and enterprises which are associated by various arrangements—such as franchise agreements (see Wadley: Chapter 10)—to particular industrial concerns. In Yugoslavia enterprises manufacturing textiles, shoes, confectionery, and other consumer products maintain their own outlets up and down the country, but in other socialist economies centralized trading agencies distribute goods from several or all producers to each marketing outlet. In general it seems appropriate to regard these as industry-related activities rather than ones that should be included within the industry sector itself. In practice in several countries the official statistics allocate to the industrial sector only those selling activities that take place at the factory concerned, such as timber sold at a sawmill, cloth at a textile plant, and butter or cheese at a dairy factory.

It would seem useful, then, to treat organizations as belonging to one of three categories:

(a) *industry*, being activities wholly or dominantly concerned with the processing of materials by physical or chemical means into more valuable products;

(b) *industry-related*, being non-industrial as an activity in itself but closely linked to those that are;

(c) *industry-environmental*, being activities that do not fall into the previous categories but that help shape the environment within which industry operates.

Having said this it must be noted, however, that in socialist countries the term 'industry' is used in its economic and planning aspects to embrace

a sector of the economy concerned with the extraction of natural resources (e.g. all branches of mining) and with the processing of raw materials also containing human labour, and of semi-finished products (manufacturing industry). It also includes certain industrial services (public utilities such as electricity, gas and thermal heating systems, as well as repair and maintenance services). In its practical sense, industry is to be understood as the operation of industrial organizations, primarily economic units performing industrial activity (Bora, 1977, p. 1).

Systems

This definitional discussion illustrates that industry does not operate in isolation but rather as part of a very much more complex arrangement, or 'system', of activities. The relevance, application, and complexity of a systems approach to geographical enquiry has been examined by, among others, Chisholm (1967) and Walmsley (1972). Here it is sufficient to note that a system consists of a set of 'actors' that (a) functions together, (b) through various types, degrees, and directions of linkages, demands outputs from and supplies inputs to other actors, and (c) behaves in particular ways as a result of interactions between either the whole set of actors or between certain groupings of them on the one hand, and the 'environment' on the other. The acknowledgement of the existence of an external environment is a recognition that the system itself is not closed and that, although cohesive and interdependent as a whole, it comprises subsets of actors which to a greater or lesser extent interact with the external environment.

ELEMENTS OF INDUSTRIAL SYSTEMS

An industrial system comprises the operating units (i.e. the actors), the functional relationships between those units, and the interactions between the units and the external environment. Each of these elements must be considered in turn.

Operating Units

The operating units in an industrial system can be identified as follows:

(a) *production units* in which inputs are converted by physical or chemical means into higher valued outputs;

(b) *associated units* within industrial organizations—including offices, laboratories, and research and development facilities—where policies, strategies, and technologies are developed and determined. These decisions directly influence the function, size, and location of all units in the organization and the relationships between them, and other units in the system, and the external environment;

(c) *industry-related units* including those producing raw materials, transporting inputs and outputs, selling manufactured goods, and providing after-sales services.

Research on industrial systems should be concerned both with the location of individual units and with the spatial distribution of specific groups or types of units (such as those engaged in a particular kind of manufacturing, or those supplying inputs to a specific manufacturing enterprise, or those that have franchise agreements to distribute a certain product). For most analyses it is important to consider not only the location of the units but also the magnitude of their operations which, depending on the purpose, can be quantified in terms of single measures like employment, floor space, value of tangible fixed assets, value of net or gross production, or in terms of ratios such as net production or turnover per employee. Such measurements enable geographers to observe relative and absolute differences between subsystems and between places. In capitalist and mixed economies, the analysis can focus on units managed by an individual industrial organization which, either as a capitalist firm or a government-operated enterprise, may be concerned with a particular branch of industry or be involved in several industries and industry-related activities. In socialist economies the focus may be on individual production units or on ministerial-level state organizations that are responsible for all the operations of entire industries such as iron and steel, or textiles or pharmaceuticals.

Functional Relationships Between Units

The functional linkages between units in an industrial system also involve connections between the organizations responsible for those units. This can be illustrated by first considering organizational relationships and then technological–economic relationships.

Organizational relationships between industrial units are greatly influenced by the characteristics of the particular socio-economic milieu in which they operate and, in particular, whether this functions as a capitalist or as a socialist system. The organizational characteristics of each are different but in both cases they are very complex and not at all stereotyped. Thus in socialist economies much depends on whether, and how far, control is centralized or decentralized, for Council for Mutual Economic Assistance (CMEA) and non-CMEA socialist countries exhibit a substantial gradation of levels of centralization or decentralization which is, on a more restricted scale, analogous to the range between developed and developing countries.

In a fairly or highly centralized socialist economy, executive management for an entire industry normally resides in a central government ministry or ministerial-level organization while day-to-day routine administration takes place at the operating unit. Linkages between individual units may vary according to the functional scope of the organization concerned. Thus if a ministry of ferrous metallurgy also has responsibility for mining and minerals and generating its own power, the vertical relationships are likely to be more complex than in a ministry which is solely concerned with the production of iron and steel. Whatever the precise detail, the ministry will impose horizontal (and possibly some vertical) relationships concerning the functional specialization and output (or share of national and export markets) on the operating units.

There are less centralized socialist countries in which economic associations of operating units play an important role, particularly where the units themselves can derive advantages (such as the reduction of uncertainties) through this form of co-operation. They may, for instance, plan vertical linkages or they may make agreements about the horizontal division of the national and regional markets by product or geographical specialization. Some economic associations form subsystems within a particular ministerial-level organization; more significantly, others form inter-ministry subsystems that cut across strict vertical relationships in the organizations concerned.

Finally, there are highly decentralized socialist economies in which a wider range of significant decisions relating to a particular unit is made by elected councils of workers who are thus involved in self-management (*samoupravljenje* in Serbo-Croatian); the development and operation of these councils in Yugoslavia has been discussed by Hamilton (1974b). In the formative stages the units may operate like single-plant firms, undertaking managerial and production functions on the spot but depending to a considerable extent on other units for the supply of inputs and the disposal of outputs. Later, units may come together to form enterprises having basically the same characteristics as the 'economic associations' previously described.

In the capitalist system the key organizational unit is the firm, company, or corporation. It is difficult to categorize these since they vary greatly in complexity. At one extreme are *single-unit, single-function firms* which may be highly specialized and thus greatly dependent on other units for the provision of goods and services; at the other, are *multi-unit, multi-function, multi-location firms* which through vertical and horizontal linkages may achieve considerable internal cohesion even if still relying on other firms for some supplies and services. Yet, whatever its size, the capitalist firm differs in four important ways from its ministerial counterpart in a socialist economy. First, it does not as a matter of policy have a production or market monopoly within the nation but is usually horizontally associated with other producers through competition for sales. Nonetheless a firm may move into a monopolistic position temporarily (such as by introducing a new product protected by patents) or more permanently (by a process of acquisition and takeover). However in several capitalist economies governments have enacted legislation giving them power to prevent mergers, various trade practices, and other anti-competitive arrangements judged to be against the public interest. Second, capitalist industrial undertakings are not restrained from diversifying into other industries and sectors that they consider would best serve their interests. In socialist economies, by contrast, undertakings strictly limit their activities to the organizational sphere of the ministry to which they are responsible. Third, firms in capitalist economies are able, fairly readily, to extend their activities into other countries, for instance to secure raw materials or develop markets, whereas socialist undertakings confine their activities to the national or subnational space for which their ministry has responsibility. Finally, capitalist firms are in business to make a profit rather than to achieve specified national or regional economic and social goals as is the case with socialist industrial undertakings. (Although some capitalist firms use part of their profits to fund social and cultural activities, such philanthropy is seldom the prime motivating force behind the original investment decision.) Nonetheless, capitalist firms in some countries may be subsidized in one way or another for social welfare reasons. Some may be assisted to enable them to maintain production at high levels in a region with a record of chronically high unemployment; others may allow firms in a declining area to phase out their activities without undue hardship to the local community (Linge, 1978a, b).

In both the socialist and capitalist systems the organizational relationships between industrial units are, in reality, much more complex and variegated than suggested in this summary. However, the most striking differences between the organization of industry under the two systems concern market relationships and spatial boundaries. In capitalist economies, large organizations compete, basically, either by distributing each of their wares nationally from specialized production units or by establishing a multi-product unit in each regional market. This results in a hierarchy of subnational overlapping market areas, the boundaries of which are constantly changing. In a centrally planned socialist economy, however, there is no segmentation of the national market between competing government organizations. In some cases, units producing identical goods each serve a distinct region; in others, the national market is supplied by units each making a particular product. Sometimes elements of both these approaches are combined, but the key point is that all producers are financed by, and are ultimately accountable to, only one central organization. In some countries these elements of wholly competitive and wholly segmented markets tend to become blurred: for example, in Australia cases are known where firms in particular industries (such as brewing) have written or tacit agreements to divide up markets geographically among them.

In theory the spatial 'boundaries' of both capitalist and socialist industrial undertakings are identical: the total world sets the upper limit. But in reality such undertakings have an 'industrial action space' within which they derive their inputs and undertake their productive activities, and a 'commercial action space' within which they market their products. Commercial space is strongly influenced by an external environment which may distort distance through such impediments as tariffs or quotas or such assistance as trade agreements and freight rate concessions. Here the concept of 'psychic distance' (Wiederscheim-Paul, 1972) is useful since it embraces various factors—language, culture, level of industrial development, political systems, and so forth—which prevent or interrupt information flows between firms and their potential commercial space. Psychic distance is likely to be strongly correlated with actual distance but, as Johanson and Wiederscheim-Paul (1975) point out, exceptions are not hard to find: Australia is close to the United Kingdom in terms of psychic but not geographical distance whereas the reverse is true of the United States and Cuba.

The industrial and commercial action spaces of capitalist firms can be—and for the transnational corporations certainly are—geographically much wider than those of socialist industrial organizations. There are two main reasons. On the one hand, capitalist enterprises have a long history bound up with colonization and development in the world at large. A typical sequence would be for a firm to open up a market in another country by selling its products through independent agents or representatives (which minimizes its commitments); if sales reach a satisfactory level the firm would open up its own sales subsidiary and later, in turn, its own manufacturing facility. Although in recent years many host countries have imposed stricter controls on external investments of this kind (Stopford and Haberich, 1976), there is still scope for the expansion of transnational corporations even if these are increasingly taking the form of 'joint ventures' with locally owned and controlled companies (Gullander, 1976). On the other hand, socialist enterprises, being managed by state ministerial-level organizations, are identified with national political and administrative interests and thus, like their state-owned counterparts in capitalist economies, they have been unable to establish production facilities in other countries. Nevertheless there are indications that the action space of socialist enterprises may become less restricted in future; countries in the CMEA area are anxious both to earn (or save) hard currency and to acquire Western technology (NATO, 1976). Although these aims are mainly being pursued by buying (or leasing) complete plants or production lines from Western countries or establishing joint ventures in the CMEA area in partnership with capitalist firms, there are now several instances of socialist enterprises (or their export/import agencies) which have set up production and/or marketing facilities in Western countries (Perlmutter, 1971–72; Meyer, 1977). As a case in point, Tracteroexport established a plant in Sydney in 1978 to fit out Soviet-built Belarus tractors and agricultural machinery for the Australian market. As a further example, a joint venture has recently been established between a Hungarian trading organization and a subsidiary of a British trading company to facilitate not only bilateral trade in specialized chemicals between the United Kingdom and Hungary but, in effect, also to act as a 'clearing house' between industrial producers and industrial consumers of chemicals in Western Europe and North America (such as ICI, Courtaulds, or Monsanto) and those more widely located in the CMEA countries.

There is another aspect of these differences in the action space of capitalist and socialist enterprises. The former tend to be heterogeneous in both function and scale, and they decline, survive, or expand as their managements neglect, exploit, or create opportunities. Thus capitalist enterprises may be essentially local, regional, national, or international but, generally, the larger they are the more varied the action space of the constituent units becomes. By contrast, most socialist industry is specifically organized into national or regional units under central ministerial-level control: where market scale permits or political-administrative organization demands, there may also be regional or republic units under republic control. In every socialist country there is also some local industry (for example producing building materials or processing farm products) under the management of district, country, or city authorities. Even farm managements are now engaging in industrial activities in these countries. For example, horizontal integration between farm co-operatives in Bulgaria has facilitated the creation of some 150 vertically integrated agro-industrial complexes which draw their inputs from almost 90 per cent of the country's cultivated land (Wadekin, 1977). The action space of a socialist industry is thus related both to its scale and to its place in the administrative hierarchy: hence the growth of a small-scale local industry into a regional one would necessitate a change in the status of its administrative arrangements.

Technological–economic relationships between units form a second set of linkages within industrial systems. Much of the literature on industrial geography and plant location has focused on these kinds of linkages which fall into three broad categories. First, linkages can take the form of vertical or diagonal integration between successive or related production stages to yield technical, physical, and economic advantages. In practice these manifest themselves in a great diversity of forms ranging from fairly loose *ad hoc* arrangements through to the kind of pre-planned, tightly structured 'territorial-production complexes' being established in Siberia (Karaska and Linge, 1979). Second, there are 'commensal' linkages between industrial undertakings which use the same infrastructure (such as that available in an industrial 'estate' or 'park') but which have little else in common. Finally, there is a broad range of economic linkages between spatially separate industrial organizations. This latter kind of linkage has generated a wealth of analysis, much of which has been couched explicitly or implicitly in a Weberian framework emphasizing the costs of bringing raw materials and components to a factory and distributing the end product(s).

In recent years, however, two circumstances have contributed to a shift in emphasis. On the one hand, advances in transport and distribution technology have very considerably reduced the relative significance of the costs involved in physically assembling inputs and marketing outputs. On the other hand, locational analysts have begun to pay much more attention to the costs of bringing together and disseminating various kinds of information ranging from daily routine statistics to monthly boardroom edicts. Some of the control and communication problems *within* a large organization like Unilever (which has between 400 and 500 subsidiary companies in 60 countries) have been discussed by Weingardt (1971–72) who draws attention to the balance needed between decentralized decision-making to achieve flexibility in the market place and centralized control to maintain the essential unity of the whole enterprise. Important, too, are the information linkages *between* organizations. Fredriksson and Lindmark's study (Chapter 9) of the relationships between AB Volvo and its subcontractors illustrates some of the spatial implications of these kinds of linkages. Subcontractors supplying components subject to frequent design modifications are likely to be chosen because of their proximity and accessibility whereas those making long runs of standard parts are more likely to be selected on the basis of their proven ability, reliability, and price competitiveness.

Relationships with the External Environment

The 'environment' of an industrial system can be regarded both as a source of inputs and as a destination for outputs. These terms are not used here in the restricted sense of physical inputs and outputs but, rather, to embrace wider notions which may perhaps be designated as 'influences' and 'effects'. The 'quality' of the interrelationships with the external environment varies between levels in the industrial system: for example the local and regional environments have a less significant impact on the national and international levels of the system (see Figure 1.1).

Inputs can be broadly categorized as 'opportunities' or 'constraints' affecting the nature, scale, pace, or locational pattern of industrial development. At one level they can take the form of economic organizations (such as the United

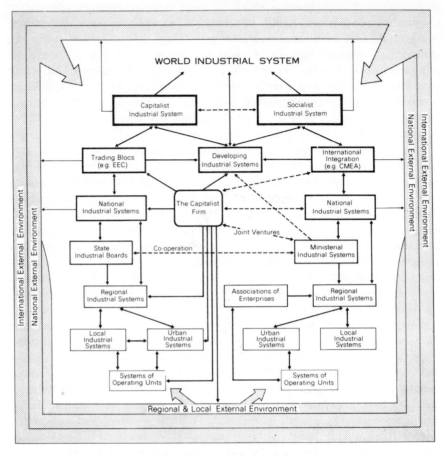

FIGURE 1.1 The world industrial system

Nations Industrial Development Organization, the European Economic Community, the Council for Mutual Economic Aid, and the Association of South-East Asian Nations) which reflect and help mould international attitudes towards industrialization and affect the distribution of operating units and the linkages between them. At another level there are differing national attitudes towards industrial activity which find expression in policies relating to tariffs, quotas, subsidies, taxation, investment incentives, bureaucratic controls and, indeed, the whole gamut of public and private sector behaviour which collectively makes up the 'climate' in which industrial organizations must operate. Then there is the availability, suitability and cost of labour and capital, of raw materials, components, and equipment, and of infrastructure ranging from transport and communication services to research facilities.

Outputs from the industrial system to the environment consist of 'goods' and 'bads'. By the former is meant the comforts, conveniences, technology, and infrastructure which contribute to the material well-being of society. The 'bads' include pollution of land, air, and water; the production of wastes—scrap metal, plastic wrappings, used paper, and contaminated chemicals—ranging from the dusty to the deadly; and the consumption of the world's non-renewable resources.

The environment is not, of course, fixed so that the industrial system is constantly adapting itself to new opportunities and constraints. Indeed Terreberry (1967–68) argues that organizational change is increasingly externally induced and that organizational adaptability is a function of ability to learn and to perform according to changes in the environment. Some changes (such as attitudes to the control of pollution or more equal opportunities for male and female workers) are fairly gradual and can be accommodated by adjustments within the system. Others, like the 1973 decision of the Organization of Petroleum Exporting Countries to raise crude oil prices overnight or the introduction of legislation by the Indian Government in 1974 to force foreign companies to reduce their equity in their Indian operations to between 40 per cent (in low priority branches) and 74 per cent (in export and high technology branches), represent sudden significant 'shocks' to the system which result in feedbacks to, and changes in, the environment itself. These sorts of changes—becoming known in systems terminology as 'turbulent environments'—demand short-term adaptation by organizations (Emery, 1969; Hamilton, 1974a; Western and Wilson, 1977; Goddard, 1978). Thompson and McEwen (1958) outline four organizational strategies for dealing with the environment: one is competition and the others (bargaining, co-option, and coalition) are various forms of co-operation involving interaction among organizations. For example, government-owned and private corporations may bargain with a trade union to make *their* perceived environment more amenable (even if it makes that of others more hostile). The rise of industry lobbies in many capital cities—perhaps epitomized by the formal procedures required for registering pressure groups in Washington DC—is another tangible expression of this kind of activity. Some such groups are established on a fairly permanent 'watchdog' basis while others briefly bring together highly competitive organizations to support—or oppose—some particular perceived benefit or threat (such as an important vote in a legislature). Sustaining these interactions with the environment adds another dimension to the costs of the information flows discussed earlier in terms of intra- and inter-organizational contacts. As Boddewyn (1976–77) points out, transnational firms in particular expect their senior executives to devote a great deal of time and effort to such tasks as conferring with governments, trade unions, academics, and community groups; obtaining approval and support for past and pending actions from decision-makers and opinion leaders; and attempting to tone down the hostility displayed by critics.

Even this brief discussion raises doubts about whether the environment can be defined as something strictly external to industrial organizations. Sales (1972–73) has suggested that the activity, location, and other characteristics of an organization effectively place it in an environment over which it can have varying degrees of control:

> In this sense, the degree to which the environment is a determining factor is relative to the firm under study. But one must add that the firm (that is, the entrepreneur in the larger sense) imputes his own overall meaning to his environment; and consequently, he is situated in the field in his own way (Sales, 1972–73, p. 239).

This suggestion is supported empirically by the work of Touraine *et al.* (1967) who, by classifying all new industrial establishments locating in the Paris region during a thirty-month period, showed that the greater the decision-making autonomy of the firm, the freer it is from the constraints of the immediate environment and the more its choices can be explained by its role in the overall system of production. They categorized firms into those that are tied to particular markets, those that are tied to means of production, and those that have no economic restraints regarding space; they then argue that these display, respectively, adaptive, integrative, and creative locational behaviour. For example, the latter group, consisting of firms with great technical initiative and an established research division, tends to develop industrial space in new prestigious zones which become characterized by 'modernity'. According to this view, such firms not only generate innovative products but also foster new spatial patterns, and in so doing create aspects of the environment more nearly suited to their perceived needs.

THE FUNCTIONING OF INDUSTRIAL SYSTEMS

The aggregate global industrial system consists of a hierarchy of subsystems—illustrated in Figure 1.1—which have different degrees of 'closure' and 'openness' and hence different degrees of interdependence or linkage with higher- or lower-order subsystems. Thus behaviour at any one level is influenced by the operation of the remainder of the hierarchy; in this sense part of the external environment in which each level functions is internal to the system as a whole. This can be illustrated by three examples.

First, the functioning of the aggregate capitalist and the aggregate socialist industrial system is influenced by their mutual existence: each is affected by the behaviour of the other almost like operators in a duopolistic market situation. But this analogy cannot be taken too far because the systems have become identified with groups of nations and blocs which—by design, by virtue of their internal cohesiveness, or by dint of their different laws and organizations—have erected major barriers to commercial interaction. Examples given in this chapter indicate, however, that in recent years various levels in the two hierarchies have become somewhat less insulated from each other.

Second, the industrial system of any nation in the capitalist world has to operate within a framework consisting of (a) policies of trading blocs (of which the nation concerned may or may not be a member) which facilitate or hamper flows of industrial goods and technology; (b) policies and practices of countries as trade partners or competitors; (c) activities of foreign industrial organizations competing on internal or external markets; (d) activities of foreign-owned or locally owned industrial organizations operating within the national system but whose goals may not correspond with it; and (e) national policies towards and relationships with countries in the socialist bloc and with developing nations. The industrial system of any nation in the socialist world has to operate within (a) policies of blocs (such as CMEA) which may encourage or constrain growth, linkage or co-operation between the countries concerned, and (b) the policies relating to trade in industrial goods with capitalist, developing, and non-CMEA socialist countries and the development of world markets in competition with capitalist industrial organizations. These constraints and opportunities within the existing industrial system are, of course, additional to those already discussed which arise from the external environment.

Third, an urban industrial system is influenced in its behaviour by the opportunities offered in the region in which it is situated, by the regional industrial policies of central, state or republic governments, and by the goals and performances of industrial organizations located within the system in relation to the national and international economy. Again, of course, these constraints and opportunities are in addition to those associated with the overall environment of the nation and the socio-economic system in which it is located.

This view of the world industrial system as a 'nested hierarchy', with each lower order being within the environment of the one above, needs further elaboration. Thus as illustrated in Figure 1.1. the capitalist firm, especially the large corporation, can have linkages with several levels of the hierarchy and hence provides a key but complex series of connections between various subsystems. The same applies in modified ways to a state-owned nationalized industrial board in a mixed economy or a central government industrial ministry in a socialist country. Moreover, a further dimension is added if 'industry' is disaggregated into its various sectors or branches, each of which has a set of hierarchical relationships of its own; these are known in the U.S.S.R. as territorial-branch subsystems (*territorial'no-otraslevykh podsistem*). The environment of an industrial branch in a socialist country consists of the totality of other industrial branches and their functional linkages and bargaining power for funds, manpower, and other resources, while in a capitalist country it consists of the behaviour of firms in other branches as well as government policies towards that branch.

Two actual examples will help illustrate the great complexity of the linkages between parts of the world industrial system. The first relates to an agreement for British shipyards to build 24 vessels needed by PZM (Polska Zegluga Morska) the Polish state shipping line. Early in 1977 the British government set up a £65 million 'intervention fund' that was used to subsidize the prices at which its state-owned shipyards tendered for orders. In this case £23 million (about one-quarter of the cost) was allocated from the intervention fund because it seemed likely that by reducing the total price by this amount much needed work would be secured for state-owned shipyards in Tyneside and Clydeside (in north-east England and Scotland) both of which are areas of high unemployment and electoral uncertainty. In addition, Britain agreed to raise the loans to cover the cost of construction—70 per cent being provided by the Export Credit's Guarantee Department and 30 per cent being obtained by British Shipbuilders through a Eurobond issue. As a further part of the arrangement, Poland (which lacks sufficient foreign exchange to buy the ships outright) will charter the vessels for fifteen years from a joint Anglo-Polish company formed by British Shipbuilders and PZM. On the one hand, this package provides employment for about 8000 British shipyard workers for three years (at a subsidy of about £3000 per head, which might be regarded as a welfare measure); on the other, it enables Polish shipyards to continue exporting 90 per cent of their output (60 per cent to the U.S.S.R.) and thus earn foreign exchange. The deal, however, has wider ramifications. Britain was originally allowed to establish this intervention fund by the European Economic Community on condition that it would be used to rationalize the nation's shipyards as part of a plan to halve the EEC's shipbuilding capacity. Moreover, during 1977 the EEC put pressure on Japan (which in 1976 had secured 70 per cent of all the shipbuilding contracts signed in countries belonging to the Organization for Economic Co-operation and Development) to raise its prices and reduce its capacity. Early in 1978 Japan complained that while its production had been reduced by 9.0 per cent during 1977 the tonnage from European yards—sustained by subsidies—had risen by 7.8 per cent.

   A second example of the ways in which industrial systems become linked is provided by recent circumstances involving Australia and the ASEAN countries (Indonesia, Malaysia, Thailand, Singapore, and the Philippines). Australia imposes high tariffs on industrial goods (about 13 per cent compared with, for instance, 8 per cent in the EEC) and these have helped to maintain employment in labour-intensive industries like the manufacture of clothing, textiles, and footwear. At the same time the relatively small domestic market limits the economies of scale available to the more technologically advanced industries which therefore must export to reduce unit costs. The association of Great Britain—its traditional trading partner—with the EEC has caused Australia to try to open up markets in developing countries in the Pacific Basin. Among these are the members of the ASEAN group which, faced with the need to find jobs for 100 million people during the next 30 years, have embarked on programmes of rapid industrialization which depend on expanding export markets, including Australia. The early 1970s saw increasing friction between Australia and the ASEAN group over trade matters and this came to a head during 1975–76. One particular reason was that the doubling of wage costs in Australian manufacturing during the early 1970s exposed labour-intensive industries to even greater competition from imports which, therefore, were cut back by quantitative restrictions imposed in December 1974. Escalating direct and indirect labour costs also led Australian clothing and footwear manufacturers to establish 'off-shore' capacity in countries with lower wage structures largely to make goods for sale in Australia. Early in 1977 the Australian government decided that the products of such off-shore operations must continue to be included in existing import quota arrangements. Among other reasons, it was feared that the transfer of job opportunities overseas and increased competition would place regional policies in jeopardy: since the Second World War labour-intensive industry has been encouraged to locate in inland country towns to try to arrest the long-run drift of population towards coastal capital cities. These import barriers angered the ASEAN nations, some of which took retaliatory action: the Philippines, for example, reduced its purchases of Australian steel. The loss of existing and possible potential export markets means that in this instance higher unit costs have to be passed on to domestic steel users (such as Australian motor vehicle and domestic appliance industries) which, in turn, are already becoming less competitive on external markets and less able to meet competition from imports.

These particular examples have been chosen because they illustrate the interaction between socialist and capitalist industrial systems and between those in developing and developed countries. They also emphasize the crucial role played by governments in arranging and adjusting the environment in which industry operates and the way that chains of circumstances, seemingly unrelated, provide links between quite low-ranking levels of the world industrial system. Such is the case with the shipyards and their associated industrial systems at Glasgow in Scotland, Gdansk in Poland, and Yokohama in Japan—even though they are operated by unrelated industrial organizations, draw on different sources of inputs, and operate in different socio-economic environments. Or again, the affairs of a clothing factory at Wagga Wagga in New South Wales can interact with the business of a wholly separate car plant at Adelaide in South Australia through decisions over which neither has any control (or perhaps even knowledge about) made in Manila, Kuala Lumpur, or Canberra. These complex but less obvious threads that help tie the world industrial system together have not been given adequate attention by spatial analysts and this represents a serious deficiency in the understanding of how the system actually works.

Changes in the Industrial System

Change may take the form of alterations in the number, location, scale, or activity of operating units; in the direction, type, and volume of the functional relationships between operating units within or between organizations; and in the interactions between operating units and the external environment. The modifications may come about as a result of *organizational changes*, such as when one capitalist firm takes over another or when socialist administrative control is reorganized. As one example, during the last few years the previous management structure of some industries in the U.S.S.R. has been replaced by 'production and industrial associations' which A. N. Kosygin described in 1976 as 'unified production-and-economic complexes in which science and production are organically fused and specialization and cooperation are developed on a wide scale' (*Current Digest of the Soviet Press*, Vol. 28, No. 10, p. 9). Recently Barr (1974) has analysed some examples of the progress made in implementing this reorganization of Soviet industry and has examined some of its spatial implications. Modifications may also ensue from *technological changes* which can alter the scale, processes, and inputs/outputs of existing plants, or require intra-organizational restructuring (following, for instance, the introduction of computers), or bring into being plants using new techniques or making new products. The pace of technological change can be very rapid. One recent example is the development of direct reduction electric furnace steel-making to replace conventional technology especially in applications where only small quantities (e.g. 200,000 tons annually) are required; another is the use of bacteria, yeasts, and algae to produce fodder for livestock, protein supplement for human consumption, and petroleum for transport and other applications.

Many aspects of the development of, and changes to, industrial systems deserve close examination. Among these are:

(a) The motives, incentives, and objectives of the original entrepreneur (s);

(b) the functional and spatial development of the system (such as the changes in the number, scale, and activity of operating units and their rearrangement in space);

(c) The quantitative and qualitative changes to the physical and informational flows and linkages in the system;

(d) the explanation of the flows within the system and in the external environment leading to change and subsequent iteration and feedback effects.

So far, however, research along these lines in capitalist countries has lacked an adequate conceptual framework, yet there is a good deal of evidence that would support the construction of a theory of the growth of a firm (and its extension, the transnational corporation). For example, there is evidence that the 'territory' of a large firm—when weighted with the locational economics of the organization's dominant industrial sector, and with the perceived behaviour of its competitors—consists of a 'core' and a 'periphery'. In the core area—or heartland—is its head office, research and development laboratories, major innovative production units, and central warehousing and distribution facilities. In its peripheral territory the firm may have branch factories that supply the core with inputs or that incorporate specialized items received from the core into products for sale in regional markets. Moreover in such areas the production, distribution, and service subsystems may operate with some degree of autonomy. To reach this stage, however, capitalist firms extend their industrial action space from the regional to the interregional scale within national frontiers (Pred, 1977; Hamilton, 1978b).

Capitalist firms operating in more than one country also have an 'international periphery', though in terms of sales, profits, or assets this can range from being of marginal to major importance. In this respect there are considerable differences between the expansion paths of United States and European firms (Hamilton, 1978c). Until recently, firms in the United States tended to regard the parent company as *the* profit centre and took advantage of foreign opportunities only if there were sufficient funds for all attractive domestic purposes. European firms, in contrast, often had to be internationally minded at the outset because their home markets were too small to permit economies of scale (Kaufmann, 1972). Whereas European-based companies like Unilever, Philips, Siemens, and Nestlé have at least 25 per cent of their assets and/or sales outside their countries of incorporation, American companies tend to rely less on their overseas operations: as a case in point, the General Motors Corporation, Detroit, has a mere 16.7 per cent of its total assets abroad and these account for only 14.2 per cent of its total turnover. Yet there is evidence from some West European countries, for instance Belgium (Cracco and Van Campenhoudt, 1976–77) that 'internationalization' by indigenous firms can still be in a relatively embryonic phase, even though it has been gathering momentum for several years.

The strategies used to manage activities in the international periphery vary from one organization to another. But even those that vest considerable autonomy in 'peripheral' subsystems retain the most powerful and specialized forms of control—over finance, research, design, and quality—in the core region. In this way the peripheral subsystems can be manipulated so as to dilute the risks and strengthen the advantages of international operations. As Wadley suggests (Chapter 10), it is unlikely that the boards of conglomerates (i.e. the core) long recall the problems faced at a particular time in one overseas market (i.e. the periphery).

By contrast, studies of the origins, growth, and change in ministerial-level industrial systems in socialist countries or of state-owned industries operated by boards or corporations (with varying degrees of independence) in capitalist mixed economies, focus on an entire industrial sector or branch. Most such analyses subsume the organizational background in that they concentrate on the decision-making process itself and on subtleties of the evolving relationships between the central authority (ministry, board, or corporation), the operating units, and the local or regional authorities concerned (which may desire or deplore any particular proposal). Polemics aside, only feeble attempts have been made to develop a conceptual spatial framework incorporating the origins and growth of such systems. An appropriate construct would need to embrace the processes by which inherited capitalist industrial systems were dismantled, adapted, rationalized, or enlarged in an attempt to achieve not only economic efficiency but also social, political, strategic, and other national goals. In addition it would need to take account of subnational requirements and opportunities as expressed through programmes of economic regionalism.

It might be expected, *a priori*, that such socialist systems would display a more dispersed pattern of industrial-sector facilities. The replacement of both the agglomerative forces of capitalist oligopolistic competition and the firm-centric perceptions of capitalist industrial management by a ministerial view of national space ought to result in a more 'equitable' weighting of the relative importance of all regions. But in practice it seems that the 'core–periphery' concept also has some validity in socialist countries. The continuity of the core—whether inherited or recently developed—will be assured since as an industrial system proceeds from infancy to maturity and develops spatially it will require new and more sophisticated inputs from the centre. It does not necessarily follow, however, that the core will continue to *dominate* the national spatial system of an industry.

Change occurs, of course, throughout the global industrial system, but regions (in the sense of subdivisions of national territory) appear to provide a particularly fruitful level of observation since it is there that the 'territorial-production complex' and related notions gain full expression. Much can be gleaned from comparing regional industrial systems operating in contrasting geographic and socio-economic environments. Good examples are the Ruhr in the German Federal Republic and the Kuzbass in the U.S.S.R., both of which grew up on coal and iron. Capitalist enterprise in the Ruhr and state enterprise in the Kuzbass developed similar heavy-industry sectors—thermal power, coking coal, ferrous and non-ferrous metallurgy—functionally interlinked to form regional industrial complexes. But beyond that their structures differ, the Ruhr having developed chemical industries based on oil and natural gas and the Kuzbass pulp, paper, and other timber-processing plants. Furthermore, metal manufacturing, engineering, and fabricating industries in the Ruhr have recently added greatly to the diversity of its activities. Quite different kinds of changes are taking place in the two regions. In summary, the older heavy industries of the Ruhr are stagnant or declining while those of the Kuzbass are still growing; newer kinds of industries (and related tertiary and quaternary activities) are expanding in the Ruhr whereas they have hardly begun to appear in the Kuzbass. Among the many reasons for these differences, the Ruhr (a) is much older industrially than the Kuzbass region; (b) constitutes the economic heart of the German Federal Republic whereas the Kuzbass is less important in the U.S.S.R. than the Donbass or Urals and, geographically, is not so central; and

(c) developed on the basis of a local coal industry which now faces competition from imported oil, natural gas, and coal whereas such alternative sources of energy have not been allowed to affect the development of the Kuzbass. Moreover the Ruhr, considered either as a regional industrial complex or as a set of urban-industrial places, has become less dependent on internal structural cohesion or local entrepreneurial relationships and more characterized by external linkages. This change has resulted from three main causes: the diminution of activities previously supported by regional-scale inputs; the introduction of activities new to the region by national or international firms with much wider linkage and contact systems; and the conversion of processes dependent on local resources (e.g. coal) to imported alternatives (e.g. oil and natural gas) in an attempt to meet competition from other European and overseas steel producers. By contrast the Kuzbass is still growing industrially and will develop a greater range of activities some of which may represent the production locally of manufactured goods currently brought in from other regions (such as the Urals). Thus in contrast to the kinds of changes occurring in the Ruhr, it seems probable that the linkages within the Kuzbass will become stronger and those with other regions will diminish, at least relatively, in importance.

This brief comparison between the Ruhr and Kuzbass regions illustrates the kinds of analyses that can be undertaken within the framework of the industrial systems structure that has been suggested here. Similar investigations can of course be undertaken at various levels in the hierarchy although relatively little attention has been paid to the functioning of international industrial systems and the impact of interactions at this level on lower-order systems. Indeed it is probably not unfair to suggest that until recently many industrial geographers viewed 'the international system' as more or less synonymous with the role and behaviour of transnational corporations. Moreover, most such studies, some of which have been reviewed by McNee (1974), treat transnational firms unrealistically, as though they operate *entirely* as an independent—not to say wholly maverick—system within the capitalist industrial system.

While there is no gainsaying the importance of the role played by the transnational capitalist firm as an institution, preoccupation with its behaviour may have diverted attention from other, rather more significant, changes in relationships between international industrial systems. Perhaps the most important of these—both now and for the future—is the interaction between the industrial systems of developing and developed nations (a division which should, however, be recognized as an oversimplification since it suggests two discrete groups rather than a continuum of countries at various stages of development). It is fair to suggest that by the mid-1960s the developing countries had become disillusioned about the progress being made internationally towards tackling what they perceived to be their particular trade problems—the existence of tariffs and quantitative restrictions on their exports of manufactured goods. For example, the considerable increase in the exports of clothing and textiles from South-East Asian countries during the 1950s led the governments of most major importing countries to implement protective measures of various kinds, many of which were outside the 'safeguards' that had been written into the General Agreement on Tariffs and Trade (GATT) because they discriminated against particular member states. The proliferation of 'illegal' restrictions led to the conclusion by GATT of a 'Short-Term Arrangement on Cotton Textiles' in 1961 and a 'Long-Term Arrangement Regarding International Trade in Cotton Textiles' (LTA) which came into force the following year. The LTA permitted importing nations to introduce restraints on imports of cotton goods from specific countries: Canada, for example, negotiated restraint arrangements on various items of clothing with eleven countries from 1960 to 1971 (Textile and Clothing Board, 1977).

It was in the context of events of this kind that, in November 1966, the United Nations passed a resolution to 'promote and accelerate the industrialization of the developing countries' and shortly afterwards established the United Nations Industrial Development Organization (UNIDO). Early guidelines of UNIDO were laid down at an international symposium on industrialization held in 1967. The following year UNIDO organized an interregional seminar at Minsk (Byelorussian SSR) on industrial location and regional development (the first international gathering devoted exclusively to such issues and problems). The work of UNIDO was again examined at conferences in 1971 (Vienna) and 1975 (Lima). The latter took place soon after the United Nation's 'Declaration and Programme of Action on the Establishment of a New International Economic Order' which urged the international community to make every effort to encourage the industrialization of the developing countries with a view to increasing their share in world industrial production. The result was the 'Lima Declaration and Plan of Action on Industrial Development and Co-operation' which advocated that the share of world industrial production by developing countries should increase from 7 per cent 'to the maximum possible extent and as far as possible to at least 25 per cent of world industrial production by the year 2000'. Subsequently the United Nations (resolution 3362 (S-VII)) urged developed countries to

> facilitate the development of new policies and strengthen existing policies, including labour market policies, which would encourage the redeployment of their industries which are less competitive internationally to developing countries, thus leading to structural adjustments in the former and a higher degree of utilization of natural and human resources in the latter. Such policies may take into account the economic structure and the economic, social and security objectives of the developed countries concerned and the need for such industries to move into more viable lines of production or into other sectors of the economy.

Although there are many uncertainties about whether the Lima objectives can be achieved in the time envisaged, about the meaning of the concept of 'redeployment' (which can be interpreted as ranging from investing capital or training nationals in developing countries to selling them technology, know-how, management services, or even second-hand equipment), and about the appropriate roles of government and of private enterprise, there can be little dispute that the world is moving into a period of massive industrial adjustment. Apparently abstract ideas like the 'establishment of a new economic order' or a 'plan of action on industry development and co-operation' become more meaningful when considered in terms of a hierarchy of industrial systems since, by definition, every level will be affected to a greater or lesser extent. Thinking in terms of industry systems will not only help geographers (and decision-makers) to raise their sights but also bring them down to earth.

Chapter 2

A Structural Approach to Industrial Systems in Different Social and Economic Environments

ALEKSANDR P. GORKIN AND LEONID V. SMIRNYAGIN

In most cases, research in economic geography deals with complex objects which can be thought of as *systems*. Manufacturing is one such object. Although it depends upon the aims of the research and upon the approach adopted, nevertheless manufacturing can be treated as a 'manufacturing system' at any scale, whether that be at the scale of the entire world, of the socialist or capitalist countries, or of the major regions of one country. Since manufacturing is an appropriate subject for systems analysis, its research investigation cannot be confined within the bounds of one particular science; it manifests diverse characteristics and processes which must be analysed from the viewpoint of several sciences, such as economics, management, or economic geography. Indeed, it is safe to say that manufacturing is both an economic and an economic-geographical system, depending upon which aims and research methods are adopted. Note, though, that an economic system can be regarded as an economic-geographical one only when it is typified by a spatial structure, whereas any economic-geographical system is simultaneously an economic one. Thus it is considered here that regional economics is not an independent science but only a method of organizing socio-economic research which weaves together the approaches and methods of economics, economic geography, mathematical statistics, management theory, and other sciences.

The manufacturing industry of any country is a complicated hierarchically organized, polystructural system of interconnected elements. The degree of integration in a 'manufacturing system' can be determined by the extent of its insulation from the external environment and the existence within it of system-forming linkages between its constituent elements. Any one element is a component of a system which is indivisible in the light of the research being undertaken. In economic-geographical research on manufacturing, therefore, an industrial enterprise is treated as such a basic, indivisible element, though in specific cases some plants or workshops operated by one industrial enterprise (for example in mining or timber-processing industries) can be presented as a separate object of research.

Within a polystructural 'manufacturing system' a number of objectively existing structures may be identified, of course, according to the ways in which it is divided into elements. From the economic-geographical viewpoint, an enterprise as an element of a 'manufacturing system' may be analysed variously as a productive, organizational, or spatial unit. Accordingly, a 'manufacturing system' is typified by three *basic* structures which may be termed respectively the *productive-technological, organizational,* and *spatial*. Hierarchism is inherent in a manufacturing system and within its constituent elements, so that each of these structures comprises interconnected subsystems of different levels. Each structure has its own particular kinds of internal linkages. What is meant by linkage is the relation wherein the existence, absence, or change of particular objects implies conditions of the existence, absence, or change in others. Thus the existence of linkages as a form of interaction is a typical feature of the 'manufacturing system' (as, indeed, with any other system). So flows of materials and components constitute the main linkages in the productive-technological structure of manufacturing whereas in the organization structure it is flows of information which are most important. The spatial structure comprises specific forms of linkage which reflect only a potential possibility for the existence of material and information linkages: these may be termed spatially structural linkages.

Before turning to the salient features of manufacturing systems, note that the three basic structures are formally of the same type when viewed from the standpoint of systems-structure in both socialist and capitalist manufacturing because they reflect in an objective manner the complexity of development and operation of this major economic sector. However, 'economic relations in each given society appear primarily as *interests*' (Marx and Engels, 1961, p. 271). Capitalist manufacturing contrasts with that of socialist manufacturing in that it has different goals and thus different parameters of optimization and development which, in turn, are reflected in their different structures. As a result, not only do basic distinctions occur in their content, but likewise structural differences do arise, above all in organizational structure.

Indeed, the *organizational structure* of capitalist manufacturing is, it seems, a complex of relationships between the elements (i.e. plants) and the hierarchical subsystems (i.e. divisions and branches of firms, corporations and their subsidiaries and, likewise, ministries of nationalized or state-owned industries). These relationships appear as: (a) vertical management linkages of a hierarchical type, and (b) horizontal linkages in the form both of competition between firms and of state regulation. Such a combination of vertical and horizontal linkages is specific to the organizational structure of capitalist manufacturing. However, state regulation in the shape, for instance, of indicative planning by state-owned enterprises, government tax policies, and incentives—which has enjoyed significant development in many capitalist countries—requires separate consideration and is not discussed here. Yet within the organizational structure of capitalist industry a plant must be considered as an organizational economic unit whose management linkages appear only as inputs, except in the case of the one-plant firm where they are also outputs. Normally, at plant level, decisions are put into effect which have been taken primarily at higher levels in the organizational hierarchy. As a rule, such linkages only amount to a search for optimum ways of obtaining the results desired within the firm. Horizontal linkages between manufacturing subsystems in capitalist countries appear, first and foremost, as competition between firms and their consortia—not only within single but to a degree also between different manufacturing industries. Such horizontal linkages in capitalist manufacturing are also the long-term cumulative effect of contacts among firms regarding supplies of raw and semi-manufactured materials, co-operation and the innovation of joint ventures, leading to specific forms of competition between amalgamations of firms. To an important degree such new forms result not only from tendencies inherent in the capitalist competitive process itself towards oligopoly and monopoly but also from tensions set up in the external environment by technological progress and by accelerated competition from socialist manufacturing.

Indeed, the organizational structure of capitalist industry is very complicated and is typified by great diversity or non-conformities within hierarchical levels. Thus on the level of the single firm there are, at one extreme, powerful monopolies with dozens of specialized divisions operating in various industrial sectors and each owning hundreds of enterprises (plants); at the other extreme there are small companies with only one plant. Large monopolies usually have highly developed internal structures comprising several organizational sub-systems. However, the vast majority of firms in developed capitalist countries have, as a rule, one plant, so that of course most of the intermediate stages of the organizational hierarchy are of limited occurrence. Yet while many small single-plant firms are formally independent, they are actually within the sphere of economic influence of the large firms to which they supply materials, components, or services. In this case, small firms actually become one of the lower stages of organizational structure corresponding to a large firm. It is our view that the complexities and irregularities of organizational structure in capitalist manufacturing are determined by the predominance of horizontal competitive linkages over the vertical management linkages in the evolution, growth, or survival of the firm.

By contrast, the organizational structure of socialist manufacturing within a centrally planned economy is a complex of relationships between the elements (enterprises) and hierarchic subsystems comprising production unions (or economic associations of enterprises), directorates (*Glavki* in the U.S.S.R.), and ministries of various manufacturing industries. The top echelons of this structure are the state planning bodies (Gosplan-type organizations) and state executive authorities (the Councils of Ministers). Linkages within the organizational structure of socialist manufacturing appear as (a) vertical management linkages of hierarchic type; and (b) horizontal and vertical interindustry linkages of common national economic planning. An enterprise is considered within this given structure similarly as a lower organizational economic unit with tight management linkages. However, the organizational structure of socialist manu-facturing is more regular than that found in capitalist countries or 'mixed' economies: there cannot be any instances in which the lower system elements—the enterprises—contain the top levels of the organizational hier-archy. Though socialist enterprises have some, and frequently nowadays increasing, economic independence and rights to use initiative, their activities are still governed by the *goals of socialist society in its entirety*—goals which are attained by fulfilling the state national economic plan common to all enterprises and organizations. For instance, Article 16 of the Constitution of the U.S.S.R., which was adopted by the Supreme Soviet of the U.S.S.R. on 7 October 1977, states:

> the economy of the U.S.S.R. is an integral economic complex comprising all the elements of social production, distribution and exchange on its territory. The economy is managed on the basis of state plans for economic and social development, taking due account of sector and territorial principles, and by combining centralized direction with the managerial independence and initiative of individual and associated enterprises and other organizations, for which active use is made of profit, cost price and other economic levers and incentives in management accounting (*Pravda*, 25 October 1977).

Thus vertical linkages prevail over the horizontal ones in the organizational structure of socialist manufacturing. However, it is an urgent problem to improve the structure by strengthening the horizontal linkages. Already in 1971, at the third session of the Eighth Supreme Soviet of the U.S.S.R., A. N. Kosygin pointed out the limitations of planning which embraced only vertical linkages. In particular, he noted that

> So far the planning agencies and ministries still give primary emphasis to vertical planning, i.e. from top to bottom: State Planning Commission—Ministry—enter-prise. Horizontal planning should be improved as well, i.e. by forming national technological linkages between industries and enterprises (*Pravda*, 25 November 1971).

The *productive-technological structure* of manufacturing is a complex of technological links between its elements (enterprises) arranged into hierarchical subsystems: subsectors of industries and groups of industries. This structure reflects the division of manufacturing according to the economic purpose of production; the types of consumption of fuels, energy, raw materials, and intermediate products; the technological processes and machinery applied in the productive process; the occupational structure of the labour force and specific working conditions. Here the term 'productive-technological structure' [or 'production-technology structure'] is proposed to replace the notion common in economic geography of a 'branch structure of manufacturing'. This is because the latter is really the superficial manifestation of numerous technological and techno-economic linkages between enterprises and subsystems of manufacturing which are interwoven in complex ways. In a socialist economy the branch structure of manufacturing is formed according to a plan and its goals, while in capitalist economies it comes about spontaneously as a result of structural crises (for example, the energy crisis), technological innovation, and the flow of capital from one industry into another in pursuit of a higher rate of return to profit. Nevertheless, while the principal differences between capitalist and socialist manufacturing emerge in the way in which they are organized and emanate from differences in production relationships and societal goals, the production-technology structures of manufacturing can be similar in countries with distinct socio-economic systems yet with similar natural resource endowments and levels of industrialization. Thus Revenko (1971, p. 50) notes that

> Soviet and American statisticians both adhere primarily to the criterion of allocating plants to one or other branch of manufacturing according to the type of product manufactured by the enterprise. Similar criteria are applied also in the case of enterprises manufacturing non-uniform [i.e. diversified—*Eds.*] products.

In this way an enterprise becomes an economic or production-economic unit, typified by uniform or predominantly uniform products and a particular technical unit.

The *spatial structure* of manufacturing is a complex of potential possibilities for the spatial realization of production-technological and organizational linkages offered by the location and the association of the spatial elements and subsystems—plants, industrial centres, agglomerations, and regions. Both the number of subsystems of spatial structure and their denominations are understood in conventional terms, in particular to emphasize the importance of the structural hierarchy. Here, research deals with the linkage relationships expressed in the spatial proximity or neighbourhood effect, compactness, and configuration or elements and subsystems. By itself the spatial structure or 'geometry' of manufacturing lacks specific socio-economic content. Study of that structure involves the investigation of:

(a) the position of elements or subsystems along particular co-ordinates (elements and subsystems henceforth are treated as points, lines, or surfaces);

(b) spatial interrelationships, i.e. the correlation of two or more positions expressed metrically or topologically;

(c) the degree of concentration of elements and subsystems in space, expressed algebraically;

(d) the form of the spatial distribution of elements and subsystems (clusters, uniform dispersion, random distribution, uni-nodal, and multi-nodal); and

(e) the distribution pattern of the elements and subsystems in space (linear, annular, star-shaped etc).

Earlier in this chapter three basic structures of a 'manufacturing system' were discussed. None of these in themselves can be an original object of economic-geographical research. The organizational and production-technological structures taken singly without their spatial dimensions are the research subjects of other sciences—political economy, management science, industrial economics, or any other economic science—but not of economic geography. At the same time, spatial structure alone can provide the economic geographer only with formalized constructs (even though this may be of some interest in understanding the map of manufacturing). Research in economic geography demands that spatial structure is given a particular content, and this can be achieved by superimposing the spatial structure of other basic structures into a more complex or 'synthetic' territorial (spatial)-productive and territorial (spatial)-organizational structure.

The *territorial-production structure* of manufacturing implies, first, a distribution of the production-technological elements and subsystems of the 'manufacturing system', their association, linkages and interaction within the confines of the system of an entire country, region, agglomeration, or urban centre under investigation. When the production-technological and spatial structures of the same system coincide, the geographer is particularly concerned with the analysis of factual, or real functional 'manufacturing regions' (that is, regions in which specific industries are associated or localized). But a second approach to the territorial-production structure of manufacturing can be imagined; this emerges from the combination of the production-technological manufacturing structure with the spatial structure of other systems *external* to the 'manufacturing system'. Examples of such external systems are those of state administration or economic integrations. The spatial structure of these systems represents a network of administrative-territorial divisions, economic regions, or conventional statistical regions. Again the coincidence of the production-technological structure of manufacturing with the spatial structure of external systems makes the 'manufacturing region' the object of study: in this case, the integrated economic region with a specific type of manufacturing development which influences its territorial-production structure or the analysis of administrative or statistical regions from the point of view of the development and distribution of manufacturing within them (Gorkin *et al.*, 1976; Gokhman *et al.*, 1976). These may be termed administrative-manufacturing regions.

The *territorial-organizational structure* of manufacturing implies the distribution of the organizational-economic elements and 'manufacturing subsystems' (i.e. plants, branches of firms, firms and amalgamated corporations in capitalist countries; enterprise, production unions, or economic associations, directorates or *Glavki*, ministries, and central economic planning authorities in socialist countries), and their combination, linkage, and interaction within the countries, regions, agglomerations, or centres being studied. Research on the territorial-organizational structure resulting from the superimposition of the basic organizational and spatial structure is not only concerned with the distribution of firms or ministries within physical space; of no lesser importance is the study of the influence of organizational structure on the spatial structure. Thus the peculiarities of the organizational structure of capitalist manufacturing bring about a host of specific inversions in the territorial linkages between enterprises. Commonly, for example, enterprises interact not with the nearest potential partner (i.e. another enterprise) but with a more distant one, because the latter belongs to the same firm. The very characteristics of economic space (primarily its 'friction' or 'permeability') differ among firms with varying economic capacities, since small firms encounter greater friction when functioning in space than do powerful monopolies. These peculiarities of the interaction between basic structures exert considerable influence on the territorial organization of manufacturing in capitalist countries since the intra-firm linkages between enterprises play a very important role in it. It is precisely because of this that traditional models and theories of regional economics (gravity models, central place theory, growth pole theory) fail to explain adequately the present-day geographical distribution of manufacturing in developed capitalist countries (Pred, 1976).

As has been shown, the three basic structures (and likewise, the two superimposed ones) are logically of the same type for both socialist and capitalist manufacturing. However, a basic goal of this chapter is to try to examine whether there are any distinctions in spatial structures of socialist and capitalist manufacturing and in their complex, superimposed structures (i.e. territorial-production and territorial-organizational) and, if indeed there are any, to consider their character.

First, the spatial structure of manufacturing (its 'geometry' or the draft of the planned spatial distribution) is usually passive in combination with other basic structures. As a rule, the spatial structure cannot alter productional-technological or organizational structures, while the latter actually determine the character and peculiarities of spatial structure. That is why the similarities and differences in the spatial structures of socialist and capitalist manufacturing result from the impact of other basic structures in the course of their evolution in space. Thus resemblances between the territorial-production and territorial-organizational structures of manufacturing in different socio-economic environments are determined mainly by similarities in production-technological structures; differences are determined by basic distinctions in organizational structures. This explains why territorial-production structures of socialist and capitalist manufacturing have much more in common than do their territorial-organizational structures. In reality, the development of the territorial-production structure under both capitalism and socialism is determined practically by the same location factors because usually nowadays the technological processes are the same everywhere.

Changes in the role of certain location factors occur also in similar ways. The production-technological structure of both capitalist and socialist manufacturing is becoming increasingly complicated, resulting in the gradual technological separation of industrial branches. This offers the opportunity for some activities within the same industry to be located separately and promotes the creation of interlinked, interdependent interindustry clusters as, for example, in a 'territorial-production complex' (Karaska and Linge, 1979). Geographical research into the distribution of manufacturing in both socialist and capitalist countries tackles nowadays such common problems as the creation of industrial complexes, the distribution of manufacturing in urban agglomerations, the optimization of the spatial relationships of manufacturing with other systems such as settlement, infrastructure and the environment. Moreover, the social aspects of industrial distribution and their impact on the social life of regions is becoming more urgent in both socio-economic systems.

However, second, there are some essential differences between socialist and capitalist manufacturing with regard to territorial-production structure. In general under capitalism this exhibits greater spatial concentration and greater unevenness at the international, interregional, inter-urban, and even intra-urban levels. Territorial combinations in this structure are usually represented by simple groupings of partially linked (or even totally unconnected) industrial plants: true 'territorial-production complexes' are rare and are on a small scale. Under socialism, however, the creation of giant 'territorial-production complexes' has become the main principle shaping the geographical distribution of manufacturing, particularly in recent years since the Communist Party of the Soviet Union (CPSU) incorporated the creation of 'territorial-production complexes' as an item in its economic programme. At the 25th Congress of the CPSU, A.N. Kosygin stressed that in the Tenth Soviet Five-Year Plan specific development in individual regions will be determined to even a greater extent by the fulfilment of major national economic programmes involving the creation of territorial-production complexes. The programmes that are already being implemented (Figure 2.1) include the agricultural development of the non-chernozem zone of the RSFSR, the industrial-agricultural zones of the Kursk Magnetic Anomaly, the West-Siberian territorial-industrial complex, systems of the Aktyubinskiy, Karaganda, and Angara-Yenisey complexes, the South Tadzhik complex and others (Kibal' chich, 1977). A new Timan-Pechora industrial complex is to be developed from the utilization of available deposits of oil and gas. In future, a number of complexes will be formed along the Baikal-Amur Mainline, which is at present under construction: the largest will be the Chulman-Aldan complex comprising mineral-extracting centres for several types of manufacturing (Material from the 25th CPSU Congress, 1976, p. 152).

Third, and most important, the geographical distribution of capitalist manufacturing as a process is concerned with the attainment only of goals which pertain to the manufacturing system. That is why this distribution comes about rather autonomously, being generally independent of other systems in capitalist

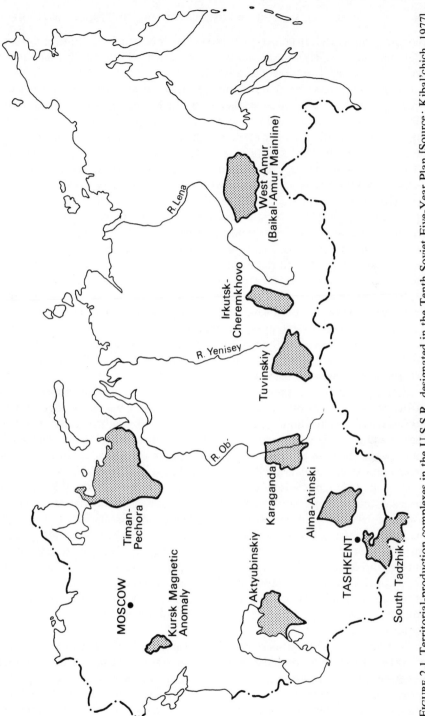

FIGURE 2.1 Territorial-production complexes in the U.S.S.R. designated in the Tenth Soviet Five-Year Plan [Source: Kibal'chich, 1977]

economy and society. In contrast, the territorial-production structure in socialist economies is decisively dependent upon goals which are directed by more broad systems functioning in society as a whole.

It is apparent, however, that it is not the territorial-production structure itself which causes these differences. Rather, in the main, they are explained by basic differences in the organizational and territorial-organizational structures. The high degree of spatial concentration in capitalist manufacturing stems from the fact that under conditions of private ownership of the factors of production, location decision-making evolves under conditions of much uncertainty, and decision-makers tend to locate plants where similar plants are already operating successfully (Webber, 1972; Hamilton, 1974a). Such uncertainty does not exist, or is less important, in socialist economies thanks to centralized national economic planning. Under socialism, therefore, such concentration can be avoided more easily. The limited development of the 'territorial-production complex' in capitalist countries is also affected by the private ownership of the factors of production: this leads to antagonism [competition—*Eds.*] between the separate firms owning technologically interconnected plants which, had they been located together, could have derived additional mutual economic benefits. The socialist mode of economic management gives broad opportunities for deriving such effect and is the reason why the 'territorial-production complex' approach has now become the major force shaping the planned geographical distribution of manufacturing in socialist countries.

Finally, the territorial-production structure of manufacturing as a subsystem of the capitalist economy has developed as a result of numerous independent decisions by many maximum profit-orientated firms, so yielding the autonomy of the structure. In socialist societies, the economy belongs to the people and is managed by them; in this case the development and modification of territorial-production structure is not an end in itself but is a means by which to solve broader, more comprehensive and mainly *social* problems. It is well-known, for instance, that an important role was played by socialist industrialization in the course of developing the backward peripheral areas of the U.S.S.R. The changes made in the territorial-production structure of Soviet manufacturing were carried out not for the sake of maximizing efficiency within manufacturing itself but were used as a key force in the social reorganization of society. This permits us to conclude that it is mainly the difference in the organizational structure of socio-economic environments that makes the territorial-production and territorial-organizational structures of socialism differ from those of capitalism.

Typically, the territorial-organizational structure in a capitalist economy has many centres where locational decisions (on the level of a firm) are made: it does not have a super co-ordinator—a high level management body. Attempts by governments in several capitalist countries to undertake management functions in some sectors of the economy do not change the main principles of the capitalist economy. Each of such decision-making centres is orientated towards its own optimum, but their sum does not take into account the optimum operation of the system as a whole. Thus from the management viewpoint, the capitalist economy can be referred to as a *multi-nodal heterogeneous system*, in which it is mainly the elements and subsystems that manage the system and not *vice versa*. On the contrary, the socialist economy is a *uni-nodal homogeneous system* where the 'behaviour' of the elements and subsystems is determined by the 'behaviour' of the whole system. That is why in the socialist economy the primacy of the *global* optimum is the main goal of development, while in the capitalist economy it is the primacy of the *local* optimum.

In practice, both the socialist and capitalist territorial-production structures of manufacturing deviate from the optimum. They are not perfect at every moment of time due to objective contradictions inherent in each of these systems. These contradictions are gradually becoming overcome in the dialectical-contradictive process of the evolving territorial-production structure. Nevertheless, the major contradictions are the following: between the global (i.e. national) and the regional optimum (what is beneficial for the region can be unacceptable for the country as a whole); between the purely economic and the purely social optimum (what is beneficial for an industry itself is likely to be undesirable for society in general); between the optimum for a certain type of industry and for a certain area; and between specialization and diversity of industrial centres and regions. Under individual capitalism these contradictions are antagonistic in character and cannot be overcome in principle; they can be only partially ameliorated. But in the planned socialist economy the contradictions cited are not antagonistic and can be overcome in the course of development by national economic planning.

There are many common features in the *spatial structures* of manufacturing in countries with different socio-economic systems, especially in countries with the same level of industrial development. The spatial distribution of manufacturing is of 'point' character, points (i.e. plants) being grouped in clusters. Clustering is the result of the gravitation of manufacturing to settlements, main transport lines, and nodes. Exceptions can be mainly explained by the gravitation of certain industries towards spatially fixed resources. The similarity of spatial structures becomes obvious when patterns of location are seen as one 'frame' in a film, but each 'frame' is the continuation of a series of past events. Yet it is in the dynamics—the evolution and development of the spatial structures of capitalist and socialist manufacturing—that the significant distinctions are exposed. If the spatial structure of capitalist manufacturing is rather inert and changing slowly, the distribution of socialist manufacturing is more dynamic and mobile. Points, plants, and industrial centres appear in new regions much more often in socialist than in capitalist economies. Clearly, in this case, the revealed differences are determined by basic distinctions in organizational and territorial-organizational structures of the socialist economy.

It should be pointed out in conclusion that traditionally it is the territorial-production structure that usually becomes the main object of economic-geographic research. But the process of regulating and managing the economy is becoming more and more complicated. The comparative role of different conditions and factors of industrial location is changing (Gorkin and Smirnyagin, 1973). The friction of space is decreasing as a result of the effects of the scientific technological revolution. In view of this, the study of the territorial-organizational structure of industry and the comparison of its development in different socio-economic environments should be treated as an urgent problem. Yet while 'a systems approach in itself does not offer an immediate solution to any problem, it does serve as a means of stating a given problem in a new way' (Yudin, 1973, p. 43).

Chapter 3

Modelling Industrial Location: Towards A Broader View of the Space Economy *

David M. Smith

INTRODUCTION

Industrial location has been a popular field for model-building during the past two decades. Geographers have been able to benefit from spatial analysis in economics, which provides perhaps the most sophisticated foundation yet developed for the study of any type of location problem. Beginning with the work of Weber (1909) and continued by Palander (1935), Hoover (1937, 1948), Greenhut (1956, 1963), Lösch (1954), and Isard (1956), this field has now attracted contributions from geographers attempting synthesis or reformulation from their own prespective (e.g. Pred, 1967, 1969; Smith, 1971; Webber, 1972). Recent collections of papers reveal something of the scope of contemporary geographical work (Hamilton, 1974c; Collins and Walker, 1975b), now heavily influenced by the statistical and behavioural approaches popularized in the 1960s as well as by modelling in the economic tradition. Added to this is the contribution of regional science and regional economics, in which plant location problems have been a major focus of attention.

The location of industry might thus be expected to be one of the better understood aspects of the space economy. Yet our ability to explain observed patterns of industrial activity with any precision remains somewhat limited. And it still proves difficult to plan industrial development with real confidence that the outcome will achieve the desired economic and social objectives. This chapter reviews major themes that have emerged in theoretical and model-building approaches to industrial location in the Anglo-American tradition, outlining their strengths and weaknesses. It is then argued that a more adequate approach requires extension and reformulation of traditional models, set within a much broader view of the production process and of the nature of its outcomes in space.

While some of the discussion relates to positive problems of explaining actual locations, the emphasis here is more on the development of normative models with planning applications. The proposals put forward are at a level of generality that should make them relevant both to public intervention in a capitalist or

* Revised and expanded version of a paper originally published (in Russian) in *Contemporary Geographical Problems* (Moscow: U.S.S.R. Academy of Sciences, 1976, pp. 235–48) and presented at the Methodological Seminar on Modelling of Spatial Organization of Economic Activity, 23rd International Geographical Congress, Moscow, 2 August 1976.

mixed economy and to location decision-making under central planning. However, it is important to recognize at the outset that very few models of human activity are free from important assumptions that relate to specific economic, social, or political situations. Certain technical relationships in production hold good universally, as do the algorithms designed to solve mathematical models, but which models are actually used, and in whose interests, is very much governed by the nature of the economic system. 'Theoretical principles of regional economics and policy cannot be universally applicable. Their dependence on the prevailing mode of production and social structure is obvious' (Nekrasov, 1974, p. 18). It is thus necessary to recognize the extent to which any location model is dependent for its operation and outcomes on particular social institutions.

THE TRADITIONAL APPROACH

The Variable-Cost Model

The traditional focus of model-building in industrial location analysis has been the individual production facility or single-plant firm. Private ownership under a capitalist mode of production is an important implicit assumption. The factory is viewed in isolation from other elements of the space economy and society, except for sources of inputs and destinations of outputs. Its individual economic success (usually the level of profitability) is the sole operative criterion of performance.

This approach originated with the work of Weber (1909). His well-known 'locational triangle' situation can readily be extended into an n-cornered 'location figure' where any source or destination of any input or output can be regarded as exerting a pull on the optimal or least-cost location (e.g. Alonso, 1967; Hamilton, 1967; Smith, 1971). While the oversimplicity of this generalized Weber model is now widely recognized, it retains a capacity to solve practical problems where the objective is to locate a single unit of production at the point of least operating costs, given a fairly simple input–output structure. This is an attribute not to be underestimated as it applies equally to the private producer and the public concern. Algorithms based on the Weber model, such as that of Kuhn and Kuenne (1962), can also be used to solve problems of public facility location in the service sector (e.g. hospitals), where the movement of clients from different destinations, perhaps weighted according to need, is analogous to the assembly of inputs from different origins (Taylor, 1975; Smith, 1977, pp. 300–43). The vast literature now available on location–allocation models (Lea, 1973) owes its inspiration largely to Weber's theory of industrial location and its subsequent extensions.

The weaknesses of the expanded Weber model are both practical and conceptual. On the practical side is the difficulty of accurately measuring the variables and parameters involved, especially those associated with external economies of agglomeration and industrial linkage. The more the production unit in question operates in isolation from others, the easier the Weber model is to apply (e.g. the study of the Mexican steel plant by Kennelly, 1954–5). But such situations are rare in the modern, highly integrated space economy—under either capitalism or socialism. More generally still, the Weber model fails to capture broader interdependencies such as the impact of industrial location on local employment prospects, levels of living and environmental quality (a criticism that also applies to most other models of industrial location). But it is two rather specific conceptual defects that have attracted most attention in the immediate development of location theory beyond the generalized Weber model—the assumption of 'economic rationality' on the part of decision-makers and the abstraction from demand or spatial variations in revenue required by the variable-cost approach. Responses to these problems must be considered before returning to the broader interdependencies neglected in the traditional approach.

Spatial Margins and Locational Choice

The suboptimal behaviour of the entrepreneur or manager and the range of locational choice open to the planner can be accommodated by a simple yet vital extension of the Weber model. This involves the addition of a 'spatial margin' (Rawstron, 1958) comprising a locus of points where operating costs are just covered by revenue. This at once shifts attention from the single elusive optimal location to the range of choice available if viability is to be maintained. If Weber's original 'isodapanes' (lines joining points of equal additional transport cost) can now be thought of as depicting a total cost surface in the generalized model (given a volume of output), the spatial margin is revealed by the intersection of this surface with one representing total revenue (Smith, 1966; 1971, pp. 188–206).

Figure 3.1 shows a spatial cost surface in a generalized form, as an inverted cone with costs rising from a point 0—the optimal or least-cost location. Revenue is depicted as a spatial constant (in the spirit of Weber's demand assumption), represented by a horizontal surface. The spatial margin (M) is where the TC and TR surfaces intersect. Projecting M onto geographical space reveals the region of viability for the plant in question. A section through the three-dimensional diagram provides the simplest possible model of the basic single-facility location problem. The space cost curve is analogous to the conventional cost curve in production theory (distance replaces output), while the margin (M and M') is the spatial equivalent of the conventional 'break-even' points.

This model adds an explicitly spatial dimension to the congruence between location theory and production theory (Smith, 1971, pp. 207–305), first recognized formally by Moses (1958). However, it has received little attention outside geographical literature, apart from passing references in regional

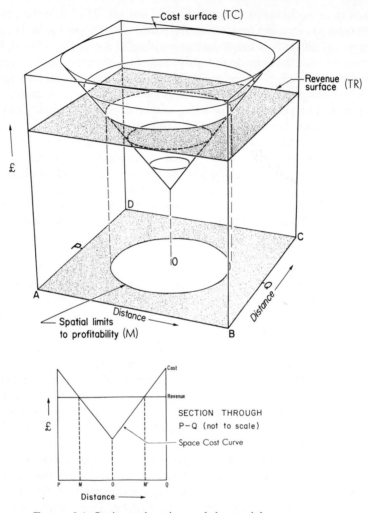

FIGURE 3.1 Optimum location and the spatial margins in a simple comparative-cost model. [Reproduced by permission of the Institute of British Geographers from Smith (1970a)]

economics (e.g. Richardson, 1969). Two considerations have limited the practical application of the concepts of space cost and revenue surfaces (or curves) and spatial margins—the difficulty of empirical identification and doubts as to their actual utility as explanatory devices.

The difficulty of empirical identification is a matter of data availability. Yet this problem can be overcome, at least for a plant with simple input–output relations. For example, Haddad and Schwartzman (1974) have identified a space

cost and revenue curve with respect to a steel mill at Itabirito (in the State of
Minas Gerais, Brazil), using records for 1905. They calculated the cost of
producing a ton of steel at all possible sites along the railway to Rio de Janeiro
(the principal marketing centre). This incorporated expenditure on the required
inputs of charcoal, iron ore, and calcium, sand and clay (spatial variables), and
on labour and capital (spatial constants), together with State export duty and the
cost of distribution. A space revenue curve was derived from data on prices and
transport costs. The result is illustrated in Figure 3.2. The actual location of the
steel mill at Itabirito is shown to be close to the optimal location—at Miguel
Burnier 25 km away. The points A and B, where SCC and SRC intersect,
represent the spatial margin to profitable operation.

Another interesting attempt to find spatial margins empirically has been made
by McDermott (1973). Margins were identified for five industries in New
Zealand, adopting the simplifying assumption that the only spatially variable
cost operating is that of transport to the market. Among other things,

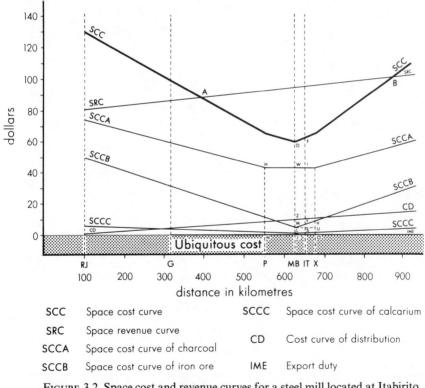

SCC	Space cost curve	SCCC
SRC	Space revenue curve	
SCCA	Space cost curve of charcoal	CD
SCCB	Space cost curve of iron ore	IME

SCCC	Space cost curve of calcarium
CD	Cost curve of distribution
IME	Export duty

FIGURE 3.2 Space cost and revenue curves for a steel mill located at Itabirito,
Brazil. [Source: Haddad and Schwartzman, 1974.] Note: RJ = Rio de
Janeiro; MB = Miguel Burnier; IT = Itabirito

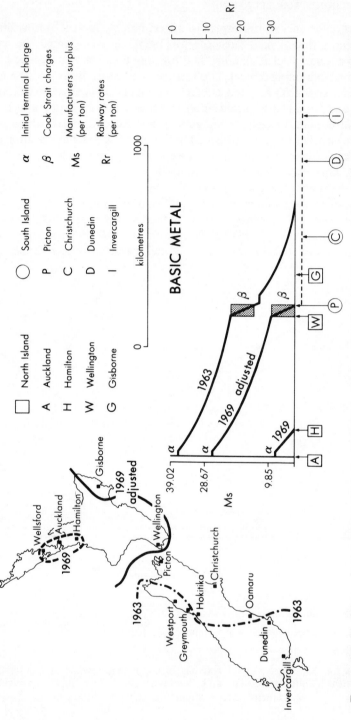

FIGURE 3.3 Spatial margins to profitability in the New Zealand basic metal industry. Note: manufacturers' surplus and railway rates are in monetary units. [Reproduced by permission of the New Zealand Geographical Society from McDermott (1973)]

McDermott discovered that the margin can shift substantially over a short period. This is illustrated in Figure 3.3 for the basic metal industry showing the graphic derivation of the margins from space cost curves and their position on the map Compared with the 1963 margin that for 1969 shows a marked contraction of the area in which profitable operation is possible, even when adjusted to compensate for an unusually low level of profit in 1969. The identification of margins offered some insights into industrial location in New Zealand, but McDermott (1973, p. 73) concluded that their instability and the assumptions upon which they are based render them 'of only limited value'.

However, the concept of the spatial margin to profitability remains helpful in drawing attention to a specifically spatial economic constraint on plant viability. Inferences as to the changing position of the margin may aid the interpretation of shifts in location patterns, as has been shown in the hosiery industry of the East Midlands of England (Smith, 1970b). Even with very limited data, simple two-dimensional graphic models drawn as sections through the spatial cost/revenue topography may assist in the analysis of the effect of changes in costs and prices. The possible impact of a local subsidy or tax introduced to influence location decisions can also be examined (Smith, 1966, p. 106). While the usual context for this type of model in Anglo-America is the private profit-seeking (or loss-avoiding) entrepreneur, it is equally applicable to the analysis of locational choice for the publicly owned enterprise.

The main objection to the concept of the spatial margin as an explanatory device is that it reveals nothing about the individual location decision other than that it is spatially constrained. In reality the margin for some industries may be very extensive—perhaps incorporating virtually the whole of a country like Britain (Taylor, 1970). Recent geographical research conducted under the rubric of the 'behavioural' approach has thus focused attention on how individual locations (within the margin) are actually arrived at under conditions of uncertainty and with different economic or personal objectives (e.g. Pred, 1967, 1969). While some interesting empirical findings may emerge eventually, this does not seem to be a particularly fruitful line of inquiry for the development of models to assist the planning of industrial location—except perhaps in the design of incentives more attuned to the personal motivations of businessmen and managers. Even as a framework for explanation, the behavioural approach has a fundamental weakness. By focusing attention on the individual entrepreneur or production facility and interpreting actual location decisions in this narrow context, attention is diverted from the broader economic structures within which the so-called 'actors' operate—a point stressed by Massey (1974) in her critiques of conventional location theory (see also Chapter 4).

Demand and Locational Interdependence

The introduction of spatial variations in demand goes some way towards accommodating the spatial interdependence of different units of production, largely neglected in Weber-type models. The original context was the recognition that space implies imperfection in the 'perfect' competition which was central to conventional (non-spatial) economic theory (e.g. Hotelling, 1929). In addition to competition, such local features as level of income, tastes, and the price of substitutes can affect the level of demand for a good and hence the revenue obtainable by a unit of production located at a given point. Thus a non-horizontal total revenue surface must be recognized. Two major difficulties arise in models where cost and revenue are both spatial variables. One is the difficulty of accurately measuring the conditions on which demand depends—including the whims and fancies of individual consumers. The other is the interdependence of cost and revenue via scale considerations (average unit cost affects the price at which goods can be sold, which affects level of demand and hence scale of output, which in turn affects average cost . . .). This renders the location problem insoluble, as Lösch (1954, p. 29) recognized, unless one of the major variables can be held constant. Nevertheless, if some simplifying assumptions are made, operational models can be constructed in which a spatially variable demand function is specified (e.g. Hoover, 1967; Smith and Lee, 1970; Smith, 1971, pp. 159–76).

As with the variable-cost framework, the data requirements for running models with demand as a spatial variable are formidable. The familiar potential formulation of spatial interaction has the capacity to generate a surrogate demand surface, but only under rather restrictive assumptions concerning the sensitivity of sales to distance from the plant (Smith, 1971, pp. 296–311). More fundamental problems arise from regarding demand for a good as somehow autonomously given—in the spirit of much neo-classical production theory. Tracing back the origins of demand requires some reference to features of economic and social structure that mould consumer preferences and differentially distribute the pecuniary wherewithal to express demand effectively in the market-place. These considerations are generally regarded as exogenous to a plant-location model.

While the variable-demand or 'locational-interdependence' school of location theory recognizes some aspects of the interconnected nature of the space economy, it clearly falls far short of providing a complete general model. For something approaching this in the economic realm one has to move to the macro-scale work of Lösch (1954) or to a dynamic interregional input–output framework. But the general equilibrium approach of conventional (non-spatial) economics, when extended into the space dimension, runs into such severe conflict with reality (e.g. imperfect factor mobility, local market monopoly) that it becomes little more than an elegant academic exercise. In addition, practical applications of input–output analysis have been much frustrated by the data requirements of this model, especially when disaggregated spatially—not to mention assumptions such as the stability of the coefficients. These problems, together with failure to penetrate basic structural relationships within society, are at the root of some contemporary disquiet with traditional location theory (e.g. Massey, 1974). The possible avenues for reformulation suggested in the second part of this chapter are in part a response to this critique. While some aspects of traditional location theory are more flexible and resilient than their critics recognize—and this includes the Weber model (Wood, 1969; Smith, 1970a)—it is certainly timely for industrial-location modelling to break free from some of its historic limitations. The directions that might be taken are many and varied, ranging from formal extensions of classical location economics to radical restructuring in the spirit of the contemporary resurgence of interest in Marxian economics. The suggestions now to be discussed comprise more of a development from the existing traditions of Anglo-American location analysis, the shortcomings of which may be more closely related to the societal context of their application (or lack of application) than to deficiencies and weaknesses of the models themselves.

SOME REFORMULATIONS

A Broader View of the Production Process

Much of the weakness of existing approaches to the modelling of industrial location arises from an unduly narrow conception of the production process. The prevailing Anglo-American view (though see Hamilton, 1974 a, c, 1978 a, b, c) is a purely technical one: of a plant assembling and processing certain inputs to generate an output in the form of material goods with 'value added' attributed to the contribution of the 'factors of production' employed. This fails to capture many important interdependencies which tie the plant or firm into the rest of the space economy. It also overlooks the broader societal context of the organization of the economy: the fact that production involves human relationships among individuals and classes in a specific institutional framework, not simply technical relationships among factors. A broader model of the production process is thus a necessary prerequisite for more complete and helpful models of industrial location.

Figure 3.4 sketches out some elements of the production process, broadly conceived. At the centre is the transformation of inputs into outputs, or what is thought conventionally to be where 'value added' takes place. The inputs (including capital) come from nature and human labour; how they are used, and in what quantities and where, concerns the familiar production decisions of scale, technique, and location. The *physical* process of transformation is a purely *technical* matter, defined formally as a production function. This will vary with the socio-economic system only insofar as different technologies are adopted. But what Marx referred to as the *value* process of production involves *social* relationships. These take on a distinctive form under a capitalist mode of production:

> The value process of production has to be with the buying and selling of output . . .
> in the market thus dissolving the specific characteristics (use value) of whatever is
> produced by reducing it to its exchange value freely translatable into another
> commodity (Desai, 1974, p. 24).

The institution of private property under capitalism enables a particular class to
appropriate surplus value generated in the production process, by virtue of
ownership of the means of production and the power that this bestows. How the
surplus is distributed is thus an outcome of particular societal formation and
institutions, as is suggested in Figure 3.4.

What is produced (the output) is traced back to human needs and wants, with
their bases in biology and culture. The conventional wisdom in neo-classical
economics is of consumer demand or desire transmitted to producers via the
intermediary of market-place 'signals', without much reference to the origin of
individual preferences. But this view is being increasingly questioned in the light
of the observed capacity of producers in a capitalist society to induce specific
wants through advertising. Capitalist producers also have power to influence
broader societal values through control of such institutions as the mass media,
which enables them to create a predisposition towards particular patterns of
consumption that serve the interests of the producers. The structure of outputs
that emerges thus reflects the prevailing preoccupation with private profits and
capital accumulation, mediated by the need to maintain and reproduce a fit and
necessarily skilled workforce. Under socialism, the population's requirements to
be satisfied via production may be traced in theory to more elevated origins, e.g.:

> They are engendered by the objective laws governing human life and reflect the
> objective necessity and historically established level of consumption at the given stage
> of development of the productive forces (Buzlyakov, 1973, p. 31).

In practice, this seems to mean the reproduction of the means of production
(including labour), with a measure of pragmatic judgement about how much
concession should be made to the more materialistic aspirations of the workforce
in the interests of preservation of social stability.

A serious omission on the output side of most economic models is consideration of negative side-effects or externalities. In Figure 3.4 this defect is
highlighted by inserting a category 'value subtracted', to complement the
conventional 'value added'. In neo-classical economics, value added is the
market-place evaluation of what output is worth in pecuniary units, less the cost
of material inputs. In other words, it is the direct or indirect contribution of
labour. If this market-place evaluation reflects consumer perceptions of utility or
satisfaction to be derived from the goods in question (as neo-classical theory has
it), it would appear necessary to adjust the value of output by some measure of
the dissatisfaction or disutility caused, for example, by environmental pollution.
Similarly in socialist accounting, the negative side-effects should properly be

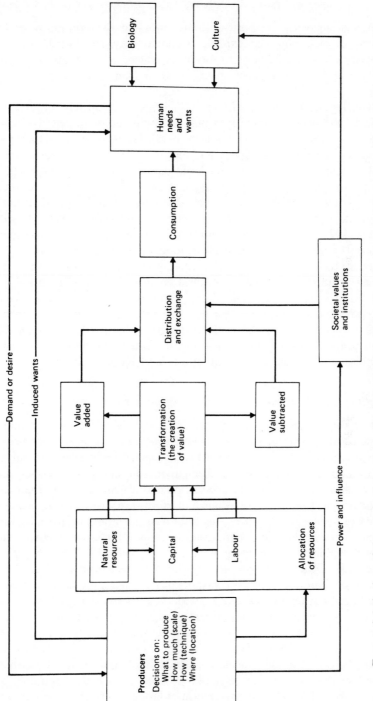

FIGURE 3.4 A view of the production process, broadly defined. [Reproduced, with permission, from Smith (1977 p.49)]

considered along with the positive contributors to the promotion of living standards, or whatever the explicit objective may be. For instance, the productivity effect of additions to means of collective consumption might be depreciated by a negative effect arising from environmental degradation as it affects physical health and mental well-being.

To date, models of industrial location have almost entirely ignored 'value subtracted' in the form of environmental pollution and other negative externalities (Beyers and Krumme, 1974; Murata, 1978). The recognition of this or some similar item as a necessary component of output is in the spirit of recent attempts to question and alter the way in which national accounting is conducted, with GNP reflecting the monetary value of goods and services, while no notice is taken of many environmental and social costs (Mishan, 1967). Proposals to replace GNP by a more general measure of economic or social well-being (e.g. Nordhaus and Tobin, 1972; Samuelson, 1973, pp. 195–7) have important implications for the criteria of performance adopted in models of industrial location. Some extensions of the conventional input–output model and its interregional version have been proposed, building the natural environment onto the usual list of sectors (Isard et al., 1972) and adding non-economic commodities such as respect, power, and even love (Isard et al., 1969). The operational problems involved in loading such models with meaningful empirical data are formidable. But even in their abstract forms they help to draw attention to economic and social interdependencies in space hitherto largely ignored.

Externalities and Distribution in the Space Economy

Most of these interdependencies are dealt with in neo-classical economics under the rubric of externalities. For a long time, unpriced benefits or penalties were regarded as awkward exceptions to the general efficiency and equity of market outcomes, but it is gradually being realized that externalities play a vital part in the general process of the production and distribution. Externalities are almost invariably spatial in both origin and expression, arising from the physical proximity of production facilities, means of transportation, households, and so on. Their importance in the distribution of human life chances is reflected in recent geographical literature (e.g. Cox, 1973; Harvey, 1973; Smith, 1977).

Harvey has drawn attention to the 'hidden mechanisms' which connect resource allocation decisions on transport development, industrial zoning, the location of public facilities, and so on, with their distributional effects upon the 'real income' (or well-being) of different groups in the population. Control of these mechanism enables certain groups in certain places to gain disproportionately from public expenditure. The activities of city governments, using public funds, can generate enormous gratuitous advantages for the owners or occupants of certain sites, just as public services such as education and health underwrite part of the cost of production of labour that otherwise falls on the private employer. If, as Lojkine (1976, p. 34) suggests, capitalist firms locate so as to enable them to reduce *indirect* production costs as much as possible, then explanatory models must clearly incorporate a set of external effects that go well beyond what is still referred to rather vaguely as economics of agglomeration.

The other side of the externality issue is the negative effect of industrial operations. Items of value subtracted, disutilities or negative externalities must be measured in some way to permit the building of models which capture the total impact of an industrial plant. In some cases, such as air pollution, this may not be very difficult, particularly if a fairly regular distance–decay function can be identified. In this connection, it may be helpful to see the consumption of disutility as analogous to the demand for 'goods' as modelled in location theory. Figure 3.5 sketches out how this might be done. Just as Lösch (1954) suggested a 'demand cone' representing the volume of sales that could be anticipated from a given production point, so it is possible to postulate a utility or a disutility cone. The level of a disutility such as noise or particulate matter in the air falls away with distance from its source, to cease at the limit of the 'disutility field' (Harrop, 1973) by comparison with market area. Given information on population density, the total volume of the cone (the value subtracted) could be estimated.

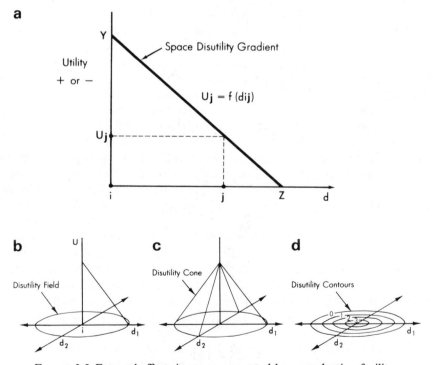

FIGURE 3.5 External effects in space, generated by a production facility.
[Reproduced, with permission, from Smith (1977)]

Changing the location could alter this figure, and hence the 'viability' of the plant in terms of its general economic, social, and environmental performance.

Only recently has the problem of integrating externalities into general spatial models been given any attention. Jackman (1975) has examined some of the implications for the Lösch model: if an externality cost is added to the conventional production and transportation costs, this can affect the optimal scale of operations and hence the size of the hexagonal market areas. But the precise impact depends crucially on how local levels of externalities are measured, which is in turn related to assumptions concerning the marginal disutility of (for example) polluted air for different groups in the population. While conventional equilibrium models are capable of accommodating additional variables such as pollution within their formal structure, the conclusions derived may appear perverse at times. For example, it is possible to argue that polluting plants should concentrate where marginal disutility is lowest, but this could mean further deterioration of already poor environments where people's perception of the pollution problem is low simply because they are accustomed to breathing foul air. Such analyses founder on the ethics of interpersonal utility comparisons, which have rendered much of welfare economics devoid of empirical relevance.

The measurement of actual disutilities must be made on some uniform scientific scale, before ethical judgements are made as to whether different people suffer differently from the same objective level of nuisance. A topical if not strictly 'industrial' example of negative externalities capable of fairly precise measurement is aircraft noise. An international airport probably has a greater capacity to generate nuisance (along with its benefits) than any other facility. The disutility field can be identified by noise contours, just as in Figure 3.5d: examples can be found in Stevenson (1972) and Smith (1977, p. 334). The general impact of a major airport is indicated by estimates from Stevenson (1972, pp. 214–7): for Chicago's O'Hare Field in 1975, 432,000 people, 142 schools, and 6 hospitals subject to 'objectionable' noise: for New York's Kennedy Airport a comparable population figure is 1.7 million. The degree of annoyance caused will vary with the location of the facility and is measured by the Noise and Number Index (NNI) which takes into account the peak noise level of individual aircraft and the total number of aircraft movements (above $NNI = 35$, some nuisance is generally acknowledged). Estimates from the Roskill Commission Report on the siting of a new airport for London showed 94,200 people within the 35 NNI contour for the Nuthampstead site compared with 28,400 for Cublington, 33,900 for Foulness and Luton, and 25,200 for Thurleigh (Lichfield, 1971, p. 165). Who *should* suffer this nuisance or bear the cost is an important question of distributive justice, which will be considered later.

At this point it is worth examining the distinction between 'industrial' plants and other production facilities. This is often rather artificial even in a conventional framework: how should the construction 'industry' be classified, and how should the manufacturing and service functions of the same firm be separated? But in the broader view of production it becomes largely irrelevant. All facilities have a capacity to generate both sources of satisfaction (value added) and sources of dissatisfaction (value subtracted—whether they are factories, mines, hospitals, or social clubs. Their overall contribution is some function of both the goods and the bads that they generate. The fact that one may produce pig iron and smoke by processing natural resources while another produces *bonhomie* and noise through inputs of alcohol and music may be less important than their similarity as facilities differentially distributing benefits and costs. As the category 'industrial' becomes less helpful, so the modelling of *industrial* location might be better subsumed under more general attempts to model spatial *production* systems in the broad sense of the concept of production advocated here.

The argument, then, is for models that can capture a much wider range of the benefits and costs generated by a facility. But this type of modelling does not necessarily mean the abandonment of all our traditional devices; far from it. The general input–output framework has the capacity to incorporate non-industrial relationships in the generation of human well-being or ill-being, as Isard *et al.* (1969) and Drewnowski (1974) show, if these can be identified empirically. The simple model of the location of a single unit of production introduced already (Figure 3.1) survives virtually intact, if costs and revenues can be redefined in broad social terms. In Figure 3.6, the optimum location for a single unit of

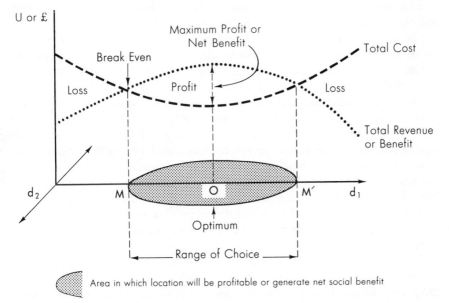

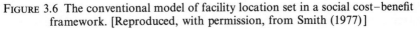

Area in which location will be profitable or generate net social benefit

FIGURE 3.6 The conventional model of facility location set in a social cost–benefit framework. [Reproduced, with permission, from Smith (1977)]

production (O) now identifies the point at which net social benefit is maximized. The spatial margins show limits to the area within which total benefits exceed total costs; beyond the margin the net contribution of the facility is negative.

A weakness of this model is its concern with *total* net benefit (or cost) as a dependent variable of the location decision. But performance cannot be adequately judged by such aggregated data alone: distribution must also be considered. Just as such economic indicators as GNP or income per capita are of very limited use as measures of social progress in the absence of distributional impact (e.g. the Gini coefficient), so are figures for more broadly defined benefits if who actually enjoys them is ignored. The question of who gets what where is crucial (Smith, 1974, 1977). The distributional outcome should be an essential feature of all general location models. This is reflected in the broad view of the production process given in Figure 3.4, where both 'value added' and 'value subtracted' enter a box labelled distribution and exchange: how distribution is accomplished depends on societal values and institutions. Thus if a 'society' (or those who control it) believe in the private ownership of land and capital, a substantial part of the 'value added' will flow to landowners and capitalists as rent and dividends. If there are no adequate arrangements to protect people from environmental pollution and the more degrading accompaniments of wage labour, these aspects of 'value subtracted' will be distributed disproportionately to those sections of the population which are too poor or powerless to avoid them. Again, these models of industrial location and of the space economy in general are incomplete if they ignore the distribution of outputs among individuals, classes, and places, and the processes that govern it.

The problem of airport noise mentioned already typifies a wide range of distributional issues concerned with facility location. While the aggregate net benefit generated may be substantial, there may be very little coincidence between those individuals or groups who gain and those who pay part of the price in the form of nuisance. There is thus a question of equity involved. Market pricing provides no mechanism for gainers directly to compensate losers, and it is doubtful whether less direct transfers such as rates rebates and grants towards double glazing are adequate to redress the situation. The losers will be identified only if the distributive impact is an integral part of facility location models. This applies under both capitalism and socialism, for differential spatial impact is an inevitable physical condition arising from the application of a particular technology. Who suffers *where* is socially determined as the location decision is made. The distributional impact of facility location is explored in greater detail in Smith (1977).

The application of such models depends critically on the prevailing socio-economic structure, of course. Under capitalism, the function of the private production facility is to make profits, and the capacity of planners to impose a locational optimality criterion relating to net social benefit is clearly limited. In a mixed economy, an overall spatial cost–benefit analysis is conceivable for public facility location decisions (as in the case of the proposed third London airport), though whether final decisions are made with such rational deliberation is another question. In a centrally planned economy there may be more scope for this approach. However, even with distributional impact built on, the kind of models illustrated in Figures 3.5 and 3.6 suffer from the traditional limitation of relating to a single facility in isolation. They do not readily adapt to the multi-plant firm under capitalism or to the highly integrated view of the space economy required for effective central planning. For this, still broader models are required.

Production Complex Analysis

Weber's model of industrial location was developed in a specific economic–historical context. Just as his emphasis on transportation costs reflected prevailing technological conditions, so his preoccupation with the viability of the individual (capitalist) enterprise in isolation reflected the prevailing mode of production and social formation. Single-facility models derived from Weber's original formulation are capable of extension to accommodate some social/environmental impacts of current concern. But focus on the isolated plant is ill-suited to the growing organizational complexity of a modern space economy, capitalist or socialist, in which the economic interdependence of production units is of paramount importance.

The most obvious attempt to broaden the economic scope of traditional industrial location models is to be found in industrial-complex analysis. First introduced by Isard and his associates (e.g. Isard, 1960, pp. 375–412) this approach combines comparative–cost analysis after the fashion of the generalized Weber model with input–output economics, to accommodate interdependencies within a planned multi-plant complex. With given resources, technology, and markets, an optimal (profit-maximizing or cost-minimizing) complex of integrated facilities can be designed.

An elaboration of this concept—the territorial-production complex (TPC)—is a focus of much contemporary research on optimizing the spatial organization of economic activity in the U.S.S.R. (Bandman, 1976; Granberg, 1976), in line with the recent Soviet adoption of input–output and programming techniques in planning. The idea of the TPC in the U.S.S.R. goes well beyond the original industrial-complex analysis in two important respects. First, it is much broader in spatial scale, embracing the entire spectrum from local relationships among productive facilities to interregional linkages within the national economic structure. Second, the objective function to be maximized in the planning version of the model relates to the standard of living of the people and not merely to the pecuniary advantage of the private (or public) industrial concern involved.

The recognition of territorial-production complexes is a major advance on the traditional theoretical approach with its focus on single-plant models. Of particular importance is the portrayal of a space economy as an intricate system of diverse activities linked by various input–output relations, stressing the interdependence of the component parts. The TPC has enormous potential benefits for a society able to plan its economy in this manner.

But even here there is a danger of overlooking important 'non-economic' interdependencies. Preoccupation with the technical production structure of a complex may divert attention from some of the human consequences of its operation. The planning objective of maximizing standards of living implies a social welfare function in which a desired consumption structure is fully defined. But we have little theoretical or practical guidance on the appropriate form of such a function. Should it include merely the material output of factories, should it also embrace the provision of services, and should it be extended to incorporate the negative side-effects of the production process? Clearly, the broader the concept the better, otherwise important components of living standards will be overlooked. An elegant mathematical resolution of the design of a territorial-production complex is of little value if what is maximized fails to satisfy basic human needs. Whatever the rhetoric of socialist planning, consumption now serves a wider purpose than simply the reproduction of the labour force. The 'objective laws' that determine the appropriate level of provision of the various contributions to living standards under socialism seem almost as elusive as a real social welfare function under capitalism, if recent Soviet writing is any guide (e.g. Buzlyakov, 1973; Nekrasov, 1974; see also Pahl, 1977).

An immediate priority is therefore the clarification of concepts such as standard of living and quality of life (Smith, 1977). This has been a focus of recent research on social indicators in the U.S.A. and other Western countries, where attempts have been made to measure quality of life as a complex multivariate condition. But measurement is no substitute for attainment. And to achieve societal goals relating to a broad concept of life quality requires the planning of industrial development in close association with other aspects of human activity. Even then one is left with the problems of how differing and conflicting preferences can be adequately met in such a system, and of how far the quality of life is really subject to positivist scientific analysis and planning.

CONCLUSION

This chapter has done no more than offer tentative suggestions as to how the modelling of industrial location might be better attuned to contemporary realities and needs. To see the location of industry in its proper perspective requires a broad view of the production process that stresses the satisfaction of human needs in a broad societal context and recognizes the distribution of those things on which human well-being or ill-being depends as a necessary part of the performance criteria. In particular, the impact of externalities must somehow be accounted for, along with the more conventional conception of output. While some traditional models (including that of Weber) remain helpful for the solution of specific practical problems, the development of more general spatial models of the entire production–distribution–consumption process seems now to be a more constructive route to take. To focus attention on individual components of this process, thus missing its essential unity, is a classic case of failing to see the wood for the trees.

Chapter 4

A Critical Evaluation of Industrial-Location Theory*

DOREEN MASSEY

INTRODUCTION: NATURE OF THE CRITIQUE

In attempting a critique of a discipline, the fundamental problem always arises that the very concept and definition of disciplines are themselves functions of a particular ideology and epistemology. From the viewpoint of this critique, the separate existence of an entity called 'industrial-location theory' is itself open to question. In different ways, many of the classical theories of industrial location have proceeded as though the object of study were an abstract firm—that is, one without effective structural relationships with the rest of the economy. The specific problem of idealized abstraction will be dealt with later. The immediate question is the connected one of the presumed separation of spatial behaviour from the economic system as a whole. In fact, of course, the two are intimately related at all levels. In the first place it is rarely valid to posit a complete distinction between the specifically locational decision of the firm (if, indeed, there is such a thing) and all its other economic decisions. Secondly, the nature of a firm's behaviour will be influenced by its position within the total economic structure. And thirdly, at a more aggregate level, the spatial shape of the economy is the result not only of specifically spatial forces but also of the non-spatial dynamic of the economic system having a spatial manifestation.

It is, then, impossible realistically to treat 'the spatial' as a closed system. Certainly industrial-location theory does not have a genuinely separable object of its own, and in that sense there could never be an *autonomous* theory of industrial location. Not all the work considered here contradicts this view, but the point needs to be borne in mind throughout the following discussion since many elements of the critique spring directly from it. Nonetheless, there *is* a body of knowledge called industrial-location theory, and the spatial expression of the economic system—and the feedback effects of spatial differentiation on that system—do have to be analysed. Given that, it is important to evaluate the approaches so far adopted for this analysis.

Most industrial-location theory is, in fact, closely related to 'economics', but in the sense that it derives very directly from neo-classical marginalist economic theory, sharing its ideology and its epistemological approach. This relationship has influenced the definition of the object for study, the methodology, and the main elements of historical development.

*This chapter is a heavily-revised version of a paper published originally in *Antipode*, Dec. 1973.

The threads of industrial-location theory examined in this chapter fall under four major headings. First is a line of development, derived from the initial work of Weber (1909), which centres on the location decision of the individual firm in a known locational environment, with no interdependence with the locational decisions of other firms. In contrast, the second group of theoretical studies, most of which sprang from an original article by Hotelling (1929), focuses primarily on small numbers of firms in locationally interdependent situations. Third, a more behavioural approach to industrial location has recently developed, in response both to changing real conditions and to contradictions in previous approaches. The fourth theoretical approach to be discussed here is that of Lösch (1954): although it started from an analysis of the individual firm, it differed in that the prime concern was to examine potential whole economic landscapes, an attempt essentially to parallel in spatial terms the economic concept of general equilibrium.

Three levels of critique are presented. At the first, and lowest, level there are those technical deficiencies which have provided the stimulus for the development of existing theory, either pursuit of particular strands or the establishment of new approaches. At the second level, there are more major problems of internal inconsistency which, not insignificantly, have generally remained unresolved—indeed largely ignored—skeletons in the theoretical cupboard. Finally, over and above all these problems, is a more fundamental epistemological critique. The following discussion implies that few problems at the first two of these levels (if the implications of these problems are correctly recognized) can be solved without attention to the third one. Moreover, few of the contemporary demands for 'relevance' can really be met without a more radical reformulation of the fundamental approach to industrial location than has yet been proposed. Yet the author is also aware that the arguments here constitute neither a fully elaborated critique nor a fully worked-out constructive alternative (see, however, Massey (forthcoming) and Massey and Meegan (1978)).

SOME FUNDAMENTAL CHARACTERISTICS AND PROBLEMS

One of the main threads of argument in this evaluation is that the most important problems of industrial-location theory exist at an epistemological level. Although separate strands of development certainly do exist, the theory as a whole lies firmly within one major, overall 'paradigm'. None of the changes in direction in the historical evolution of industrial location theory has produced a reformulation at such a basic level. The most fundamental features of the epistemology within which industrial-location theory has so far existed comprise the need to commence from building abstract models of individual firms and of their locational behaviour: this is at the root of many of the present problems in industrial-location theory. However, the criticism is *not* that the focus of theoretical attention is on the individual firm as the object to be explained, nor that it is directed at the particular content of the various assumptions that have been made about the salient features of individual firms. What *is* at issue is the fundamental methodology that has restricted the level of attempted explanation to that of the individual firm.

The basic building-block of all the threads of industrial-location theory discussed here is an idealistic, abstract model of the individual firm, a model constructed to represent either all, or a specified subset, of actual firms. Such models are built using the abstract methods of neo-classical economics, on which much critical attention has been focused. Thus Dobb (1940) debates the issue in some depth:

> Once the formal question of internal consistency is settled, the acceptance or rejection of a theory depends on one's view of the appropriateness of the particular abstraction on which the theory is based.

He then discusses two approaches:

> In the first place, one may build one's abstraction on the exclusion of certain features which are present in any actual situation, either because they are the more variable or because they are quantitatively of lesser importance in determining the course of events.

Such abstraction he sees as a necessary and justifiable structural simplification of a reality. Secondly, however,

> One may base one's abstraction . . . simply on the formal procedure of combining the properties common to a heterogeneous assortment of situations and building abstraction out of analogy.

Dobb points out that the first method abstraction is employed by neo-classical economics, and it is clearly this approach which has been directly adopted in those streams of industrial-location theory usually called 'classical', based, for instance, on the work of Weber and Lösch. Yet with its resultant idealistic models, this method of abstraction is also shared by more recent theoretical offshoots, including the behavioural school.

Here an attempt is made to distil common factors from heterogeneous real phenomena, and then use these to develop a formal model representing the 'essential firm', abstracted from the particularities of history—and of geography. Several problems arise when such models are used in empirical investigations: they cannot of course adequately represent 'real firms' since any actual firm will differ in details in its characteristics and behaviour, from the archetypal model. Questions then arise about ways of handling this divergence and of applying theory to empirical reality. As the central theoretical tool available is essentially descriptive (derived simply by the distillation of common factors), the model can only be set up against the real firm which is the object of study and permitted to account for what it can of that firm's behaviour, leaving any variation from the model to be attributed to 'additional factors'.

Such methodology seems wrong for three reasons. First, it is inconsistent epistemologically in the relationship between theory and reality, the behaviour of any real firm being split into two parts—the essential core (the abstract model) and deviations from that essential behaviour (specified in the individual case). In its relation to the reality to which it is applied, the model is thus pre-specified *a priori*, and the additional factors are derived by simple description. Second, as Dobb (1940) notes, because the model does not consist of a structural abstraction of the real phenomenon to be explained but rather a collection of characteristics common to several such phenomena, it may account for only a small part of the mechanisms at work in any particular situation. This may obscure the real structure and dynamic of a phenomenon, relegating some mechanisms to the status of 'additional factors'. For example, industrial-location theorists talk of producers and consumers, ahistorical characterizations which say nothing about the particular form of, and relationship between, 'production' and 'consumption' at any point in time. What, of course, is actually embodied in the models is a description of a specifically *capitalist* form of production and consumption which determines the structure and dynamic of the real situation being studied. Taking these two criticisms together, however, a third and more fundamental point emerges. Not only is behaviour split methodologically into two, none of it *explained*: the 'core' (or ideal) is given, as an abstract *a priori* model; the other characteristics of behaviour are 'additional factors', inexplicable because they are simply brought on to the stage as required in any specific empirical case.

The variety of entrepreneurial behaviour 'explicable' only by 'additional factors' may occur both between individual firms in any economy at a given historical stage and between firms existing in different historical periods. The lack of explanation is perhaps easiest to see in the latter case. Thus in location theory, as in neo-classical economics, idealistic models exist to represent both perfectly competitive profit maximizers and companies with a degree of oligopolistic control. In applying either model to reality the characteristics which they represent are assumed to be given. The dynamic of the system within which they exist is ignored. Although both perfectly competitive and monopolistic situations are studied, they are analysed as separate situations which might obtain in different places, perhaps, or in different sectors of the economy. Relationships between the two, particularly the development of one from the conditions of the other, are neglected. Internal contradictions and the dynamics of development are not apparent.

Yet there is contradiction even here in the pretension to trans-historical distillation and the firm's roots in the contemporary economic system. This contradiction arises not because the *particular* abstractions of location theory (neo-classical economics) are incorrect, but because the whole *concept* of an ahistorical formal model of human behaviour is a misapprehension. Forms of behaviour are themselves produced, not given. They result from particular historical conditions and from position within the total system at any point in time. Different forms of economic system, and different structural positions within any one such system, will produce different forms of behaviour. The critique is not simply, therefore, either that 'economic man', for instance, is an empirically inadequate abstraction, or that there should simply be a change from analysis at the level of the individual firm to analysis at the level of 'the system'. The critique is rather that, instead of striving towards an abstract model of behaviour from which historical and individual variation has been removed, the attempt should be always to analyse behaviour *in* its real historical context. Only thus can behaviour in all its variant forms actually be explained. Concepts of economic man, and the 'theories of the firm' discussed here, fail to do this because the starting point for their analysis is an ahistorical, self-constitutive subject. The approach should be to define the structure of an actual situation in time and space, rather than abstracting from time and space to some quintessential core of similarity.

THE DEVELOPMENT OF MAJOR LINES OF APPROACH IN INDUSTRIAL-LOCATION THEORY

The whole of the existing body of theory is confined within the same epistemological approach, and this creates fundamental problems. Industrial-location theory has not followed one continuous stream of development, rather there have been definite stages and threads in its growth. It is interesting to note the different levels at which criticism, and response to criticism, may occur. This critique attempts to make fundamental points about the nature of the approach as a whole, but when viewed, as it were, from within the ideology, the inadequacies are likely to be interpreted differently. Either they will produce minor modifications and sophistications to the given theory as often as not leading to a cul-de-sac of complexity, or they will stimulate a new line of thought though not one which breaks out of the fundamental framework.

The generally accepted founding father of industrial-location theory was Weber (1909). His analysis was of single firms, and was confined to minimizing costs, in the general case specifically transport costs. The *a priori* model was of a single-plant firm in a perfect market, a firm able to react optimally to locational factors, and with the aim of cost minimization. Weber himself did not formulate the problem in the framework of economic theory, but instead saw it in terms of a physical analogy as a problem of the resolution of various 'location pulls' or 'forces'. Later developments, however, through Isard (1956) and Moses (1958) have shown how Weberian concepts can be incorporated within the existing marginalist substitution analysis.

At the 'lowest' level of critique, this analysis was judged far too simple, both in the number and complexity of factors which might operate as forces on the location of a plant, and in that too many relationships or states (production coefficients, for instance, and size of output) were taken to be fixed. These criticisms led to further development within this line of theory. Hoover (1937) and Smith (1966) introduced new factors, made some implications explicit and transformed locational 'forces' into cost (and revenue) surfaces. Predöhl introduced methods of substitution analysis into the Weberian approach, and this was further elaborated by Isard (1956) who, however, kept 'transport inputs' as separate identifiable entities, thus limiting the dimensions of possible substitution. With Moses' (1958) article, this branch of location theory was fully integrated into marginalist economics. Such a direction of development thus involved a process of increasing sophistication and detail. Moses in some senses represents the end of the line, for although he did introduce new conceptual approaches from Isard, and his attack, therefore, was very much a reformulation of the problem, nonetheless his results, showing the total (marginal) interdependence of the system and the requirement of locational adjustment for every change in any other variable, do not provide either a basis for operational application or a framework for understanding the forces at work in shaping the space-economy. Attempts have been made, such as with Rawstron's (1958) spatial margins, to extract a simplified structure from this approach (see also Smith, 1966). As Bater and Walker (1970) point out, however, this approach is subject to many of the same drawbacks as the optimizing version, including variation between firms and the consequent problems both of aggregation and of generalization, difficulties which stem in turn from retaining as the central theoretical aim the construction of an abstract model of the individual firm.

It was two other, interrelated, criticisms of Weber which led to the development of new strands within the overall context of location theory. They were indeed much more fundamental criticisms, but were treated so that they did not break out of the existing methodological framework. First, Weber assumed perfect competition, which is at variance with the inclusion of the spatial dimension: there cannot be perfect competition over space. The implications are important and affect the extent to which location theory can play the same sustaining role as economics. Yet the recognition of the inconsistency of Weber's assumptions neither jolted the development of location theory as it might have done nor have any significant feedback effect on a-spatial economics. Because of the monopolistic element introduced into markets by space the policies of firms are interdependent, and an oligopolistic situation prevails. Locational interdependence became the next area for research and the limitations of that approach are examined below. Second, the realization of the need to relax the assumption of 'economic man' was again a recognition of a genuine inadequacy. However, the alternative approaches which have most commonly been sought reveal a misapprehension of the reasons why an assumption of 'economic man' is incorrect.

The interdependence of producers is in part a result of the existence of a monopolistic element in their competition. There are two distinct ways such an element of monopoly may enter a spatial economy. The first is a function of distance itself, the second is the normal a-spatial concept of monopoly as the concentration of capital into a few hands. The development of the branch of industrial-location theory which concentrates on locational interdependence was probably to some degree a reaction to both, but certainly much of its stimulus came from the theories of imperfect competition developing in a-spatial economics. And this development in economics was in turn a response to changing real conditions. But although much of the development of theories of locational interdependence was undoubtedly thus an indirect result of the actual monopolization of capital, with a-spatial economics providing many of the tools of the trade, the resultant theory has focused almost exclusively on certain aspects of that element of monopoly which is solely the result of distance. In fact, relatively little explicit attention has been paid in location theory (as opposed to empirical analysis) to the actual monopolization of capital.

Moreover, even examination of the effect of the element of monopoly conferred by distance has been fairly restricted. The main emphasis has been on individual locational-interdependence situations, examined either through market-area analysis (e.g. Fetter, 1924; Hyson and Hyson, 1950) or through an approach more allied to game theory (see, for instance, Hotelling, 1929; Stevens, 1961). These investigations have produced some interesting results, but the restriction to this level of analysis has prevented the real inferences being drawn and also affected the tenability of Pareto optimal equilibrium solutions. Furthermore, even within situations analysed, the actual results in terms of location decisions are usually indeterminate, both in some specific individual circumstances and as a general characteristic of this class of problems. This point is well made by Chisholm (1971), and is again essentially a result of the monopolistic character of the situation. For while market mechanisms are the controlling force in perfect competition, in conditions of imperfect competition it becomes possible for the actors to influence the environment. 'Strategies' become important. Given those, the result of any specified game situation may be predictable, but the problem is now that the choice of strategies at this micro-level is indeterminate. Increasing complexity of this approach as an analytical tool again led to a cul-de-sac: once more, the focus on the individual firm as the locus of explanation prevented any real theoretical advance being made.

The 'behavioural approach' to industrial-location theory is for two reasons of particular importance, and must be treated in some detail. Firstly, this approach represents the most recent direction of development within industrial-location theory, and it has attracted much attention and support (see, for instance, the wide-ranging collection in Hamilton, 1974c). But secondly, this approach, the attention it has attracted and the problems it is now facing, demonstrates well the failure to solve the fundamental problems which stimulated its development. Like other 'new approaches', behaviouralism has responded to the symptoms of these problems rather than to the problems themselves.

The behavioural approach developed as the culmination of a number of tendencies. It resulted from consideration of the effects of space: empirically, assumptions of perfect knowledge are obviously unrealistic as soon as concepts of distance are introduced; theoretically, in a spatial context firms are necessarily locationally interdependent, and analysis of their behavioural strategies thus becomes important. Perhaps more significantly, though, the development of the behavioural school was, even more than that of interdependence theory, a reaction to changing material conditions, that is to the increasing concentration of capital which meant that it was no longer possible to assume that behaviour was subject to the external control of the market. For this reason, too, it became necessary to consider the possibility of locational strategies not subject to the automatic determination of a perfectly competitive market.

The development of the behavioural school was, then, not a result simply of a process of intellectual refinement *within theory*. It was also a response to a changing empirical reality, i.e. to the actual situation of increasing differentiation between firms, the spread of large corporations and oligopolistic structures, and the declining influence of the market as a uniquely determining external force. As a descriptive device, the perfect-competition model was becoming increasingly unconvincing.

The fundamental critique of perfect competition (economic man/resource allocation) usually advanced by behaviouralists is that the model, in historical perspective, no longer corresponds to the real world. This is thus a historically specific and entirely empirical criticism, and at the level simply of empirical description it is, of course, correct. However, if that were the limit of the criticism, it would be possible to respond by building a similar model, but this time having the form and the characteristics that match the new reality. Thus the model in the marginalist approach was one of the individual firm as a perfectly competitive, perfectly informed, profit-maximizing unit. The behavioural school has sought to replace this with models of the firm as a complex organizational structure. Such a new model (or series of models) therefore bears the same relationship to current empirical reality as did the economic-man model to, say, the nineteenth century. It is a temporary correlation. This has two major implications. The first is the obvious criticism that neither theory can theorize the change from one-model-type-which-fits-reality to the next. There are two possible replies to this criticism: (a) that location theorists are quite content with a process of *ad hoc* reaction to a changing reality (i.e. it is not a problem) or (b) that most of the dynamic for the change between the two states (model types) derives from a-spatial forces in the economy (i.e. the solution to the problem lies outside the field of industrial-location theory). Assuming that the first response is in principle unacceptable, the implication of the second is that there can never be a closed system called a dynamic theory of industrial location.

The second, and crucial, objection to location theory's temporary adjustment to the environment concerns the way in which behaviour is conceptualized. The behavioural school limits itself to criticizing the *content* of the assumptions of the old model. Its positive response has taken a variety of forms, which can be characterized along an axis of which the two poles are purely descriptive behaviouralism, and the theory of the firm. In practice, these two approaches are not often separable; they represent possibly conflicting tendencies. Their existence signals an emerging central tension in industrial-location studies, between the evident need to deal with considerable variety, and the desire to have one central theoretical structure. At one extreme, descriptive behaviouralism is a simple recognition of variety and will not *of itself* produce a new theoretical formulation. At the other extreme, however, the attempt to develop the theory of *the* firm is just as much a misapprehension of the problem—insofar, that is, as it is an attempt simply to replace one abstract formalism with another. Differences in behaviour are both recognized as being significant and yet still handled as deviations from an ideal-type. The problem may be simply indicated by asking: how many model-types the behaviourists should construct, to represent adequately the rich variety they have so correctly recognized in the real world? Moreover, the same applies to this dimension of variety as to that of historical change; by building models one will simply register the existence of variation, not explain it. No ideal-type models such as these, posed at the level at which diversity occurs, can hope to account for that same variety. The critique that should have been made of the marginalist approach was that it even attempted to produce abstract formal models of behaviour, and that it made these the centre-piece of the theoretical structure.

Finally it is useful to examine the rather different contribution of Lösch (1954), and some of its problems. Lösch was one of the pioneers to attempt to a spatial counterpart to economic general equilibrium. From an initial even distribution of population he derived for each sector a net of hexagonal markets which fulfilled the zero excess-profit conditions. By combining sets of market areas for different goods he produced the well-known sectoral and semi-hierarchical economic landscapes which fulfilled certain welfare criteria, such as maximizing the number of purchases made locally and minimizing the sum of the minimum distances between production sites. The economic system explicitly assumed was one of competing profit-maximizing firms (revenue-maximizing with equal costs) under conditions of free entry, and with f.o.b. pricing. The implication is, therefore, that such a market system can produce the result described.

The ability of the decentralized price mechanism to sustain a general equilibrium solution and the conformity of the latter with the marginal conditions of Pareto optimality has always been a major weapon in a-spatial economics' armoury of apologetics. The purpose is to prove that a completely decentralized (perfectly competitive) price mechanism will produce an allocation which is optimal or, as Bramhall (1969) says, is 'an affirmation of the existence of internal control mechanisms in the social order'.

Even in a-spatial economics the assumptions necessary for the derivation of general equilibrium have reached heroic proportions (e.g. see Graaff, 1957), and the implications of the theory of second best and of Arrow's theorem are far-reaching (see Hunt, 1972). Nonetheless, introduction of the spatial dimension is critical. Indeed the 'abstraction' of much of theoretical economics that life takes place on the head of a pin should be regarded as one of its least convincing assumptions. Some other assumptions, already dubious in a-spatial economics, become even less tenable when space is introduced. Thus the whole set of assumptions about economic rationality and perfect knowledge become impossible to maintain over distance, even ignoring, as economic theory traditionally does, any institutional constraints. Even within one city, jobs in the suburbs go unfilled while potential employees remain out of work in the city centre. Similarly, locational inertia prevents the adjustments which 'ideally' are necessary responses to changes in other variables (and the number of variables to which locational adjustments might be required, even within the context of a single plant, is indicated in Moses' (1958) analysis).

Nonetheless, such objections in fact ask only for 'realism'. Within the context of the given location theory, they are not theoretical arguments, in that they do not prove any logical impossibility in attaining through the market a spatial equilibrium satisfying certain welfare criteria, except, of course, that to overcome them it is necessary to assume that (continuous) space has no effect. It would still be possible to argue that the market would produce the desired result if only it were allowed to operate 'perfectly'. However, serious *theoretical* problems are caused by the consideration of space.

Consider first the specific system designed by Lösch, where under a given set of assumptions, profit-maximizing firms arrived at an equilibrium satisfying some sort of welfare criteria. (These criteria are anyway not those of Pareto optimality.) Even within this simple framework, Mills and Lav (1964) have pointed out a critical inconsistency. Thus among Lösch's assumptions are the suggestions that firms are profit-maximizers, and that the locations are so numerous that the entire space if filled. Mills and Lav show that these two assumptions are not necessarily consistent, that the second is in fact a theorem which should be examined in relation to the first. They examine it and find that it will not necessarily always hold. In very similar vein, though much more rarely pointed out, is the problem of the arrangement of the final multi-commodity economic landscape. The idea is that the single-commodity sets of hexagonal market areas, having established one point at which they all have a plant, then rotate about this central metropolis until the number of locational coincidences is maximized. Obviously such was not the economic process intended; Lösch was explicitly designing an optimal system with normative implications. But as 'Palander has shown . . . agglomeration economies cannot cause towns to form unless the model postulates some mechanism whereby firms can co-ordinate their choices' (Webber, 1972, p. 27). In other words, although Lösch's system was in some sense normative, it did nonetheless assume that, given the right conditions, the market economy could produce the desired result. These arguments show that even within this very restricted formulation this is not necessarily the case. Both points imply a need for economic mechanisms of control or co-ordination not included within the model. It is often precisely to disprove the need for such mechanisms that equilibrium is cited in a-spatial economics.

In fact the end state produced by the Löschian equilibrium itself does not fulfil even those welfare criteria acceptable to a-spatial neo-classical economics. F.o.b. prices equal average cost and delivered price, therefore, exceeds marginal cost plus transport cost. This is again the result of the monopoly element inherent in any discussion of space in these terms. (F.o.b. pricing is here considered throughout, though a Löschian system can be derived with uniform pricing—e.g. McCrone, 1969—with different distributional implications.) Thus Böventer (1963b, pp. 164–5) writes,

> The main difficulty in locational theory is that in order for a general equilibrium model to have an optimal solution which the market or theoretical solution process necessarily approaches and which fulfils the usual welfare conditions of production, it is necessary to assume linear homogeneous production functions. Indivisibilities and agglomeration economies, which are basic for locational analyses, in particular for urban analysis, cannot be incorporated in such a model. If they are included, the substitution principle, *if it is applied at the margin only*, loses much of its force and becomes useless in finding the optimal spatial structure. For this reason, the marginal principles have to be supplemented by the *total conditions* of equilibrium.

And Richardson (1969, p. 102), writing on a general theory of location, says:

> Thus the dilemma is that it is difficult to formulate a determinate general theory of location without adopting the pedagogic device of the equilibrium concept, yet if this concept is adopted complications arise from the probability that general equilibrium is inconsistent with the implications of the space economy.

THE SPATIAL DIMENSION AND INTERNAL INCONSISTENCIES WITHIN NEO-CLASSICAL ECONOMICS

Some elements of the relationship of industrial-location theory to neo-classical economics emerged in the last section. Industrial-location theory is thus vulnerable to many of the same criticisms that can be made of that subject. For location theory, however, this is only the tip of the iceberg. The discussion of Lösch, for example, showed that his system could not guarantee to produce the equilibrium he described without higher-level control mechanisms: that the aggregation of individual decisions cannot be guaranteed to produce the required welfare solution. Moreover, even if such a solution were to be produced, it would not, without very restrictive assumptions, fulfil Pareto optimality criteria. In both these cases, the introduction of the spatial dimension produces internal inconsistencies within the usual body of neo-classical economic theory.

The purpose of the brief section that follows is to explore this in more structured form and is thus restricted to problems of internal inconsistency within location theory.

The discussion of Moses (1958) demonstrated how the introduction of space enormously complicated the analysis and, because of the difficulty of assuming complete spatial mobility, its applicability. With the introduction of a definitive spatial dimension, in fact, the need becomes apparent for a rigorous but structured form of analysis which does not depend on the 'over-precision' of marginalism. Richardson (1969) examines this point and its relationship to a meaningful concept of spatial general equilibrium.

The spatial dimension complicates the arguments of economics through its introduction of an element of monopoly. Most significantly in the context of this section it has been seen how the apparently comforting welfare conclusions of a-spatial general equilibrium become much less easy to draw. This monopoly element may be illustrated in a variety of ways. The preceding paragraphs focused attention on the existence of interdependence between producers, since that was the one theme taken up by location theory. But there are alternative ways of demonstrating the point which link in with theoretical criticisms already made.

The degree of monopoly conferred by space is particularly important to industrial (as opposed, for instance, to residential) location theory in the control it allows of the area *surrounding* the point of location. Here the intra-sectoral context—the geography of market areas—is most important. The level of analysis may be intra-urban still, or interregional, or international; the point is the same. One condition of perfect competition is that, in equilibrium, consumers will be indifferent between producers because their prices and products are indistinguishable. Such conditions can no longer hold, under normal pricing assumptions, when the economy is distributed over space since distance and concomitant transport costs amount for the consumer to a form of product differentiation. Producers may, therefore, raise prices without losing all their custom, may extract monopoly profits, and may indulge more easily in various forms of price discrimination. Another instance in which the misconceptions of economics become critical when applied to spatial location theory is that of the static and partial nature of the conceptual approach. In a-spatial economics the normal restriction to a static view prevents analysis of the dynamic forces within capitalism.

The restriction is even more crucial in a spatial context because the spatial and a-spatial concentration of capital may be seen as mutually reinforcing mechanisms. The a-spatial concentration of capital itself has spatial effects. Thus Parsons (1972) illustrates empirically the reinforcement of tendencies to spatial agglomeration which may be produced by the increasing dominance of large corporations. Yet space itself may be the active element in the dynamic: in industrial-location theory one of the most important of such 'spatial forces' is agglomeration economies. But these are usually studied within a conceptual structure which causes their full significance to be missed. In most cases the structure is that of partial analysis, with only one or at most an oligopolistically small number of firms being studied. Such is the case with Weberian analysis and most of its derivatives.

The likelihood of individual firms agglomerating is noted but the effects of this on the system of economic activity as a whole are not studied. Lösch, however, does consider location at a more aggregate level and includes the more macro-level effects of (inter-sectoral only) agglomeration economies. Apart from the other problems already mentioned (including that of the means by which numerous private decision-makers can actually take maximum advantage of agglomeration economies), this approach fails—because of its static equilibrium nature—to appreciate the cumulative effects of such economies. It does not even attempt to feed back information to change the initial state assumed at the beginning of the process.

Externalities, as a general category which includes agglomeration economies, are not part of the main stream of very precise mathematical neo-classical economic formulations. But for location theory or spatial economics this cannot be treated merely as some 'aspect' or 'imperfection' which has been ignored. Externalities are, or should be, central to any theory of locational arrangement. Again, the transfer from a-spatial to spatial reinforces the inadequacies of neo-classical economics.

These misconceptions and contradictions have not been totally ignored in industrial-location literature as the contribution of Mills and Lav demonstrates. There are, moreover, several rigorous illustrations of the deficiencies of the decentralized price mechanism in achieving and maintaining a non-trivial equilibrium solution to certain problems in spatial allocation (e.g. see Koopmans and Beckmann, 1957, for the case where profitabilities rely not only on individual location but are interdependent). Again, Beckmann (1972) demonstrates in each typical case of the single firm monopoly/multiple firm monopoly/free entry continuum how the market falls short of welfare maximization. Much of this work is, however, given only peripheral attention. Koopmans and Beckmann initiated a debate (see, for instance, Reiter and Sherman, 1962; Mills, 1970) but few of its central implications for the standard body of location theory are ever fully evaluated or, if quoted at all, are presented as problems requiring modification of the basic theory. In fact, in many cases they constitute elements of a much more fundamental technical critique.

HINTS TOWARDS A POSSIBLE REFORMULATION

None of these developments has overcome the fundamental problems that are clearly recognized as issues within location theory. The first difficulty is the empirical evidence about variations in individual behaviour and the 'aggregation' or 'generalization' problems this has posed. Second, and as another result of the continued commitment to an abstract-model approach, there has been a growing divergence between increasingly high-flown technical/theoretical work and empirical description. So long as 'theory' is conceived of as necessarily abstract and formal in the sense discussed here this divorce will continue, and empirical work will be reduced to empiricism.

One way to solve these dilemmas is to reformulate the method of explanation in industrial-location theory—to interpret behaviour as the product of the overall structure of the system in which the individual firm is set, and of its place within that structure. This links to a further theme which has been underlying much of the evaluation so far—the connection between spatial and non-spatial economic phenomena. Industrial-location theory cannot itself account for spatial behaviour, or for historical changes in such behaviour, because the ultimate causes lie outside the realm of spatial analysis. It is as an aspect of a process geared to production and accumulation that location factors and spatial differentiation are taken into account in company decisions, and from which differential spatial impacts result. And it is in this a-spatial—rather than in the simply spatial—sphere that the primary causal links exist between the wider economy and the individual company.

Some elements of a possible alternative approach must now be obvious. A structural approach is demanded because behaviour must be explained, not assumed, because it cannot be explained at the level at which it occurs, and because historical change and development must be understood together at 'micro'- and 'macro'-levels respectively. These considerations demand a *theorized* relationship between the nature of locational behaviour and the structural context within which that behaviour is produced.

These points are probably better made by illustration rather than by abstract exhortation. A recent research project (see Massey and Meegan, 1978), attempting such a form of explanation took as its empirical focus the spatial implications of the financial restructuring carried out in British electronics and electrical engineering industries in the second half of the 1960s. This financial restructuring (mainly mergers) was itself an effect of the contemporary economic situation in the United Kingdom. The crucial problem was therefore to design a framework for explanation which allowed locational changes to be understood in relation to the general characteristics of the recession. The method adopted was really a disaggregation of the overall question into three discrete steps, much simplified here. These assessed respectively:

(a) the effect of the crisis on them: the particular reason for restructuring;
(b) the nature of the reorganization of the production and labour processes;
(c) the spatial implications of this reorganization.

Several points are relevant to this framework. First the 'spatial dimension' was introduced only in the last step of the causal sequence; spatial change was thus understood predominantly as an effect of the response to non-spatial developments. In that sense, no autonomy was accorded to the spatial dimension. The more general implication is that, when studying locational patterns, behaviour or changes for any period, the essential first step should be to understand the operative structural economic processes which are the underlying causes of spatial phenomena. These processes may, and in fact probably will be nonspatial. Part of the aim of the location theorist should be to analyse these processes so as to distinguish those which are spatially effective or significant.

Second, in this framework there is no attempt to use abstract models of individual firms. There is in that sense no 'application' of a preconceived theory, and consequently no divorce between a formalized and abstract theoretical structure and the description of empirical reality. The form of abstraction used in this approach was of the first type referred to by Dobb—that of isolating the determining structure of the actual situation under study. Only within the context of a severe national economic crisis, and its implications for the production process and consequently for locational requirements, could the spatial behaviour of the individual firms be understood.

Third, this approach also allowed the differences which clearly existed between the locational responses of different firms to be analysed, rather than merely described. Such differences were considered to result from the combination of general national economic effects and characteristics of the recession with the specific characteristics of particular sections of the economy and particular companies. Thus in the first of three groups of cases identified in the research, the crisis took the specific form of over-capacity and the need to cut costs within the production process. But although all the firms in this group were subject to these pressures, and although their general locational responses were similar, the precise locational effects of the mergers varied between individual firms. At an inter-sectoral level, the cost-cutting measures undertaken in the aerospace industry differed from those in power-engineering because of dissimilar production technology. Further, within the single subsector of power-engineering the reorganization of production varied between individual firms. One reason was the contrasting structures of the companies concerned: where power-engineering formed a small percentage of the output of a major multi-product company, the ability to move into more profitable lines of production was an important determinant of the reorganization. Such circumstances can facilitate cuts in capacity and consequently closures. Where power-engineering dominated production, cost cutting to increase competitiveness formed a more important component of the reorganization.

It would be possible to multiply these examples for each case studied. Such differences in behaviour between firms would be hard to explain by looking only at the individual companies. Factors such as company structure (a central feature of the behavioural approach) have been invoked but in the present case, company structure was only a meaningful part of the explanation because it influenced the form of reaction to an already specified set of external pressures. To have grouped the whole sample of cases according to company structure would have yielded no insights at all. The only way to *explain* differences in behaviour thus was to analyse, first, the general economic pressures to which they were all subject and, second, how these overall conditions were differentially articulated in specific situations.

So-called 'structural explanation' is frequently thought of as concentrating its attention entirely at the 'macro-level'. This certainly need not, and should not, be so. The objection to the preoccupation with the individual firm is not that it is a focus for *attention*, but that it is the only locus of *explanation*.

The final point concerns historical specificity. The study referred to concerned the spatial effects of mergers. However, the categorization resulting from the form of explanation adopted (i.e. the three groups of cases) was not based on (a) an abstract catalogue of managerial motives, or (b) formal descriptions of the 'nature' of the mergers (such as whether they were horizontal or vertical), or (c) a simply sectoral distinction. The three groups of cases were defined according to their relation to the economic crisis in Great Britain in the present period, and this was the dominant determinant of their locational behaviour. Historical specificity was thus at the very basis of the structure of explanation.

This does, however, raise the problem as to whether the question asked concerned the spatial effect of mergers or the spatial effect of the mergers carried out in the United Kingdom in the second half of the 1960s. The authors tried to allow for the possible existence of certain 'timeless' effects of mergers by attempting to distinguish between the effects of mergers which resulted from their causes and those effects which resulted in a sense from the merger itself. In the latter category fall phenomena flowing from the simple integration of two organizations such as the rearrangement of control functions and the elimination of duplicated facilities. However, even in those instances where it was possible to make such a distinction empirically, it was found that the actual spatial forms which resulted were themselves largely conditioned by the historically specific reasons for which the merger took place. The only way to explain the effects discovered was to relate them to the wider, and specific, conditions in which the mergers occurred. But most importantly, *any* attempt to answer empirically questions about the spatial effect of mergers *must*, like the present study, be historically specific. This applies to any question about location. It is the search for eternal—and thus philosophically *a priori*—statements about behaviour which has produced the theoretical difficulties and inconsistencies which, it is argued here, constitute a fundamental criticism of industrial-location theory. We cannot, as industrial-location theory persists in trying to do, normalize for history.

Chapter 5

The Impact of Energy on the Regional Economy of Louisiana

Peggy A. Lentz and H. Wade VanLandingham

The energy crisis of the 1970s is not caused by a lack of potential energy resources but rather is the result of a technological milieu dependent on a limited, non-renewable energy base. Although crude oil reserves in the United States have been progressively declining since 1967, public recognition of a problem did not begin until the temporary petroleum shortage in 1973. The severe winter of 1976–77 which resulted in natural gas shortages and concomitant industrial slowdowns and shutdowns also motivated the Federal government to develop a formal national energy policy. The primary federal objective is to change habits in energy usage. Until alternatives such as sea thermal and solar power become economically feasible, industry will continue to depend on coal, petroleum, and natural gas. This, in turn, raises questions about the prospects for underdeveloped areas since the lack of plentiful cheap energy is yet another problem they have to overcome. Ironically, some oil- and gas-exporting areas in the United States are likely to suffer from this additional development problem.

This chapter focuses on Louisiana, which has one of the lowest per capita income levels in the South. This State is a major national supplier of fossil fuels but even so its development has not kept pace with that of the United States as a whole or of the South in particular. The recent decline in its gas and oil reserves, and the current awareness of its vulnerable economic position, has sparked an intense debate (Traigle, 1975). While there is some agreement that the obvious path is to take advantage of the remaining potential benefits of the localized fossil fuels, the choice of development strategy is being argued by growth advocates, environmentalists, and others. Currently, the Federal government, as part of its energy policy, is trying to control all oil and gas reserves: if it succeeds, most of Louisiana's remaining localized advantage in fossil fuels could be negated.

This chapter reviews various aspects of the energy problem and then examines several strategies for State development including those that are of concern to both the traditional growth and the environmental advocates. These scenarios are analysed by means of an input–output model which describes the flows between sectors in terms of energy units (BTUs) and dollars. The most readily available Louisiana data for the input–output matrices pose important problems which are described in the last section of this chapter. While these data problems would be critical if State policy formulation were based on the results discussed here, they are adequate for present purposes of methodology development.

LOUISIANA AS AN ECONOMIC AND ENERGY REGION

A Regional Definition

To the casual observer the State appears to be part of a much larger unit—the Sunbelt States (see Rees, 1978)—but this consists of a set of disparate regions related only by their mild weather and attractive environments. Not only are the swamps of Florida and Louisiana and the deserts of New Mexico and Arizona quite different physical environments, but there are also considerable differences in economic and political structures, urban development, and agriculture. The Gulf Coastal Plain is a logical region within the Sunbelt in which to place Louisiana (Figure 5.1 and Table 5.1) since the components of this area share similar histories, coastal-wetlands development problems, and resources. The area is rather like a doughnut with affluent Florida and Texas (second and first in income, Table 5.1) surrounding Alabama, Mississippi, and Louisiana (ninth, eleventh, and seventh in Table 5.1) which, in terms of income and type of agriculture, would form a coherent subregion for analysis.

This present chapter, however, concentrates on Louisiana as the region of interest because of political constraints and data availability. Regions are useless unless logical. Federal programmes, such as coastal zone management (U.S. Congress, 1972, 1976: Section 305 planning, and Section 306 implementation) and comprehensive planning (U.S. Congress, 1974, 1977: Section 701 comprehensive planning), are aimed at the individual States. By tradition and now by federal money, States are by definition logical regions. As in the case of other contiguous States, Louisiana, Mississippi, and Alabama rarely find it advantageous to associate in their development strategies; they compete for the same limited federal programmes, which do not require or encourage co-operation. Thus the economic data used in this study are limited by the same problems of State, rather than regional, orientation at all levels of government.

Louisiana is actually two regions held together by political glue. Figure 5.1 shows the cultural dividing line between the Catholic South with its French heritage and Protestant North with its Anglo origins. Numerous other criteria can be used to demonstrate the split between North and South Louisiana, such as the wetlands boundary (Figure 5.1), the location of urban population (63.1 per cent of whom live in the 29 southern parishes), and median family income ($U.S. 7077 average for the southern parishes versus $U.S. 5766 for the 35 northern parishes in 1969). This internal division will be taken into account in the development scenarios proposed for the State in the following analyses.

Energy Resources and Problems

The Louisiana economy has been twice blessed in energy supplies. Like the other Gulf Coast States, this State has large known reserves of fossil energy and

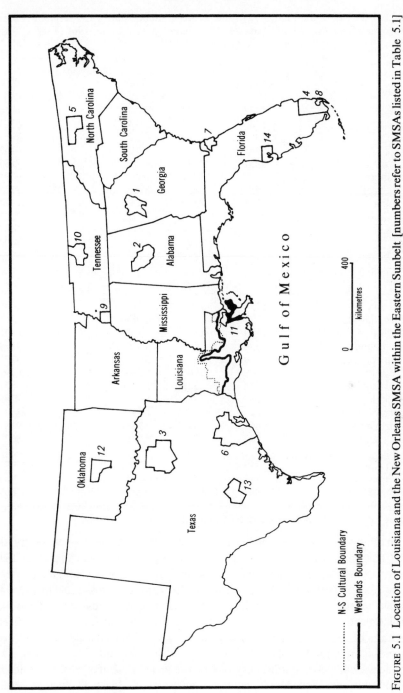

FIGURE 5.1 Location of Louisiana and the New Orleans SMSA within the Eastern Sunbelt [numbers refer to SMSAs listed in Table 5.1]

TABLE 5.1 Population and income for the Eastern Sunbelt States and largest Standard Metropolitan Statistical Areas. [Sources: *U.S. Bureau of the Census*, 1961 (Tables 33 and 36) and 1972 (Tables 2, 13, 57, and 89)]

State	Population (000) 1960	1970	Median family income ($U.S.) 1960	1970
Alabama	3267	3444	3937	7266
Arkansas	1786	1923	3184	6273
Florida	4952	6789	4722	8267
Georgia	3943	4590	4208	8167
Louisiana	3257	3641	4272	7530
Mississippi	2178	2217	2884	6071
North Carolina	4556	5082	3956	7725
Oklahoma	2328	2559	4620	7774
South Carolina	2383	2590	3821	7621
Tennessee	3567	3924	3949	7447
Texas	9580	11,197	4884	8490
United States	180,671	204,879	5488	9256
SMSA				
1. Atlanta	1017	1390	5758	10,695
2. Birmingham	721	739	5103	8295
3. Dallas	1119	1556	5925	10,405
4. Ft. Lauderdale	334	620	4996	9539
5. Winston Salem	520	604	5417	9291
6. Houston	1418	1985	6040	10,191
7. Jacksonville	455	529	5345	8671
8. Miami	935	1268	5348	9245
9. Memphis	675	770	4903	8542
10. Nashville	464	541	5332	9187
11. New Orleans	907	1046	5195	8670
12. Oklahoma City	512	641	5740	9345
13. San Antonio	716	864	4766	7981
14. Tampa	772	1013	4490	7883
All SMSAs[a]	116,969	139,418	5928	10,469

[a] There were 212 SMSAs in 1960 and 243 SMSAs in 1970.

also an abundance of renewable (or natural) energy resources. Concurrently, the Gulf Coast is in an enviable position of having known reserves greater than present needs but, less desirably, it is also the region most dependent upon natural gas and petroleum. Table 5.2 shows 1970 and 1975 fossil fuel production by State in the Eastern Sunbelt: the Atlantic Coast States had little or no recorded production and the main sources were Texas and Louisiana. Whereas two-thirds of the United States' energy needs are supplied by gas and oil, these sources account for four-fifths of the demand in the Gulf Coast States. This dependence has become a liability due to the growing shortage of gas and oil.

Given national and local demand continuing at least at current levels,

TABLE 5.2 Eastern Sunbelt fossil fuel production by State (on and off shore)[a]. [Source: Lange, 1977, pp. 112 and 118]

State and year	Crude oil and lease condensate		Natural gas	
	barrels per day[b] (000)	per cent of U.S. total	cubic feet per day (million)	per cent of U.S. total
Alabama				
1970	20	0.2		
1975	37	0.4		
Arkansas				
1970	49	0.5	497	0.8
1975	45	0.5	318	0.6
Louisiana				
1970	2485	25.8	21,338	35.5
1975	1796	21.5	19,426	35.3
Mississippi				
1970	178	1.8	345	0.6
1975	127	1.5	204	0.4
Oklahoma				
1970	613	6.4	4370	7.3
1975	447	5.3	4398	8.0
Texas				
1970	3424	35.5	22,898	38.1
1975	3347	40.0	20,509	37.2

[a] Separate production amounts were not recorded for Florida, Georgia, North Carolina, South Carolina, or Tennessee.
[b] A barrel is equivalent to 159 litres.

Louisiana now faces the reality of its fossil energy reserves being completely exhausted by the year 2000. Production of gas and oil peaked in 1971 (Table 5.3) and it is estimated that output will decline at a rate between seven and ten per cent from 1976 through 1980 (Beard and Scott, 1975, p. 2). Revenues continued to rise until 1976 (due to an increase in severance tax rates in 1973), but the diminishing supplies of cheap, plentiful fossil energy and the declining revenue derived from this source will have important impacts on both private and public sectors of the State economy.

Louisiana has a poorly developed regional economy. In some ways the State is similar to many South American or African nations in which a highly capital-intensive, extractive sector has been superimposed on a traditional rural economy; this presents it with both advantages and problems.

Labour is plentiful and relatively cheap but much of it is unskilled and rurally located. Further, while a large amount of land, mineral, and renewable resources

TABLE 5.3 Louisiana's fossil fuel production (on and off shore) and associated severance taxes [Sources: [1] Lange, 1977, p. 112. [2] Lange, 1977, p. 118. [3] Division of Administration, State of Louisiana (1970–71 through 1975–76). About 97 per cent of these taxes are revenues from oil, condensate, and gas]

Year	Crude oil and lease condensate[1]		Natural gas[2]		Louisiana severance tax[3]		
	barrels per day (000)	per cent of U.S. total	cubic feet per day (million)	per cent of U.S. total	fiscal year	$U.S. (million)	per cent of State revenues
1970	2485	25.8	21,338	35.5	70–71	254.8	14.1
1971	2562	27.1	22,142	35.9	71–72	242.3	12.0
1972	2455	25.9	21,783	35.4	72–73	265.3	11.6
1973	2278	24.7	22,582	36.4	73–74	387.8	15.4
1974	2018	23.0	21,243	35.9	74–75	548.2	20.3
1975	1796	21.5	19,426	35.3	75–76	553.0	17.3
1976	1696	20.9	19,407	35.8	76–77[a]	528.0	15.0

[a] Preliminary figures.

remains untapped, the social and physical infrastructure necessary for exploitation of these resources is also underdeveloped. Just as Louisiana has a relatively low median family income (Table 5.1), it also ranks in the bottom decile among the 50 States for other typical measures of social and economic progress such as education and health. Additionally, the lack of functional integration within the industrial sectors is indicated by the low level of manufacturing employment which was only 49 per cent of the per capita national average in 1970 (Bobo and Charlton, 1974, p. 315).

Unskilled labour, the lack of co-ordinated infrastructure, and the absence of industry itself have prevented Louisiana from competing successfully for the recent immigration of money, people, and industry to the South. In the past, one of the primary attractions offered by the State has been the lowest tax rates in the nation. Low taxes on income and property have been compensated for by the State severance tax applied to natural gas—currently 7 cents per thousand cubic feet $(28.3m^3)$—and crude oil and condensate—12.5 per cent of the value at the time and place of severance. However, the Louisianan main resource is natural gas, and the decline in extraction will reduce State revenues by $U.S. 165 to $U.S. 200 million during the 4 years through fiscal year 1980 (Beard and Scott, 1975, pp. 3–4).

Moreover much of Louisiana's reserves are on the continental shelf with offshore production accounting for one-third to one-half of the State total. From 1956 until 1975 the State disputed the jurisdiction and control of the outer continental shelf with Federal government, but on 16 June 1975 the Supreme Court limited a State's jurisdiction to the area within 3 miles (4.8 km) of its coastline. Given the division of legal control over production shown in Table 5.4 the State collects only a small proportion of the revenue from the continental shelf. Even the currently favourable tax climate may thus be changed in a direction which would be less conducive to migratory growth.

A final consideration is national and State inattention to renewable energy

TABLE 5.4   Louisiana outer continental shelf oil and gas production.
[Source: U.S. Geological Survey, 1976, pp. 89–90]

Year	Crude oil and lease condensate			Natural gas		
	barrels per day (000)	per cent State	Federal	cubic feet per day (million)	per cent State	Federal
1970	1091	16	84	7672	19	81
1971	1217	13	87	8820	18	82
1972	1240	14	86	9536	17	83
1973	1177	13	87	9904	15	85
1974	1066	12	88	10,608	14	86
1975	969	11	89	10,471	13	87

resources of which Louisiana has an abundant supply: solar energy due to its southern location; natural or biological energy, both cultivated and wild, with a year-long growing season; wind, tidal, sea thermal, and deuterium resources (heavy hydrogen, the fuel for nuclear fusion) due to its coastal location. Out of the 1976–77 Federal budget devoted to energy research and development, only eight per cent was allocated for the development of renewable energy resources. This calculation is based on a broad interpretation of funded programme activities which include solar and geothermal energy development ($U.S. 90,000), environmental research and development ($U.S. 124,800), life-sciences research and biomedical applications ($U.S. 36,900), and basic energy sciences ($U.S. 108,000). In comparison, 1976–77 funds for fossil energy development were $U.S. 237,900 (5.3 per cent) and for nuclear related activities they were $U.S. 1,681,000 (37.6 per cent). The 1977–78 Federal budget allocates 10.5 per cent of the request for energy research and development to renewable energy sources (Executive Office of the President of the United States, 1977, p. 617).

The abundant natural energy resources could also result in constraints as well as inducements for development. Environmental advocates have delineated the serious impacts on the natural environment that urbanization and development produce. Louisiana's most ecologically fragile areas are also the most susceptible to development: the wetlands concentrated along the Gulf Coast have the greatest potential for growth sparked by New Orleans but are also among the most productive, in terms of biological energy, in the world. The environmentalists argue that the costs associated with development in the wetlands are seriously underestimated. Wagner and Durabb (1976), disputing the U. S. Army Corps of Engineers, present evidence against the extension of flood protection to a potential urban development area east of New Orleans in the marshlands. Their analysis shows that the real benefit:cost ratio is closer to 1:1 rather than the Corps' estimate of 12.6:1. They argue that:

(i) it is fallacious to estimate the cost of urban flood damage on currently unprotected and undeveloped marsh;

(ii) the Corps ignored the loss of productive estuarine marsh; and

(iii) the costs of subsidence of the organic soils in the wetlands development area (estimated by the authors to be $U.S. 120 per household per year) were ignored by the Corps.

THE BACKGROUND TO DEVELOPMENT ALTERNATIVES

Two Positions on Development

Neglect and obsolescence have been the hallmarks of Louisianan social and economic infrastructure: while severance tax revenues appeared guaranteed, there was little need to give much thought to the State's future. But when fossil fuels are no longer available to prop up the public and private sectors, tourism and sugar cane will not be sufficient to support the State. Advocates of economic base theory are now calling for more public spending on the kinds of infrastructure that will attract other types of industry besides the existing petrochemical complexes. Some take an opposite view to this development solution, arguing that, when the fossil fuels are gone, it would be advantageous to retain the marshes and marine fisheries which supply natural energy. Effectively, they favour some mechanism to encourage income development without growth. Thus it is an interesting dilemma. The easiest area for enhancing the infrastructure and attracting industry is the coastal zone but this is also the most ecologically fragile area in which indiscriminate development would have serious environmental consequences.

Indicators of Economic Development

Environmental concerns have begun to constrain development decisions, if only because environmental impact statements must now be filed with any plans. Moreover activist groups have learned the fine art of court suits and lengthy litigations to delay development. The usual approach to development, however, tends to ignore this concern. Following the economic base strategy, employment and personal income multipliers are determined for major sectors within the region. The multipliers for Louisiana, shown in Table 5.5, indicate that

TABLE 5.5   Louisianan multipliers. [Source: Saussy *et al.*, 1976, p. 38]

Industry	Rank	Employment	Personal income
Transportation equipment	1	3.3858	2.8283
Fossil fuels	2	2.8447	2.5165
Stone, clay, glass	3	2.5984	1.9248
Paper	4	2.5915	2.0028
Petroleum refining and related products	5	2.4693	1.9260
Machinery	6	2.3910	1.8862
Finance, insurance, real estate	7	2.3390	2.4603
Fabricated metals	8	2.3297	1.8786
Food processing	9	2.2743	2.4908
Chemicals	10	2.1462	1.6099
Primary metals	11	1.9224	1.6835
Federal enterprises	12	1.8970	1.2413
Contract construction	13	1.8765	1.6560
Printing	14	1.8014	1.6646
Apparel	15	1.7502	1.9953
State and local government	16	1.6694	1.3563
Services	17	1.6609	1.7183
Lumber	18	1.6604	1.5718
Transport, communication, utilities	19	1.6561	1.1509
Wholesale, retail trade	20	1.4279	1.6149

manufacturing activities have a greater impact than service activities. While other methods of regional analysis might be utilized to elaborate these results, generally the conclusion would be to encourage the top-ranking industries in Table 5.5.

This type of analysis ignores the fact that energy is a rapidly growing expense and that, given current technology, much manufacturing consumes large quantities of fossil fuels, particularly natural gas and petroleum. To make development decisions, further information is needed to determine energy efficiency and effectiveness: the remainder of this chapter proposes a methodology useful for an energy-constrained analysis of development.

ENERGY EFFICIENCY, EFFECTIVENESS, AND DEVELOPMENT

An input–output study for the Louisianan economy (Burford and Hargrave, 1973, pp. 33–6) has shown the importance of four sectors, of which the most important is, of course, fossil fuels extraction. This sector provides the major stimulus to the second most important sector—financial services. Yet these sectors provide very few jobs for Louisiana (Bobo and Charlton, 1974, pp. 197–200). In third place is miscellaneous services—the third largest category of employment in the State, followed by the chemical industry, which is based on the petroleum industry and a minor employer. Other important sectors are wholesale and retail trade, utilities and communications, and transportation and warehousing. The Louisianan input–output study demonstrates the dominance of the oil and gas industries in a local economy. Inspection of the structural matrix developed by Burford and Hargrave (1973) indicates a lack of linkages between these industries and other sectors of the economy: as discussed previously, Louisiana in many ways resembles an underdeveloped nation, being mainly a primary materials supplier for the industrial States.

Energy considerations are incorporated in this analysis by comparing direct total dollar outputs and energy outputs for Louisiana and the United States. These comparisons required the derivation of energy flow matrices for Louisiana and the United States and also a simplified structural matrix for the United States economy comparable to the Louisianan structural matrix (VanLandingham, 1975).

Because the State is a net energy exporter, it has a large comparative advantage in the energy sectors (Table 5.6), but since this advantage is expected to disappear, these sectors have been excluded from the following discussion. Using population as a basis of comparison, Table 5.6 shows that Louisiana has a comparative advantage in terms of dollars in non-metallic mining, paper, chemicals, transportation and warehousing, and retail and wholesale trade; and a comparative advantage in terms of energy in forestry, fish, and agricultural services, non-metallic mining, lumber and wood, paper, chemicals, and finance, insurance, and real estate.

TABLE 5.6   Direct dollar and energy output comparisons of Louisiana to United States (population ratio of Louisiana/United States = 0.018). [Source: Derived by authors]

Sector	Dollar output ratio Louisiana/U.S. (1)	Energy output ratio Louisiana/U.S. (2)	Dollar to energy ratio (1) ÷ (2)
Crude oil and natural gas	0.400	0.200	2.00
Petroleum refining	0.090	0.056	1.61
Electric and gas utilities	0.030	0.040	0.75
Livestock	0.008	0.011	0.73
Other agriculture	0.014	0.012	1.17
Forest, fish, agriculture services	0.020	0.048	0.42
Non-metallic mining	0.083	0.035	2.37
Construction	0.014	0.017	0.82
Food processing	0.019	0.009	2.11
Textiles	0.003	0.002	1.50
Lumber and wood	0.015	0.050	0.30
Paper	0.037	0.023	1.61
Chemicals	0.038	0.027	1.41
Glass, stone, clay	0.016	0.015	1.07
Primary non-ferrous metals	0.013	0.015	0.87
Metal fabrication	0.011	0.009	1.22
Machinery	0.003	0.004	0.75
Transportation equipment	0.017	0.017	1.00
Transportation and warehousing	0.024	0.011	2.18
Retail and wholesale trade	0.021	0.017	1.24
Finance, insurance, real estate	0.015	0.042	0.36

An important aspect of Table 5.6 is the dollar to energy ratios. In considering development strategies, it is preferable to have a high dollar to energy output ratio: on this basis non-metallic mining, food processing, textiles, paper, chemicals, metal fabrication, transportation and warehousing, and retail and wholesale trade are the most advantageous sectors for State economic development. These activities are rather diverse because they reflect manufacturing, urban services, and rural materials processing. While useful for determining direct impacts, the data in Table 5.6 do not delineate linkages in the regional economy, nor give direct answers to questions about the overall energy efficiency and effectiveness of any development strategy.

These objectives can be accomplished by inspecting the multipliers produced by an *energy* input–output model. Each element in this model represents the sales of products, valued in energy units (10^{12} BTUs), from one sector to another (VanLandingham, 1975). For each sector included in the following analysis, it is assumed that energy final demand is doubled implying also that the constant dollar amount of output demanded has doubled. Since the primary purpose of this analysis is to propose a methodology for including energy constraints in development scenarios, the actual increase in final demand is of secondary importance. The following scenarios propose doubling final demand: this permits an efficient mechanism for multiplier calculation. The actual amount of final demand increase would depend upon decisions reached by the State Planning Office and the business community.

To evaluate energy efficiency the model uses a 'primary energy ratio' based on the change in total energy output in the primary energy sector (natural gas and crude oil, ΔE_1) given a hypothetical change in final demand for energy in the chosen development sectors ($\Delta F.D.$). The closer this ratio is to one the greater the energy efficiency of the scenario.

Efficiency is not the only criterion for development choices. For planning purposes, it is also important to maximize the amount of production for a given amount of energy input. An 'energy–work multiplier' also calculated in the model is the ratio between the change in total energy output by all sectors ($\Delta \sum E_i : i = 1, n$) and the change in total energy output in the primary energy sector (ΔE_1). This multiplier indicates the change in economic activity in the system caused by a change in energy final demand; the higher this is above one, the more effective the development strategy.

Finally, a total-output multiplier is also derived. Similar to any input–output model, it indicates the relative impact that a unit change in final demand in any sector (or combination of sectors) has on total output. The larger this multiplier becomes, the greater overall impact a development strategy will have on the regional economy.

Using the results presented in Tables 5.5 and 5.6, three development alternatives for Louisiana are now analysed, using the energy multipliers (see Table 5.7). The first follows economic base theory and emphasizes industrial growth for export purposes; the second concentrates on the processing of local raw materials; and the third proposes an urban-orientated strategy by concentrating on activities in the tertiary sector. Each development strategy is analysed in two parts, a minimum approach and an extended approach. If the State Planning Office alone decided to adopt one of these strategies, budgetary limitations might constrain a development programme to the minimum approach, but co-operation between business and government might make the extended strategy feasible. By considering various combinations of sectors for development, Table 5.7 also demonstrates the complexity of the interindustry linkages. The minimum strategies have greater impacts in terms of energy effectiveness and increasing total output but tend to be less energy efficient; in contrast the extended scenarios are more energy efficient but have less impact per unit of energy expended.

TABLE 5.7 Energy impact analysis. [Source: Derived by authors]

Development strategy	Primary energy ratio $\Delta E_1/\Delta F.D.$	Energy–work multiplier $\Delta \sum\limits_n^{i=1} E_i/\Delta E_1$	Total–output multiplier $\Delta \sum\limits_n^{i=1} E_i/\Delta F.D.$
1. Urban-economic base			
A. Minimum: metal fabrication; machinery including electrical; transportation equipment.	4.58	3.63	16.61
B. Extended: minimum plus primary non-ferrous metals; miscellaneous manufacturing	3.11	2.98	9.26
2. Rural materials processing			
A. Minimum: forest, fish, agricultural services; wood, lumber, furniture; paper and paper products	1.97	3.12	6.15
B. Extended: minimum plus other agriculture; food processing	3.70	2.85	10.53
3. Urban-tertiary			
A. Minimum: transportation and warehousing; wholesale and retail trade; financial services	1.76	2.84	5.02
B. Extended: minimum plus textile products; other services	2.03	2.80	5.68
4. Combined materials–tertiary			
A. Minimum: 2A plus 3A	1.89	2.82	5.34
B. Extended: 2B plus 3B	2.55	2.78	7.07

First Development Alternative

The economic base development scenarios proposed here for Louisiana start with doubling final demand in metal fabrication (barge and ship building), machinery (including electrical), and transportation equipment. Despite a worldwide decline in the shipbuilding industry, it could be expanded in Louisiana to meet the growing demand for barges, tugboats, and other specialized vessels on the Mississippi River system, to service the oil and gas rigs in the Gulf of

Mexico, and also the deep-water oil terminal being constructed by a group of oil companies. A major growing base industry in the New Orleans metropolitan area is the shipyards centered on Avondale, with Avondale Shipyards Inc. being the fourth largest in the United States. These sectors rank eighth, sixth, and first, respectively, in Table 5.5 and fabrication has a high dollar to energy ratio in Table 5.6. This initial part of the first strategy has the highest total-output multiplier and also the largest primary energy ratio—the least energy-efficient strategy in Table 5.7.

The second part of the economic base strategy adds primary non-ferrous metals and miscellaneous manufacturing. Louisiana is currently a net importer of the products of both these sectors, and it is assumed here that the State will be able to reverse this and become a net exporter. These are logical additions since the State lacks a ferrous metals sector, and they improve the energy efficiency of this strategy (as the lower primary energy ratio indicates) even though lowering the total-output multiplier. Because Louisiana lags behind the nation in economic base industries, these strategies would require considerable new development, which could produce large increases in population and in urbanized areas in southern Louisiana and thus, in turn, the conversion of more wetlands into urban uses.

Second Development Alternative

The second strategy of doubling demand for local materials processing is assumed to be rural and small town in orientation. The minimum-change strategy includes forestry, fish, and agricultural services; wood, lumber, and furniture; and paper and paper products. This strategy has the second lowest primary energy ratio and the second highest energy–work multiplier in Table 5.7. The extended-change strategy adds other agricultural activities apart from livestock raising and food processing. This extended strategy has the second highest total-output multiplier and the second highest primary energy ratio. Paper and food processing ranked fourth and ninth, respectively, in Table 5.5, and had high dollar to energy ratios in Table 5.6. The other three sectors were included in these scenarios since they complemented the rural materials processing idea. If energy were not a problem, this might be the best development choice since Louisiana already has a firm base on which to promote it. Moreover most of these activities do not disrupt the environment. Since basically it is emphasizing past trends, this scenario—if managed properly—would not induce changes in the existing population or urban growth trends. Both the minimum and extended strategies would affect the entire agricultural structure of Louisiana and the spatial impacts would probably be distributed rather evenly.

Third Development Alternative

The third set of scenarios initially proposes doubling final demand in the tertiary sectors of transportation and warehousing; wholesale and retail trade;

and financial services. The first two have high dollar to energy ratios in Table 5.6, and financial services ranked seventh in Table 5.5. This scenario is the most energy efficient in Table 5.7 but also has the lowest total-output multiplier. The extended analysis for the urban–tertiary scenario adds textile products and 'other services'; textiles had a high dollar to energy ratio in Table 5.6, while 'other services' help to complete the tertiary aspect of this strategy. Four of these five are currently Louisiana's strongest urban sectors. Of the sectors chosen here, only the production of textile goods is not well established in the State, but it would be reasonable to encourage this activity because of the nearby raw materials (cotton, petrochemicals), reasonably cheap labour, and currently available urban locations. In addition, textile products manufactured in the United States are likely to capture a larger share of the American market in the future if oil imports continue to cause an unfavourable balance of payments and this in turn leads to higher tariffs on many classes of imported goods. Because these sectors are urban in orientation, most of the development impacts would occur in southern Louisiana. Give this expectation, a prime advantage of this scenario is that little urbanization of the wetlands would occur since there are sufficient urban resources in existence to support these sectors. The multipliers associated with this scenario are not distinguished within Table 5.7.

A Combined Strategy

A review of these scenarios indicates that the second and third would have the least negative impact on the environment. By itself, the extended second strategy was far more energy consumptive than the other two but had the best development results. The minimum third strategy had the best energy efficiency. Thus the last scenario developed here is to combine the second and third schemes as a unified plan. Table 5.7 shows that the result of this fourth scenario is perhaps the best. The primary energy ratio is not much greater than the lowest value, the energy–work multiplier is low but the total-output multiplier is fairly large. As an overall plan, this last extended scenario combines energy conservation with reasonable development results.

CONCLUSIONS

If the input–output matrices used to derive Table 5.7 were reasonably accurate descriptions of Louisiana today, the results could provide policy guidance to both public and private managers. Before pursuing this analytical direction, however, the quality of the data must be imporved. The 1963 data used here are probably outdated; in many cases it was difficult to achieve agreement between the United States and Louisiana sectors; and the level of aggregation necessitated is often too broad for extensive conclusions to be drawn. Despite these problems, the analyses are indicative of development potentials in Louisiana. Of the three multipliers used in these analyses, the energy–work multiplier has the least variation (from 2.78 to 3.63). When energy final demand is changed, this causes both the output of the primary energy sector, E_1, and the sum of all sector outputs to change, although not proportionally. The amount by which each changes will depend upon the linkage between the sectors in which changes were introduced and all other sectors. In these analyses the linkages are apparently similar—generally, a lack of linkages through the regional economy.

This discussion indicates three basic problems. First, fossil fuels are not a long-run basis for development in Louisiana. While necessary as input to industry, further direct development of this sector of the economy is considered unlikely. Nor are the renewable energy sources feasible as rapid expansion of urban areas will endanger the valuable natural energy resources. And, finally, given the low starting point, the development path should produce a rapid improvement in the economic well-being of the populace.

These analyses, however cursory, indicate that the gloom of the environmentalists need not deter economic progress in Louisiana and that the prophecies of economic disaster can also be overcome: it is not necessary to make an unappealing choice between the death of the wetlands and the economic death of the State.

Interestingly, after examining the structure of the Louisianan economy from an energy-conservation viewpoint, economic base theory does not provide the only answer to a Louisianan future. This analysis indicates that a future based on Louisiana's current strengths is feasible. It appears that the national economy has diverse requirements: not every region will automatically profit from manufacturing, nor are non-manufacturing sectors definitionally unprofitable. With careful planning by both public and private managers, Louisiana can survive its crisis of fossil fuels depletion.

Chapter 6
Industry and Labour Markets in Great Britain

WILLIAM F. LEVER

There appear to be two main approaches to the study of industrial location in Britain. The first is concerned with employment measured in numbers of workers engaged in various industries in a specified area or set of areas such as the standard regions; the second examines numbers of establishments defined in area, product, size, or ownership. The choice between these approaches may be made on methodological grounds or upon the nature of the problem being analysed: a study of entrepreneurial behaviour, for example, would tend to focus on establishments rather than aggregate employment totals. On occasion, however, the choice will depend to a large extent on the availability of data. Workforce information is most likely to be generated by government departments concerned with employment or industry whereas establishment data may initially come from various agencies (such as the Health and Safety at Work Executive—formerly the Factory Inspectorate), but will almost certainly need to be augmented by empirical investigation.

The analysis of aggregate data can take several forms. It may, for example, be used cross-sectionally as location quotients to identify spatial concentrations of particular industries, or over time by the use of entropic measures to assess whether there is convergence or divergence between the various regional or subregional components of the national industrial structure. Again, over time, the analysis may use a shift-share calculation to identify the national, structural, and local components in employment change. Useful as these methods are, they have often been criticized on the grounds that they take insufficient account of entrepreneurial behaviour and decision-making. Establishment-based studies have taken several forms including the investigation of factors influencing locational choice, of linkages between firms, and of decision-making within corporate structures.

The business environment within which firms or establishments operate may be defined at several spatial scales. At the national or even international scale, changes in the levels of world trade, the aggregate level of economic activity nationally, and government activity to increase demand for goods and services will all have an effect upon output and employment in individual establishments. At this level, however, the firm or establishment is unlikely to be able to influence events and must merely respond to these exogenous forces. At the regional level, firms are more concerned with the availability of supplies of inputs and the

89

serving of regional markets. Some large firms at the regional level may be able to affect aggregate regional income levels both directly and through multiplier effects based upon their purchase of inputs, and to influence capital expenditure upon roads, housing, and infrastructure. It is at the level of the local labour market, however, where the impact of large plants can best be seen. This impact will take several forms. By definition, most of the plant's labour force will reside within the area of the spatially defined local labour market so that the impact of redundancies, recruitment, and wage expenditure patterns will all be limited to the local labour market. This in turn may be reflected in inter-urban migration, income levels, and the prices of such goods as housing. These local effects will be intensified where there is a high level of linkages between plants within the local labour markets. Together these three spatial scales, the national–international, the regional, and the local labour market, form an interlinked system for the study of the geography of the industrial environment. Seldom, however, do studies encompass all three levels. The importance of studies at national and regional levels has long been recognized but now increasing emphasis is being placed upon local labour-market studies, for it is at this scale that the relationships between entrepreneurial decision-making and the workforce as a whole can best be analysed.

Rarely has research encompassed the total impact of such decisions upon the overall labour market. But, among exceptions are Salt (1967) who studied the consequences of the decision by Ford and Vauxhall to establish motor vehicle plants at Liverpool, Greig (1971) who examined the effect of a pulp and paper mill on the economy of Fort William, and Lever (1974) who tried to ascertain the impact of various manufacturing establishments on the economy of the Clydeside conurbation.

Studies which have sought to examine the multifaceted relationship between the individual establishment and the local labour market within which it operates have been handicapped because, it is argued, the former is very small relative to the size of the latter and thus the impact is insignificant. There are, however, many local labour markets in Great Britain which are dominated by a single mining or manufacturing establishment. These form the focus of this study. It can be argued that in a number of respects these dominant plants are significantly different to other plants in their ability to influence local levels of unemployment or excess labour demand, their power to influence local prevailing wage rates, and their ability to attract potential suppliers of inputs and consumers of their output. The methodologies adopted to test the hypothesis that there are significant differences, however, must be applied to all local labour markets. While the study is therefore essentially a case study of *dominated* labour markets, in order to assess the differences between such labour markets and the balanced labour markets which are more common, it inevitably calls into question the functioning of all local labour markets.

The study is divided into six sections. The first two define and identify, respectively, local labour markets in Great Britain and local labour markets whose employment structure is dominated by a single large non-tertiary enterprise. The next two examine the characteristics of these labour markets and the enterprises which dominate them and discuss *a priori* why such labour markets might behave differently to 'non-dominated' labour markets. The concluding sections investigate in detail both the nature of changes over time in employment and unemployment in dominated and non-dominated labour markets and of functional linkages between dominant plants and the rest of the local economy.

DEFINING LOCAL LABOUR MARKETS

The Journey to Work

In studying the nature of relationships between a dominant plant and its labour market, it is essential to define spatially the labour market within which it operates. For some linkages, such as the purchase of material inputs, the appropriate scale of analysis may be the whole national economy, although at least one study (Lever, 1972) indicates that significant linkages exist at the subregional level. For other linkages—such as recruitment of labour, the spatial impact of redundancies, and second-round employment multiplier effects resulting from the demands for goods and services required by the dominant plant's workforce—the appropriate analytical scale is the local labour market. This can be defined as the spatial range of employment opportunities open to a worker without requiring a change in his or her place of residence. It will be affected by income, by the availability of transport, and by the extent of knowledge about alternative employment opportunities (Vance, 1960; Goodman, 1970). From the viewpoint of the management of the dominant plant, the local labour market is 'the geographical area containing those members of the labour force, or potential members of the labour force that a firm can induce to enter its employ under certain conditions' (Robinson, 1968, p. 66). In both cases the key criterion is journey to work and it is on this that most definitions of local labour markets in the United Kingdom have depended (Hall *et al.*, 1973; Smart, 1974).

The definition requires that journeys to work across the labour-market boundary be below a certain maximum and that the local labour market be highly integrated. As Goodman (1970) indicates, the choice of the actual percentage of non-resident workers and non-locally employed resident workers is a matter of empirical judgement. Smart (1974) amalgamated two census units into a single labour market if more than 25 per cent of the workers residing in one area had jobs in the other. Hall *et al.* (1973) applied the U.S. concepts of the Standard Metropolitan Labor Area (SMLA) and the Metropolitan Economic Labor Area (MELA) to England and Wales yielding, in each case, 100 labour markets. Smart's aim was to divide the whole of the United Kingdom into contiguous labour markets; consequently many contained too few people for present purposes—some in fact being merely rural areas. The SMLAs of Hall's study are non-contiguous and, while all have a central urban focus, many are too extensive to be described as 'local' labour markets.

Definitional Criteria

Accordingly, five criteria were applied to define a set of non-overlapping and non-contiguous local labour markets. These were:

(a) at least 70 per cent of all workers resident within the labour market were employed within it;

(b) at least 70 per cent of all workers employed in the labour market were resident within it;

(c) the resident population of the labour market must exceed 10,000 in 1971;

(d) the area should not exceed 50,000 acres (20,660 ha);

(e) population density should exceed one person per acre (2.4 persons per ha).

These criteria ensured that the resulting local labour markets would be relatively self-contained according to relatively short journeys to work and have a reasonably sized urban centre.

The procedure for creating labour markets was similar to that used by Smart. Where a single local authority area in 1971 conformed to the five criteria, it was defined immediately as a local labour market. If the self-containment levels were below 70 per cent for either the inward or outward movement of workers, local authority areas were amalgamated until the 70 per cent minimum criterion was reached, subject to the total area not exceeding 50,000 acres. The chain of amalgamation was based on the proportional sizes of flows of workers between local authority areas. A few labour markets were defined which did not precisely meet these criteria, such as underbounded towns in which suburban growth linked an urban centre to a large rural hinterland and towns whose commuting patterns were distorted by the presence of a single large employer just outside the administrative boundary. In such cases the urban centre was defined as the local labour market.

By applying the five basic criteria to the 1971 census Journey to Work tabulations, the 301 local labour markets forming the basis of this study were identified (see Figure 6.1). These resemble the SMLAs used by Hall *et al.* (1973); in contrast the MELA incorporate large rural areas (excluded in this study) and Smart's labour markets include many which are entirely rural (and lack the urban focus required by this study).

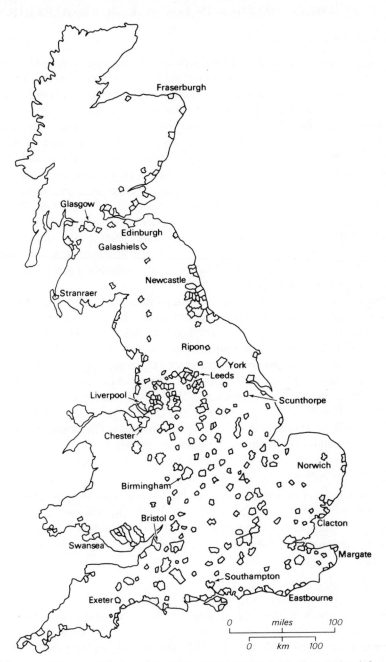

FIGURE 6.1 Labour markets in Great Britain (Northern Ireland is omitted from the analysis)

DEFINING DOMINANCE IN LOCAL LABOUR MARKETS

Data Requirements

To ascertain which of these 301 local labour markets are dominated by a single employer, data on establishment size are required. Most studies of establishment size have been executed at national or regional levels (Armstrong and Silberston, 1965) for which published data are available (Business Statistics Office, 1975). Research on local labour markets has required more intensive data searches such as those carried out by Spooner (1972) in Devon and Cornwall, and by Moseley (1973) and Sant (1970) in East Anglia. Since such methods are clearly inappropriate to a national study, attention here focused on data collected—but not usually published—by official departments. Foremost among these are the records of the Factory Inspectorate (Lloyd and Mason, 1976; Gudgin, 1976) and the Employment Record II files of the Department of Employment (Keeble and Hauser, 1971). Along with information from trade directories (Gripaios, 1977), these records helped generate data about plant size. Most of the details relate to 1973 but Factory Inspectorate information simply reflects the most recent plant inspection by one of its officers.

There are two broad approaches to defining dominated labour markets. One simply classifies as dominated those labour markets in which more than a certain proportion of the labour force is employed by one firm. The other is more complicated and requires the identification of some 'normal' distribution of plant sizes against which it is possible to recognize a discrete group of labour markets where a 'dominated' plant-size distribution exists. The first approach only needs information about total employment in the largest plant; the second requires entire plant-size distribution data. For the latter approach, information was available for 74 local labour markets covering the largest 10 employers and for 21 local labour markets covering all non-service employers.

Plant-size Distributions

Perhaps the most direct analogy with the identification of dominated plant-size distribution is the rank-size rule—particularly the concept of the primate city. Regular relationships between the size of towns and their rank in the urban hierarchy were noted first by Auerbach (1913) and can be summarized in the expression:

$$P_n = P_1 (n)^{-1} \qquad (6.1)$$

where P_n is the population of the nth town in the series 1, 2, 3 . . . n in which all towns in the system are ranked in descending size order, and P is the population of the largest city. The 10 largest non-tertiary employers in each of the 26 local labour markets in the Yorkshire and Humberside Region were ranked by size. The largest plant was given an index number of 100 to allow for absolute differences in size. In general, the mean rank-size line, for all 26 shown in Figure

6.2, does demonstrate a smooth log-linear relationship but the slope is less than that in equation (6.1). Some labour markets, Huddersfield for example, do show a plant-size distribution very similar to that described in equation (6.1) while others, such as Hemsworth, Mexborough, and Scunthorpe, exhibit a primate distribution. Others, again, such as Doncaster, York, and Pontefract, indicate no strong rank-size nor primate distributions and fall typically into an 'intermediate' category (Berry, 1961).

One problem about the rank-size approach is that, by reducing the largest employer to an index number, the absolute size effect is concealed; there is thus no measure of how important the plant is within the labour market as a whole, merely an indication as to how important it is relative to the next largest plants.

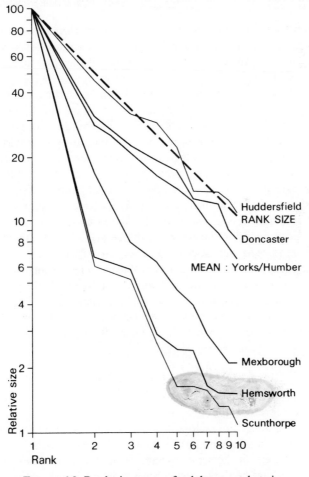

FIGURE 6.2 Rank-size curves for labour markets in
Yorkshire and Humberside

The index values for Ripon, for example, are 100, 32, 25, 14, 14, 12 . . . , which suggests plant dominance, but in fact the largest manufacturing plant employs only 7.2 per cent of the total labour force. If the index number problem is resolved by using proportional values, only the extreme cases such as Hemsworth (39.3 per cent), Mexborough (51.3 per cent), and Scunthorpe (44.2 per cent) are clearly and unambiguously identified as dominated labour markets.

The same problems are encountered if the definition is based upon coefficients of concentration, such as the Gini coefficient, or upon graphical representations like the Lorentz curve (Collins, 1973). Deficiencies in size distribution data nullify conventional usage of either of these methods. If only the 10 largest plants for which data are available are included, their total contribution to all employment in the local labour market is concealed (as in the case of Ripon cited above).

A modified form of concentration curve was developed to overcome these problems. This is shown in Figure 6.3 which demonstrates, for several Scottish local labour markets, the cumulative percentage of the workforce employed in the 10 largest non-service establishments. The average figure for Scottish labour markets is shown where the largest plant employs 12.6 per cent of the total workforce, the second 7.8 per cent, the third 4.2 per cent and so on. Against this mean curve 5 archetypal cases are shown. Fraserburgh is dominated by two plants, but the third- to tenth-ranking plants are all proportionally larger than the regional average; the slope of the curve is thus steeper and the right-hand axis intersect indicates that a high proportion of the labour force is in non-service occupations. Stranraer is the exact opposite, for all plants are small and a very high proportion of the labour force employed in service occupations; Paisley and Motherwell represent labour markets dominated by one and two plants; and Galashiels typifies a labour market in which the largest plants are all very similar to one another in size so that the concentration curve forms almost a straight line. Useful as the concentration curve is in graphically representing the relative sizes of the largest plants one to another and to total employment, it does not distinguish a discrete class of dominated labour markets.

Weaver's statistic (1954), which has been applied in several studies of industrial concentration (Lever, 1975; Kenny, 1977), seeks to identify the value of n when m is a minimum in the expression:

$$m = \sum \left(\frac{100}{n} - 1 \ldots n \right)^2 + \sum (n + 1 \ldots x)^2 \qquad (6.2)$$

where $1 \ldots x$ represent the proportions of the labour force in each of x manufacturing plants, or sectors, in the labour market ranked by size. Dominated labour markets might be defined as those in which $n = 1$ when m is a minimum. Treatment of the service sector raises some problems: a firm in this sector may sometimes be the largest employer as in Ripon and Stranraer, but in such regions a manufacturing plant only becomes 'dominant' if service-sector employment is excluded. If the workers employed in service establishments are omitted from the ranking while using total labour force as the deonominator to calculate proportionate size, the leading non-tertiary employer must employ approximately 37 per cent of the labour force before $n = 1$ when m is a minimum in equation (6.2) (though it depends partially on the size–rank characteristics of

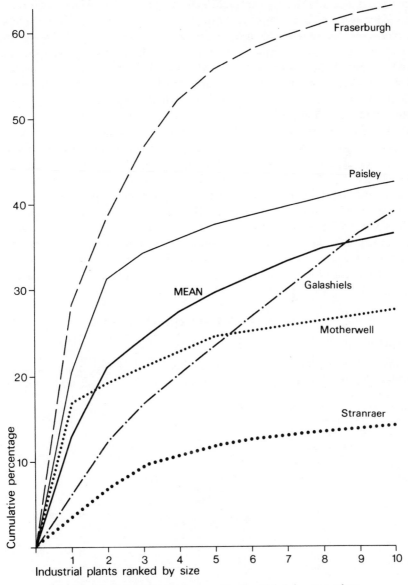

FIGURE 6.3 Concentration curves for Scottish labour markets

the smaller employers). A cut-off point of this order yielded too few dominated labour markets to suit the purposes of this study.

A Definition Based on Largest Plant Size Alone

The inadequacies of these approaches led to the adoption of a simpler and more pragmatic solution: a threshold percentage of the total labour force was selected above which an employer could be said to 'dominate' the local labour market. This represented a compromise between choosing a relatively high figure (which might yield very few dominated labour markets) or a relatively low figure (which might identify dominant plants that were too small to have a substantial effect on their respective labour markets). The percentage employed was calculated in 159 local labour markets for which data were initially available about the largest non-tertiary employer. The mean value is 12.3 per cent and, reflecting the skewed distribution, the median is 9.4 per cent, with an interquartile range of 5.1 to 15.8 per cent. Over the range as a whole the extreme values are found in Leeds and Coalville (East Midlands) where the largest employers have, respectively, 1 per cent and 66.6 per cent of the total workforce. Using the 159 local labour markets and assuming them to be typical of all 301, Table 6.1 indicates the likely number of dominated labour markets for a range of threshold values. On this basis, the threshold value of 12.5 per cent was selected. Of these 159 local labour markets, 46 were found to be dominated by this criterion; analysis of the remaining 142 local labour markets from Employment Record II, Factory Inspectorate and directory data identified a further 49 with a dominant plant.

DOMINATED LABOUR MARKETS

Plant-dominated Labour Markets

This definition thus yielded 95 dominated local labour markets, three of which—Crewe, Fraserburgh, and Llanelli—contain 2 firms both employing

TABLE 6.1   Threshold values

Threshold value (per cent)	Dominated	Non-dominated
5.0	229	72
7.5	180	121
10.0	141	160
12.5	116	185
15.0	88	213
17.5	61	240
20.0	45	256
22.5	33	268
25.0	29	272

more than 12.5 per cent of the workforce. The 98 establishments together employ approximately 570,000 workers: 6 employ fewer than 1000, the largest has almost 25,000 and the average size is just under 6000 workers. Table 6.2 and Figure 6.4 indicate that dominated labour markets are more common in the Depressed Regions (Wales, Scotland, and North), where they make up 44 per cent of all labour markets, and the Intermediate Regions (North West, South West, Yorkshire and Humberside, and East Midlands) where the figure is 32 per cent: the figure for the Prosperous Regions (West Midlands, East Anglia, South East) is only 22 per cent.

Table 6.3 reveals the wide diversity of major industrial groupings within which the dominant plants fall, although a third of them are engaged in coalmining and

TABLE 6.2   Regional distribution

Region	Labour markets	Dominated	Per cent
Depressed regions			
Wales	19	9	47
Scotland	31	14	45
North	27	10	37
Intermediate regions			
North West	36	9	25
South West	40	12	30
Yorks/Humber	26	7	27
East Midlands	26	13	50
Prosperous regions			
West Midlands	22	6	27
East Anglia	12	3	25
South East	62	12	19
Total (or average)	301	95	32

TABLE 6.3   Industrial type

Standard Industrial Classification group	Number	Standard Industrial Classification group	Number
II Mining	16	XI Vehicles	18
III Food	8	XII Other metal goods	3
IV Petroleum products	1	XIII Textiles	2
V Chemicals	5	XIV Leather	0
VI Metal manufactures	12	XV Clothing	3
VII Mechanical engineering	9	XVI Bricks, etc.	2
VIII Instrument engineering	0	XVII Timber	1
IX Electrical engineering	11	XVIII Paper	2
X Shipbuilding	4	XIX Other	1

FIGURE 6.4 Dominated labour markets in Great Britain (Northern Ireland is omitted
from the analysis)

vehicle manufacture. The only Standard Industrial Classification (SIC) groups unrepresented are instrument engineering and leather manufactures. Inevitably, industries which enjoy considerable scale economies such as shipbuilding, vehicle and aircraft manufacture, the manufacture of domestic electrical goods, and iron and steel production, are over-represented among the 98 plants.

Their relative size is shown in Table 6.4. Forty-three per cent employ between 12.5 and 17.4 per cent of their local workforces, the median value for the 98 plants being 19.3 per cent and the largest single value being 66.6 per cent. It was thought that the type of ownership of the dominant plants and the locus of decision-making might be important in explaining company behaviour: Table 6.5 thus divides the 98 plants into 5 ownership types—U.K. local-owned, branch plants of U.K. companies, foreign-owned branch plants, State-owned, and quasi-State-owned (such as British Leyland and Rolls Royce). With recent extensions of nationalization (e.g. most of the U.K. steel industry) and merger

TABLE 6.4   Relative size

Relative size* (per cent)	Number of plants
12.5–14.9	19
15.0–17.4	23
17.5–19.9	12
20.0–24.9	13
25.0–29.9	9
30.0–34.9	6
35.0–39.9	4
40.0–44.9	6
45.0–49.9	1
50.0 +	5
Total	98

*Per cent of local labour-market workforce.

TABLE 6.5   Current ownership type

Ownership	Number
U.K. local-owned	12
U.K. branch plant	39
Foreign-owned branch plant	10
State-owned	28
Quasi-State-owned	9
Total	98

activity within the private sector, several plants changed from one category to another during this project.

Industry-dominated Labour Markets

Finally, it may be interesting to compare the performances of those local labour markets which are dominated by a single plant both with non-dominated labour markets and with labour markets in which a single industry is dominant but in which no one plant predominates. From the Employment Record II lists, it has been possible to identify 34 labour markets in which one industry, here defined as a single Minimum List Heading (MLH) in the 1968 classification, employs more than 12.5 per cent of the total labour force and in which no one plant is dominant. Two problems arise. First, as Table 6.6 indicates, the MLH in which industry domination occurs tend not to be those in which plant domination occurs because of differential scale economies, and this makes comparisons difficult. Second, one local labour market, Chippenham, falls into both categories, being dominated by a large plant making electrical equipment and industry-dominated by MLH 214 (meat and fish products) manufacture.

TABLE 6.6   Industry-dominated labour markets

Minimum List Heading number	Industry	Labour markets
214	Meat and fish products	1
218	Fruit and vegetable products	1
271	General chemicals	2
311	Iron and steel	1
332	Machine tools	1
335	Textile machinery	1
339	Miscellaneous machinery	1
370	Shipbuilding	2
373	Aerospace equipment	2
399	Miscellaneous metal industries	2
413	Cotton weaving	2
414	Woollen and worsted	5
415	Jute	1
417	Hosiery	2
450	Footwear	5
462	Pottery	1
469	Building materials	1
472	Furniture	1
481	Paper and board	2
Total		34

CHARACTERISTICS OF DOMINATED LABOUR MARKETS

Employment Changes

There are several ways in which it might be anticipated that plant-dominated labour markets would differ from non-dominated ones: in overall performance, unemployment rates, and vacancy rates, the former are likely to be less stable over time. Thompson (1965) has suggested that smaller labour markets and those with the least diversified employment structures are more prone to wide unemployment fluctuations. However, so far most empirical research has focused only on interregional differences in temporal unemployment fluctuations (Brechling, 1967; King *et al.*, 1972) or on 'leading' and 'lagging' labour markets (Bassett and Haggett, 1971; Fearn, 1975). The relationship between the extent of fluctuations in unemployment and the industrial structure of the local labour market measured in plant-size distribution has been neglected. The study by Mackay *et al.* (1971) coincidentally treats 'Smalltown' in north-east Scotland which is known to be a dominated labour market. There is evidence that much greater shifts in the unemployment rate occur in 'Smalltown' than in other labour markets, although the shifts appear to have a high seasonal, rather than cyclical, component. Other studies have analysed, non-comparatively, the effects of the closure of a single large plant on its local labour market including the 1956 closures in the British car industry (Kahn, 1964), the 1953 closure of the railway-vehicle manufacturing works at Mount Vernon, Illinois (Wilcock, 1957), and redundancies in coalmining in Ashington and Bedlington (Boon, 1974). All suggest that where a major plant closes down or substantially retrenches its workforce, the capacity of other employers in the labour market to absorb the displaced workers is a function of the relative sizes of the major employer and the other employers: where the major one is a dominant plant, the impact upon the level of unemployment is likely to be particularly severe.

In most instances problems of employment instability show up as a decline in demand for labour. But even where there is a rising demand in unbalanced and dominated labour markets, the large firm may experience recruiting problems simply because it is so big in comparison to the total available labour supply. This may lead to labour being 'poached' by the dominant establishment from other firms, rising wage levels and distant recruitment. Salt (1967) has described how large car-manufacturing plants arriving on Merseyside under the aegis of regional policy in the early 1960s recruited much of their labour from existing firms. Although Bunting (1962) has suggested that dominant plants are in a near-monopsonistic position for hiring labour and could therefore drive down the prevailing wage rate, Bronfenbrenner (1956) and others have argued that a large firm will pay above average wages to build up a notional queue of labour from which vacancies can be selectively filled, thereby qualitatively improving its workforce over time. Lastly, Beaumont (1977) shows how rapid increases in the demand for labour by the British car industry in towns like Luton and

Dagenham, beyond the capacity of the local labour supply, have driven employers to seek distant sources of labour in the Depressed Regions.

Multiplier Effects

Merely relating the size of the dominant plant's redundancy or recruitment to the remainder of the local labour force understates the total impact of the resulting changes. Through the employment multiplier effect a change in the dominant plant's workforce may affect total demand for labour in two ways (Moseley, 1973). First, there are the structural effects of changes in the output (employment) of the dominant plant on local suppliers of inputs to the dominant plant (the indirect multiplier). Second, there is the induced multiplier effect through the purchases of local goods and services by the dominant plant's workforce on the suppliers of these goods and services. Estimates of local-employment multipliers vary widely but 1:2.5 is a reasonable mean value from a number of studies (Hildebrand and Mace, 1950; Thompson, 1959; Greig, 1971). In other words, a change in the labour force of the dominant plant of 100 will generate an additional change of 150 in the rest of the labour market—an overall change, therefore, of 250. There is little empirical evidence as to whether multipliers within those local labour markets dominated by one plant are likely to be higher or lower than in non-dominated ones. The induced multiplier effect, which depends upon wage spending by the workforce, is unlikely to differ except insofar as dominant plants may draw their employees from a larger hinterland: in these circumstances some retail and other spending is likely to take place away from the workplace and this, in turn, may lead to lower induced multipliers. One study of a dominant plant by Sadler et al. (1973) indicated that the higher wages paid at the Rio Tinto zinc plant at Holyhead in Anglesey led workers, previously in low-paid employment, to start purchasing more expensive goods which were not available locally, thereby transferring part of their spending to centres like Chester (60 miles—95 km—away). The evidence about the indirect multiplier effect based upon the spatial distribution of backward linkages is ambiguous. In general, input-supplying sectors are drawn to significant concentrations of certain industries at the level of British economic subregions (Lever, 1972) or SMLAs in the United States (Richter, 1969). Two other studies, however, have indicated that the existence of a dominant plant in a local labour market may have a deterrent effect upon potential suppliers. James (1964) noted the reluctance of local firms to supply the dominant Rootes (now Chrysler) car-manufacturing plant at Paisley, and Barlow (1977) has suggested that the presence of a large plant in a local labour market may deter smaller plants—possibly suppliers—from setting up there because this situation is often associated with high wages and a tight labour market.

These two major fields—cyclical fluctuations in the unemployment rate and backward linkage patterns—must now be examined to test the hypothesis that in both cases there are significant differences between plant-dominated and other labour markets.

CHANGES IN THE UNEMPLOYMENT RATE OVER TIME

Hypotheses

For reasons already suggested, it is likely that unemployment rates in plant-dominated local labour markets will show greater temporal fluctuations than in industry-dominated ones, and will vary more widely in industry-dominated local labour markets than in those that are not dominated. This is based on the probability that a smaller range of products will be made in an industry-dominated labour market and that the range in a plant-dominated labour market will be even narrower. Consequently, the impact of changes on the demand for a given product will be greatest in labour markets where it is being manufactured by a large plant. This effect is likely to be amplified by the 'law of proportionate effect': if a firm employing a third of an area's labour force dismisses 25 per cent of its workforce, other firms in the area can absorb all the displaced workers by expanding their workforces by 12 per cent, but a similar reduction by a plant employing a thirtieth of an area's labour force would require other firms to expand the numbers employed by only 0.8 not 1.2 per cent. Other firms in the area may be unable to absorb all the workers dismissed from a dominant plant. On the one hand, some of the other employment in the particular labour market may be tied to the activity in the dominant plant by direct or indirect multipliers: a reduction in the need for workers at the dominant plant may be accompanied by an associated weakening in the demand for employees at other establishments. On the other hand, the expansion or entry of other employers in the local labour market may be hindered by the existence of the dominant plant. Bronfenbrenner (1956) argues that the higher-than-average wages which the majority of dominant employers pay act as a barrier to the entry or growth of other employers within the local labour market.

To establish that significant differences in the extent of unemployment fluctuations in plant-dominated, industry-dominated, and non-dominated local labour markets are a function of employer concentration, it is necessary to ensure, as far as possible, that they are not better explained by other factors, such as the industrial structure of the labour markets or their regional distribution, or by company policies about recruitment, redundancy, work-sharing, and labour retention in the face of fluctuating demand. Large enterprises, indigenously owned and managed as single-plant companies, are likely, for paternalistic and socially responsible reasons, to try to retain as many workers as possible during a recession, thereby reducing fluctuations in levels of unemployment. At the other extreme it is hypothesized that where the large plant represents a branch of a non-locally owned company, the adjustment of labour to output will be more precise so that local labour markets dependent on such an establishment at the margin of a company's productive needs may be particularly vulnerable (Atkins, 1973). Where the dominant plant is a branch of a multinational company the opportunity to switch blocks of work to other countries may make it even more vulnerable, both to closure and to large swings in employment levels (Hodges, 1974). A company's ability to retain labour for social reasons during a recession will depend upon the competitiveness of the industry in which it is engaged: low profit levels may prevent firms acting for social reasons even if they wish to do so. Competitiveness is not an easy characteristic to measure, but some studies (e.g. Needham, 1970) have used indices of product market concentration as a proxy, the assumption being that where an industry comprises a small number of large firms some form of price fixing may reduce the degree of competition. Thus it can be hypothesized that there will be a negative relationship between the index of product market concentration and the extent of fluctuations in the unemployment rate in the local labour market.

Data and the Index of Change

Most time-series analyses of unemployment data have indicated four separate components: the long-run trend, seasonal fluctuations, cyclical fluctuations, and random elements (Thomas, 1973, pp. 195–6). Concern here was to identify the extent of the seasonal component and thereafter 'deseasonalize' the data to fit the best log-linear long-run trend line, and then to measure the extent to which individual values diverged from it. The basic hypothesis was that the mean divergence for labour markets dominated by a single plant would be significantly higher than that for non-dominated labour markets.

The basic data were supplied by the Department of Employment as Employment Record V totals of monthly registered adult male unemployed, excluding those 'temporarily stopped'. The values for January, April, July, and October were recorded for each year from 1951 through 1975. The data cover 298 local labour markets—records for three—Gainsborough, Louth, and Skegness—being incomplete.

Alternative methods of 'deseasonalizing' the data were tried—for example, moving averages, seasonal dummies, and seasonal weights—to select the most appropriate method. Some, such as the annual coefficient of variation, were useful in their own right in yielding a measure of the extent of seasonal fluctuations. But analyses of this measure indicated that the size of fluctuations was best explained by local employment structure, especially where—as in Clacton, Eastbourne, and Margate—seasonal tourism yielded high values, rather than the size distribution of employers within the labour market. The data were deseasonalized using moving averages.

These data were then fitted to the best log—linear long-run trend line by the least-squares method and the degree to which each of the value for the one hundred quarters diverged from the long-run trend was calculated. One complication is that the fitting of a single smooth trend line conceals any major shift at one point in time, the existence of which would raise the values of the r ean divergences as shown by Figure 6.5. The model of employment change over time at the national level, constructed by the National Institute of Economic and Social Research, indicates major upward shifts in the unemployment rate in 1963 and more especially in 1966 (Gujarati, 1972; Taylor, 1972). To allow for the possible impact of a major discontinuity, the largest single shift in unemployment in each local labour market in a period of eight quarters was identified and separate curves fitted before and after this jump. Although this process reduced the mean divergence value, it did not have a major impact on the ranking of local labour markets in terms of mean divergence size.

By comparing the mean divergences of the observed values of male unemployment from the long-run trend line, significant differences between various types of labour market could be identified. The mean divergence, termed DISP for convenience, was insignificantly correlated with labour-market size (in terms of

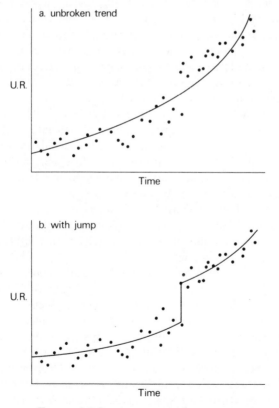

FIGURE 6.5 Long-run unemployment trends

workforce) although the sign, as anticipated, is negative. It is significantly negatively correlated with the extent of commuting independence, since labour markets subject to considerable fluctuations in unemployment are likely to look for more distant employment in recession years. DISP is significantly correlated with the rate of unemployment growth during the 1951–75 period. Lastly, DISP is significantly correlated, as anticipated, with a high proportion of male workers in manufacturing, as opposed to service employment.

The Employment Change Hypothesis

In testing the basic hypothesis relating the extent of unemployment fluctuations to the existence of a dominant plant, the value of DISP for plant-dominated labour markets (0.297 per cent) is significantly higher (1 per cent level of confidence) than that for non-dominated labour markets (0.25 per cent) but the mean value of DISP for industry-dominated labour markets is significantly (1 per cent level of confidence) higher still (0.350 per cent). Thus there is a significant difference between the types of labour markets as hypothesized, but this may not be related to dominance *per se*. The first alternative suggestion is that the difference is explained by variations in economic structure: those labour markets dominated by a large plant have a disproportionately great share of industries which nationally have higher than average employment fluctuations. Five SIC groups (mining, coal and petroleum products, metal manufacture, shipbuilding, and vehicle manufacture) are significantly over-represented amongst dominant plants. Using data on unemployment rates by industry for the period 1951–75 (and allowing for the SIC definitional changes in 1958 and 1968), these 5 sectors are ranked respectively seventh, eighteenth, first, seventeenth, and sixth, of the eighteen mining and manufacturing sectors as ordered by their national employment instability. It does seem unlikely, therefore, that the higher levels of DISP in dominated labour markets can be explained by industrial structure, and the same conclusion holds when the analysis is repeated at the MLH level. Comparison between plant-dominated and industry-dominated labour markets is possible in 11 of the 18 mining and manufacturing SIC groups. In all but two (shipbuilding and paper manufacture) the generally higher levels of DISP are found to hold at the industry level.

The second possible explanation of the significant differences in mean DISP is that it is regional. Brechling (1967) exposes significant differences between regions in Britain in the rate of change in unemployment levels. Possibly, therefore, the higher levels of DISP in plant-dominated labour markets result from their disproportionate location in regions with higher-than-average unemployment-rate fluctuations. If DISP is calculated for all labour markets and the mean calculated for each of the 10 standard regions (Northern Ireland being omitted from the analysis) there are significantly lower mean DISP values in the 3 Depressed Regions, North (0.256), Scotland (0.237), and Wales (0.236) whilst the highest values are found in the East Midlands (0.345) and the West Midlands

(0.339). These figures concur with Brechling's findings of high fluctuations in the Midlands and low ones in peripheral regions. However, it is known that plant-dominated labour markets are most common in the Depressed Regions (see abⲓ ve). Thus plant-dominated labour markets with their high DISPs are not typical of the peripheral regions with their low DISPs, despite their greater proportionate numbers there. On this basis it appears most unlikely that the higher rates of DISP in plant-dominated labour markets are a regional effect.

The third possible explanation of the higher levels of DISP in plant-dominated labour markets is that the type of establishment, as defined by ownership characteristics, is a better explanation of the DISP value than the dominance effect. Plants, irrespective of their absolute or proportional size, which are locally owned, are less likely to discharge workers when demand slackness than branch plants of companies with more remote headquarters. Belief in the instability of employment in branch plants of the latter type has not been dispelled by Atkins' (1973) recent finding that mature branch establishments were better at maintaining employment than their parent plants. When the mean DISP values for the 5 types of dominant plant ownership are compared, significant differences do occur. The values for U.K. local-owned (0.262, $n = 12$) and foreign-owned plants (0.270, $n = 10$) are significantly lower than those for U.K. non-locally owned branch plants (0.305, $n = 9$). It thus seems possible that the managements of single-establishment, locally owned dominant plants and of those operated by foreign-owned companies are better able to avoid the severest swings of the business cycle, or to adopt schemes that minimize their employment impact. The quasi-State-owned group have the highest levels of DISP and it may be this instability, together with their importance in their local labour markets, that has led to them being taken over by State agencies like the National Enterprise Board.

Thus labour markets whose employment structure is dominated by a single mining or manufacturing concern do have significantly different patterns of adult male unemployment-rate changes than non-dominated ones. The possibility that these dissimilarities stem from either industrial structure or interregional differences can be discounted, but the type of plant ownership does have a significant effect on the scale of unemployment fluctuations. The analysis can be extended by contrasting unemployment-rate fluctuations in plant-dominated and industry-dominated labour markets. The significantly higher values of DISP in the latter, once industrial sector has been taken into account, are explicable by two types of hypothesis: one relates to the internal operation of the dominant plants and the other to the relationship between the dominant plant or industry and the rest of the labour market.

Comparison between Plant- and Industry-dominated Labour Markets

Large, dominating plants within an industry are probably better able to reap the benefits of scale economies, and demonstrate greater productive efficiency, than small plants within the same industry; therefore they are less affected by downturns in product demand and have less need to lay off workers periodically. Moreover, dominant plants may be more aware of their significance to the well-being of the local community and take greater steps to avoid large-scale redundancies by operating schemes like work-sharing and overtime restriction. Other factors may also be involved. For example, large plants may be more unionized and this may lead to greater resistance to substantial redundancies; in contrast the operation of the redundancy payments scheme since the early 1960s may have led small employers to restort to frequent lay-offs and re-recruitments to avoid making substantial redundancy payments to long-serving workers. Dominant plants are more concentrated in industrial sectors with higher product market concentration ratios: as there may be less competition in this group it is possible that dominant plants are able to adopt more socially responsible attitudes when product demand declines. Alternative hypotheses suggest that in labour markets which are plant-dominated, substantial lay-offs by the dominant plant are partially countered by processes in the rest of the labour market. Major redundancies have to be notified in advance to the Department of Employment and special 'placement' offices may be set up to provide additional employment information.

There does therefore appear to be a significant relationship between the existence of a dominant plant within a local labour market and a relatively high rate of fluctuations over time in the male unemployment rate which is not explained by sectoral or regional effects. The ownership characteristics of the dominant plant have an effect upon changes in levels of unemployment in a way which suggests that locally owned plants and, more surprisingly, branch plants of foreign-owned companies are better able to protect their local labour markets from wide swings in unemployment. When standardized by industrial type, plant-dominated labour markets have lower fluctuations in unemployment than industry-dominated ones, suggesting that internal rather than external scale economies are more important to plants faced with a national or inter-national downturn in demand. All these relationships may be exacerbated where there is a high degree of interdependence between the dominant plant and other employers within the local labour market. Alternatively, if there are few linkages between the dominant plant and the rest of the labour market a radical change in employment levels at the former will have relatively little effect on the latter.

DOMINANT PLANT LINKAGES

Evidence on the degree of attraction exerted by dominant plants upon potential suppliers of inputs is ambiguous. To resolve this, input–output data from the 1963 Census of Production (Central Statistical Office, 1970) were linked to unpublished employment information to test the hypothesis that the existence of a dominant plant in a local labour market exerts a significant attractive force upon suppliers of inputs.

Location Quotients of Suppliers

Each of the 98 dominant plants was allocated to the appropriate industry group as defined in the input–output tables of the Census of Production. In each case the 3 most important inputs to the relevant industry group were identified and the proportion of the workforce employed in these 3 supply industries was calculated from the 1973 Employment Record II lists. Comparisons between these proportions with those employed nationally in the supplying industries generated the location quotient for each of the 3 supply industries for each of the 98 plants. The mean value of these quotients, 1.237, is greater than the random value of 1.000 to an extent which is significant at the 1 per cent level of confidence. Thus dominant plants are an important attraction to potential suppliers of inputs.

If the calculation is repeated for the 34 local labour markets in which a single industry dominates the employment structure, the mean value of the 104 location quotients is considerably greater at 2.431. Much of the difference between these mean location quotient values is explained by the industries concerned. Many of the industry-dominated labour markets are concerned with cotton textiles, woollen textiles, and footwear, all of which are long-established and spatially concentrated industries in which suppliers have traditionally been close; the location quotients of suppliers are therefore high. If the 14 industry groups are isolated in which comparison between plant-dominated and industry-dominated labour markets is possible, the mean location quotients show no such bias in favour of the latter labour markets. As Table 6.7 demonstrates the mean location

TABLE 6.7 Location quotients of supply industries

Industry group	Mean location quotient	
	plant-dominated	industry-dominated
9. Other foodstuffs	2.26	2.29
18. Other chemicals	0.71	0.15
19. Iron and steel	0.84	2.77
29. Non-electrical machinery	2.97	0.42
38. Metal goods	1.16	8.64
39. Shipbuilding	0.52	0.82
40. Motor vehicles	0.86	0.97
41. Aircraft	1.57	0.05
44. Cotton manufacturing	2.06	5.55
46. Hosiery, lace	7.60	0.00
48. Miscellaneous textiles	1.41	4.07
51. Footwear	5.44	4.02
54. Pottery and glass	1.17	0.35
57. Paper and board	0.48	0.47

quotients for these 14 groups are significantly higher in plant-dominated labour markets in 6 industries, significantly lower in 4 industries, and broadly similar in the remainder.

Although there appears to be a significant relationship between the presence of a dominant plant in a local labour market and the concentration there of industries which supply it with inputs, the mean location quotients of those supply industries vary widely in value as between dominant plants: in Table 6.7 it can be seen that the range of mean location quotients by dominant plant industry extends from 0.48 to 7.60. High location quotients are usually associated with industries such as knitwear, footwear, and cotton textiles which are spatially concentrated into few areas of Britain and where there has been time for suppliers to grow or locate close to them; low location quotients are associated with such industries as paper and board products, oil refining, timber products, light metal and rubber manufactures, all of which depend upon imported raw materials as a major locational factor.

Product Market Concentration and Spatial Concentration

Two hypotheses were developed to explain differences between the apparent attractive powers of dominant plants engaged in different industries. Suppliers will be more likely to locate near potential purchasers either because they are few in number or because they are spatially concentrated. The first idea can be tested by comparing the mean location quotients for the 32 industrial sectors in which dominant plants are engaged with the indices of product market concentration from the Census of Production. These indices range between 100 where all production in an industry is in the control of one organization (as in coal-mining: the National Coal Board) and values around 30, as in footwear manufacture, timber products manufacture, and cotton spinning where production is divided among a large number of small companies. The rank correlation between the mean location quotients of supplying industries and the index of product market concentration is -0.179, which is not significant where $n = 29$, as 3 industries had to be omitted because no measures of product market concentration were computed. Thus the null hypothesis that industries whose structure is dominated by a small number of large companies are no more likely to attract suppliers than industries whose structure comprises many small companies must be accepted. The most probable explanation is that, while the product market concentration ratio measures corporate size, it does not measure establishment size. It is thus possible for an industry to be dominated by a few large companies whose production is spread among many small factories which do not act as a magnet for suppliers of inputs.

The rank correlation between the mean location quotient of supplying industries and the degree of spatial concentration of the industries in which the dominant plants are engaged requires some index of the latter parameter. Using

1966 census employment data disaggregated to 61 economic subregions, the percentage of the total workforce employed in the 6 most important subregions was calculated for each industry group. The percentage employed ranged from 78.4 per cent in highly localized industries such as hosiery to 43.2 per cent in dispersed industries such as drink manufacture. A rank correlation test between these two indices yielded a value of $+0.33$ which, where $n = 32$, is statistically significant at the 5 per cent level of confidence. It is just possible, therefore, to accept the hypothesis that where dominant plants are found in a spatial concentration of their industry (indeed they may themselves in some cases represent the entire concentration) there is a significant clustering of supplying industries. If the same calculation is undertaken for the 18 industry groups which comprise the industry-dominated group of local labour markets, the value of the rank correlation coefficient is $+0.19$ which is not significant. Thus it is the existence of a dominant plant rather than a spatial clustering of a group of smaller establishments engaged in the same process which acts as a locational focus for input suppliers. James (1964) has argued that the existence of establishments in industry groups which are important suppliers of inputs to a dominant plant does not necessarily lead to functional linkages between those establishments and the dominant plant. But the particular dominant plant described by James was a recent immigrant to the region and employed industrial practices uncommon there. More usually the dominant plant has evolved slowly over time and there is a much greater probability that suppliers will have developed near it. In that case, it does seem that indirect-income multiplier effects in local labour markets whose employment structure is dominated by a single employer will, *ceteris paribus*, be higher than in other local labour markets. This in turn would help to explain the higher levels of fluctuation in unemployment rates since instability in employment in the dominant plant would be echoed by other local industrial establishments with which it was functionally linked.

CONCLUSION

An omission from industrial geography has been the paucity of studies which relate the manufacturing establishment to its local labour market. Most individual manufacturing establishments are so small relative to the size of their local labour markets that their impact on unemployment, recruitment, wage determination, or linkages is undetectable. This present study suggests that plant-dominated labour markets do experience significantly higher levels of fluctuation in unemployment rates than balanced labour markets to an extent which cannot be explained by either industrial composition or regional effects. The degree of fluctuation is in part related to the ownership type of the dominant plant; locally owned plants and branch plants of foreign companies prove to be more stable employers than branch plants of U.K.-owned companies and State concerns. Industry-dominated labour markets have even higher levels of unemployment fluctuations resulting from levels of both competitive efficiency and product market concentration. Dominant plants are more likely to be associated spatially with backward-linked industrial sectors than are industry-dominated or balanced local labour markets. The consequences of these stronger linkages may be significant in higher income and employment multipliers in plant-dominated labour markets. The study of aggregate data on plant-size distributions, employment structure, input–output flows, and ownership types has led to formulation of certain hypotheses which can be tested only by qualitative data gained directly from the plants concerned. One seeks to explain the lower levels of unemployment-rate fluctuations in locally owned plants by a paternalistic attitude of management to workers; the other suggests that branches of non-U.K. companies are less likely to be spatially associated with suppliers of inputs because of the differing economic spaces in which purchasing is undertaken.

The need is for more rigorous hypothesis testing within the area of industrial geography. Aggregate studies of changes in the level of total employment or of changes in the structure of employment necessarily can only infer causality. Regularities in changes in employment, unemployment, and industrial structure are 'explained' in terms of regional or subregional components or industrial structural factors, when in reality such changes occur because of entrepreneurial decisions taken at establishment or company level. Establishment-based studies of entrepreneurial decisions are often faced with the problems of just how representative the sample establishments are of broader industrial processes and whether the decisions are based on real understanding of these processes and measuring the extent of their outcome. The matching of qualitative data on entrepreneurial decision-making with aggregate studies of local labour-market performance over time, in a rigorous hypothesis-testing framework, does appear to represent one of the more promising avenues for future research into industrial geography.

Chapter 7
Towards a Theory of Location and Corporate Growth

LARS HÅKANSON

INTRODUCTION

In 'mixed' or capitalist industrialized economies, the firm, whether private or corporate, provides the organizational framework within which tasks are defined and employment is created or lost. It is the mould in which economic development is shaped. This is recognized in regional economic policy, which attempts to create conditions for promoting the growth of the firms in certain areas or localities rather than in others. The theoretical concepts on which such policies have been designed derive largely from the static 'theory of the firm' and are based on assumptions and postulates of neo-classical economic theory, the inadequacy of which has become increasingly obvious. Thus the aim of much recent work on location theory has been to replace the static concepts of traditional analysis with dynamic and process-orientated models. This endeavour has entailed a fundamental shift in perspective and in approach (Hamilton, 1974a; Collins and Walker, 1975a). Whereas, traditionally, location theories have set out to define causal relationships believed to exist between geographical environment and industrial activity, more recent writers tend to examine industrial location from the viewpoint of the individual firm (McNee, 1958, 1960; Keuning, 1960). Industrial location patterns emerge and develop as the result of the founding, growth, and decline of business firms. Explanations are sought which refer to the nature and logic of this process.

Changes in the size, structure, and locational arrangement of a firm's employment result from decisions, although these need not necessarily involve the consideration of a range of alternative locations for a given activity or of the most suitable activity for a given location (Böventer, 1963a; Krumme, 1969; Ahnström, 1973, pp. 125–51; Back et al., 1974, pp. 24ff). However, empirical evidence supports the assumption that such decisions display sufficient common characteristics, on which to base a taxonomy of locational behaviour (North, 1974; see also Hamilton, 1978a). Broadly, changes in the locational arrangement and structure of employment within a firm are of two types. First, they can occur through the setting up, acquisition, movement, sale, or discontinuance of geographically and functionally separate establishments. Since they often involve the long-term allocation of a large share of the firm's resources, such events are sometimes associated with decisions or decision sequences of a strategic nature, including the selection of products and markets for future expansion. Second, they may result from the growth, decline or reorganization of existing establishments. Although each single decision may be marginal to the overall employment of the firm, the effect of a series of such decisions can, of course, be quite substantial. The aggregate outcome of the two types of decisions is reflected in the size and structure of regional employment.

The purpose of this chapter is to indicate how location theory may fruitfully be connected to the *theory of the growth of firm*, as developed by Downie (1958), Penrose (1959), Marris (1964), and others. This provides a useful conceptual basis on which to construct a theory of corporate behaviour in space. The first part examines the rationale for substituting the traditional profit-maximization postulate with one of growth-maximization, and briefly discusses the motives for corporate growth. Then follows the outline of a simple conceptual model of corporate growth, identifying a number of restraints on the growth rates of firms. A set of growth strategies is available to overcome these restraints and it is assumed that the firm will select and pursue the strategy (or combination of strategies) which is expected to maximize growth in the ensuring period. Growth may be accomplished internally by means of investment in new capacity, or externally by means of acquisition or merger. In the process, mutative changes in organizational structure, production technology, and location patterns evolve. The final section, on the spatial dimension of growth, defines a set of tentative expectations as to the geographical patterns of corporate development typically associated with the basic strategies of growth.

THE MOTIVES FOR GROWTH

The 'Corporate System'

In capitalist economies in Western Europe and Anglo-America, private capital, organized in large industrial enterprises, has long been a primary agent of economic and social change. The growth and geographical extension of such firms began in the last quarter of the nineteenth century. Large firms with several geographically separate establishments began to appear. Before the industrial revolution such organizations were generally not very successful and hence short-lived (Pollard, 1965, pp. 25–60). Now, technical and organizational innovations created economies of scale, increasing the economic size of both plants and firms. Changes in the technology of transport of goods, people, and messages promoted the creation of vast integrated industrial organizations to serve expanding national and international markets. In short, the emergence of multi-plant firms was based on the technical, institutional, and organizational changes which mark the breakthrough of modern industrialism.

Among these changes was the advent of the public, joint-stock limited liability company. The corporate form promoted the mobilization of capital—a prerequisite for the successful exploitation of mass-production techniques and large-scale marketing—and made possible the financing of growth on a much larger scale than previously possible. It facilitated the legal transfer of the ownership of firms; external growth through acquisition and merger became a common mode of expansion. The growth of large corporate enterprises was accompanied by the development of modern capital markets and a concomitant dispersion of ownership. Increasingly, control passed into the hands of a new class of professional managers. The separation of ownership from control and the dominance of large corporations in many sectors of the economy are prominent features of what Berle and Means (1932) termed 'the corporate system'. The emergence to predominance of this new mode of economic organization raised questions about the very fundamentals of economic theory. Berle and Means (1932, p. 9) wrote:

> The explosion of the atom of property destroys the basis of the old assumption that the quest for profits will spur the owner of industrial property to its effective use. It consequently challenges the fundamental economic principle of individual initiative in industrial enterprise. It raises for reexamination the question of the motive force back of industry, and, the ends for which modern corporation can be or will be run.

Subsequently, several competing models were put forth in the discussion, but no general agreement as to the exact nature of the relevant 'objective function' has emerged to replace the maximum-profit postulate of neo-classical theory. The evidence of empirical studies concerning the goals of business executives is far from conclusive and has left the issue unresolved (Starbuck, 1971; Curwen, 1974).

Profit versus Growth-maximization?

As demonstrated in an illuminating article by Loasby (1971), the debate on profit-maximization and the theory of the firm can usefully be analysed within the conceptual framework developed by T. S. Kuhn (1962) in his study of theoretical innovation in the natural sciences.

> Profit-maximization [Loasby (1971, p. 867) argues] is not a hypothesis but a paradigm; and whereas a specific hypothesis embodying some version of profit-maximization can, in principle, be tested, the paradigm of profit-maximization cannot. Only in long-period static equilibrium with perfect knowledge is its formulation unique; and no such experimental conditions can be found.

Moreover, the question of the 'truth' of the paradigm is irrelevant; as Friedman has stressed, economic theory cannot be evaluated on the basis of the descriptive realism of its assumptions. 'Truly important and significant hypotheses will be found to have "assumptions" that are wildly inaccurate descriptive representations of reality . . . .' (Friedman, 1953, p. 14). To him the primary test of theory is the accuracy of its predictions. However, as Kuhn (1962, p. 147) emphasizes, predictive accuracy is not a sufficient criterion: 'All historically significant theories have agreed with the facts, but only more or less.'

The model set forth here assumes that firms seek to maximize the rate of growth of sales revenue subject to a security restrain. Development of this approach is associated with the writings of Penrose (1959), Baumol (1959, 1962), Williamson (1966), and Galbraith (1974). The formulation presently adopted closely follows the theory elaborated by Marris (1964). The growth-maximization postulate does not imply that growth is the only goal that large corporations pursue, not that it is always attained. The legitimacy of the assumption lies not in its descriptive accuracy: 'it is the . . . ability to generate a variety of hypotheses to explain, if not everything, yet a large body of important phenomena, which is the essential virtue of a paradigm.' (Loasby, 1971, p. 867). However, a growth-maximization postulate is not imbued with the same superficial validity as the profit-maximization postulate, firmly rooted in the image of the self-seeking and avaricious capitalist entrepreneur. It can be asked why large modern corporations should be expected to pursue growth rather than profits, and profits primarily as a means to growth.

Reasons for Growth

Organizational growth is not a spontaneous process, but the result of decisions made and actions taken by individuals employed in the organization. It can occur only if increased size is positively related to the goals of the organization or to those of its individual members. Although growth may be an end in itself, Starbuck notes that

> there is usually an implicit assumption that size is correlated with the attainment of goals which have more basic relevance to the organization's purpose or which are more immediately of interest to some sub-unit of the organizational membership (Starbuck, 1971, p. 14).

Of the various reasons for growth propounded in the literature, three main types of motives stand out.

Pecuniary and personal interest This interest of the executive group is often assumed to be more closely associated with growth than with profitability. Whereas profit-maximization as a goal requires the executive to subordinate personal interest to those of a largely anonymous group of stockholders, there are several reasons to expect growth to be more directly relevant to personal motives. Executive salaries are more strongly influenced by the absolute level of sales than by profitability (Roberts, 1956; Baumol, 1959; Dent, 1959; Patton, 1961; McGuire et al., 1962). The urge for power and prestige associated with the supervision of many subordinates is also a powerful motive for growth (Gordon,

1945, pp. 305ff). Job security is generally greater in an expanding firm and the addition of new work represents important career opportunities:

> When a man takes decisions leading to successful expansion, he not only creates new openings but also recommends himself and his colleagues as particularly suitable candidates to fill them (Marris, 1964, p. 102).

Furthermore, growth—as opposed to profitability—is an accepted, clearly understood and easily measured indicator of success. As Galbraith has noted,

> No other social goal is more strongly avowed than economic growth. No other test of social success has such nearly unanimous acceptance as the annual increase in the Gross National Product (Galbraith, 1974, p. 181.)

In working towards the expansion of their firms, managers not only further their own self-interest but may rest assured that they are simultaneously pursuing a social good of the highest order.

Reduction of uncertainty and risk This reduction is associated with large size and is often an important inducement to growth. Through the acquisition of competitors, customers, and suppliers, the firm may extend its authority to ever larger sections of the (potentially hostile) environment. The vagaries of the market are replaced by an increased scope for planning and control. This is the essential basis of monopolistic or monopsonistic power—historically important factors in the rise of large corporations. Similarly, growth by diversification is frequently motivated by the concern for security as, for instance, the wish to increase the number of baskets in which to put one's eggs. These considerations apart, for purely 'statistical reasons' large firms tend to be more stable than small ones:

> the greater the number of similar items involved the more likely are deviations to cancel out and to leave the actual average results nearer to the expected results (Sargant Florence, 1972, p. 61).

The existence of unused or under-utilized resources This is often an important motive for expansion. Production may have to reach a very large scale to allow indivisible and specialized resources to be utilized at maximum capacity. The determination of the optimum scale of operation according to the principle of the lowest multiple has generally been discussed as a source of economics of scale. However, in a dynamic analysis, the problem of balancing resources takes on added significance. To take advantage of presently 'idle' or under-utilized resources the firm must generally acquire new resources. These, in turn, tend to create new imbalances and further inducements to growth (Penrose, 1959, pp. 68ff). Such 'economies of growth' may exist regardless of the possible benefits associated with a larger scale of production (Penrose, 1959, p. 102). The motive for growth is frequently an 'entry advantage' which enables the firm to enter new product markets more efficiently than its competitors. At times, the original economies disappear as the newly acquired resources become progressively more specialized in their new use, limiting the scope for positive 'synergy' with the firm's old activities.

Goals, Behaviour, and the Environment

The validity of the growth-maximization postulate is limited not only to the institutional conditions of the corporate system, but also by the character of the larger economic environment. However, the relationships between goals, behaviour, and the environment are complex and little understood. Obviously, the existence of growth-orientated motives is not a sufficient condition for growth. Adverse changes in the external environment may render the realization of these goals more difficult or impossible. Moreover, the goals of the corporation are the outcome of a learning process. As Starbuck notes,

> people learn to pursue realistic goals. If growth is difficult, the organization will tend to pursue goals which are not growth-orientated; if growth is easy, the organization will learn to pursue goals which are growth-orientated. What one observes are the learned goals. Do these goals produce growth, or does growth produce these goals? (Starbuck, 1971, p. 33).

In conditions of general economic expansion, growth will tend to be more easily achieved than in a stagnating or declining economy. In the latter situation, or in other adverse conditions, the minimization of a forced decline in total revenue may be assumed to be the relevant goal.

RESTRAINTS TO GROWTH

The rate of growth that a corporation manages to achieve during any period depends on an indeterminable number of factors. Some tend to promote expansion (inducements to growth), others have the opposite tendency (re-straints on growth). Each set of factors contains an indefinite number of elements which, in various degrees, influence the actual rate of growth. However it will be presumed that growth is principally determined by a limited number of identifiable factors, and that therefore causal explanations may be defined (Brockhoff, 1966, p. 18).

The present discussion focuses on long-term structural changes or parametric shifts in the firm's production function. Such shifts can occur in large disjointed steps, *mutative growth*, as a result of the introduction of new techniques or the adoption of new products (Gutenberg, 1961, p. 286). They may also be the gradual result of successive adaptation to changing external and internal circumstances, *continuous growth*, such as the progressive extension of capacity in the face of growing demand. The mutative introduction of 'new combination of the means of production' conforms to the Schumpeterian definition of 'innovation'—the basis of economic development:

> To produce means to combine materials and forces within our reach. To produce other things, or the same things by a different method, means to combine these materials and forces differently. In so far as the 'new combination' may in time grow out of the old by continuous adjustment in small steps, there is certainly change, possibly growth, but neither a new phenomenon nor development in our sense. In so far as this is not the case, and the new combinations appear discontinuously, then the phenomenon characterising development emerges (Schumpeter, 1934, p. 65).

A review of the literature on the theory of the growth of the firm indicates four major types of factors which may induce mutative changes in the firm's production function. They are conceived of as restraints on the rate of growth of the firm, and their interplay determines the maximum attainable rate of expansion in any period. Mutative changes are induced as the firm strives to overcome these restraints. Utilizing the 'product life cycle' concept the restraints may be combined in a dynamic model of corporate growth and location change (Albach, 1965, pp. 53ff).

The Demand Restraint

Expansion, measured by sales and output, is related to the growth of demand. This relation is the basis of Downie's (1958) analysis of the rate and dispersion of technical progress. Given the right assumptions—a given product market and given technology—the maximum rate of output growth is equal to that of the market. By lowering its price, the firm may attract customers away from competitors and, for a time, grow at a faster rate than the total market. Depending on the elasticity of demand the rate of profit may initially increase but at some point, further reduction of prices brings negative returns. As the rate of profit declines, the firm's ability to raise capital for investment in additional capacity is reduced. Since the pace at which capacity can be expanded is positively related to the rate of profit, but the rate of profit ultimately will tend to decline as customer expansion accelerates, an upper limit exists to the possible rate of growth. In equilibrium, the rate of growth of the firm is equal to that of the market: when the desired pace of growth exceeds this rate the *demand restraint* comes into force.

The argument is consistent with the neo-classical assumption that by setting its price the firm determines its position on the demand curve, but that the shift of the curve, i.e. the growth in demand, is externally determined and outside its control. Although, in most cases this may be a sound and reasonable assumption, in the context of mutative change it may no longer be tenable. The very act of lowering the price may under these circumstances trigger processes which induce a more rapid shift in the demand curve, e.g. when price to a significant extent determines the range of functions to which a particular good may economically be employed. This is often the situation with the new products for which no clearly defined market exists:

> Innovations have almost always created their own market to some extent; indeed they have very often created it completely (Dahmén, 1970, p. 68).

Given the restrictive assumptions of Downie's theory, the only way in which the firm may increase its maximum sustainable rate of growth is by increased efficiency, such as by technical innovation. According to the postulates of this model, the more efficient firms in an industry will continue to grow at the expense of the less efficient ones—unless something occurs to disrupt the process— leading to a gradual concentration of the industry. According to Downie, the concentration process will be disrupted by technological break- throughs which redistribute the pattern of technological advantage in the industry. Such breakthroughs, he contends, are most likely to occur in the least efficient sector of the industry, that is by firms which are losing ground to their more efficient competitors and which are forced to regain competitive strength (Downie, 1958, pp. 59ff). It is not necessary to concur with this hypothesis on technological innovations to accept the conclusion that the emulation of technological progress is an intrinsic part of the competitive process, and that mutative changes may be induced as firms strive to overcome the restraints on growth imposed by the market.

The Managerial Restraint

Real-life firms are not bound to specific products and markets. One obvious means to increase the rate of growth is to search for and enter new product market combinations. By the same token, the most serious threat to the growth and survival of the firm is not competition from firms in the same industry, marketing more or less the same products, but from new products, which more efficiently accomplish the functions of the existing ones or make the old functions obsolete. In the process of 'creative destruction', long-run survival and growth require almost incessant diversification:

> ever since the industrial revolution, firms have been able to grow by successively marketing products they had not previously offered, thus enabling themselves to progress by successive 'jumps' to appropriate positions among an ever-growing family of otherwise static demand-curves (Marris, 1964, p. 120).

As Penrose emphasized, the demand relevant to the decision-maker is not limited to the products and markets where the firm is currently engaged, but rather to a subjectively perceived 'productive opportunity':

the "demand" with which an entrepreneur is concerned when he makes his production plans is nothing more nor less than his own ideas about what he can sell at various prices with varying degrees of selling effort . . . (Penrose, 1959, p. 81).

In consequence of this view, the focus of Penrose's analysis is shifted from the external world and the restrictions imposed by the market to the internal factors which determine the direction and rate of change of the firm's 'productive opportunity', i.e. 'the productive possibilities that its "entrepreneurs" see and can take advantage of' (Penrose, 1959, p. 81). Her analysis proceeds on the assumptions that the firm can always manage to finance profitable expansion investments, and that opportunities for these exist in the economy. With these assumptions the limits to growth in Downie's model are removed. In Penrose's theory, the limits to the rate of expansion are set by the capacity of the 'management team' to perform the tasks associated with the planning and co-ordination of growth—the *managerial restraint*.

Although the firm might be faced with numerous opportunities for profitable expansion, there are still limits to the rate of growth:

the firm cannot, and in general will not attempt to, extend its expansion plans, and with them its 'management team', in an effort to take advantage of *all* such opportunities. It *cannot* do so because the very nature of a firm as an administrative and planning organization requires that the existing responsible officials of the firm at least know and approve, even if they do not in detail control all aspects of, the plans and operations of the firm; it *will not* even try to do so if the officials of the firm are themselves concerned to maintain its character as an organized unit (Penrose, 1959, p. 45).

As in all productive processes, the capacity of the administrative organization to handle the planning and execution of growth can be increased in two ways: by increased productivity or by additional input. As the officials of the firm gain more experience their efficiency will tend to increase, but acquiring experience takes time. Similarly, an upper rate exists at which the size of the management team can be increased by recruiting new members. The new members lack the competence which comes from working in a particular group in a particular firm and thus, initially, their efficiency will be low.

External expansion—growth through acquisition or merger—represents a means to raise the limits on the rate of growth imposed by the managerial restraint. By acquiring another firm it is often possible to obtain immediately a complete and experienced management team to which the operations of new unit can, at least temporarily, be entrusted. The effect is to release managerial capacity for the planning of growth. Successful operation of the enlarged firm after merger requires the activities of the two units to be co-ordinated and their organizations administratively integrated. To achieve such integration—a process which often involves extensive organizational adjustments—requires considerable managerial effort so that, for a time, the share of managerial capacity which can be devoted to further expansion is reduced:

> In principle internal growth must be either a reasonably smooth curve or a step-like curve in which each step bears a close relation to the base from which it rises. Growth through acquisition, on the other hand, can proceed in very large steps relative to the base, but the "plateaus" after periods of extensive expansion will tend to be longer (Penrose, 1959, p. 194).

As the firm grows larger and more diversified changes in the organizational structure are sometimes critically important. Lest the whole of managerial effort be absorbed in day-to-day operations, decisions tend to become progressively more decentralized. As Chandler has demonstrated, the resultant organizational structure is closely related to the manner and direction of growth:

> Expansion of volume led to the creation of an administrative office to handle one function in one local area. Growth through geographical dispersion brought the need for a departmental structure and headquarters to administer several local field units. The decision to expand into *new types of functions* called for the building of a central office and a multidepartmental structure, while the *developing of new lines* of products or *continued growth* on a national or international scale brought the formation of the multidivisional structure with a general office to administer the different divisions (Chandler, 1962, p. 14: italics added).

To some extent, the corporation may evade the managerial limits to growth by refraining from integrating the constituent parts of the organization. However, unless managers are willing to transform the organization into an investment trust and forgo all advantages of co-ordination, they will retain final control over the allocation of funds inside the organization.

Mutative changes are thus induced as the firm strives to raise the limits to growth imposed by the managerial restraint. Acquisitions and mergers, of course, are mutative only for the individual firm; for the economy as a whole the long-run effects are likely to be more gradual. In Penrose's model, the limit to the growth of the firm—internal as well as external—is set by the managerial restraint. However, the conclusion holds only under the assumption that the firm is in a position to raise the funds necessary to finance expansion.

The Financial Restraint

The assumptions made by Penrose imply that the firm will continue to grow as long as its management perceives investment opportunities with an expected net return exceeding zero. As Marris (1964) has argued, a management pursuing such a policy will generally not stay in power for long. Like Downie, Marris assumes that the sources from which a firm may finance expansion—borrowing, new share issues, and retained earnings—are finite and positively related to its rate of profit. Adopting the managerial restraint developed by Penrose, Marris explores how 'the institutional framework, as specifically represented in an organised market for voting shares, restrains managerial independence in general and, more particularly, the freedom to grow' (Marris, 1964, p. 45). To overcome the demand restraint, a growth-maximizing management will typically pursue a policy of diversification. However, because of the managerial restraint, as the rate of diversification increases profitability will tend to decline. The converse of the managerial restraint, Marris demonstrates, is the *financial restraint* imposed by the discipline of the stock-market.

The amount of borrowing a firm can undertake is limited by the size of its equity capital, because the risks incurred by borrowers as well as lenders increase as a function of the ratio of borrowed to equity finance ('the leverage ratio'). One way to secure additional equity is to issue new shares. As long as the marginal rate of return of the proposed expansion is expected by shareholders to exceed the average rate of return on the capital already employed—and earnings per share to be maintained or increased—there will be takers of the new issue and no financial limits to growth will be operating (Marris, 1964, pp. 210ff). Yet when the new investment is expected to fall short of average profitability, earnings per share will decline and market price of shares will fall—the process known as 'dilution'. Since the effect on earnings per share after the issue depends not only on the expected profitability of the proposed expansion but also on the size of the new issue, the amount of new equity which the firm can obtain in this manner is finite; at the limit, the market price of shares is zero. In practice, of course, the discipline of the stock-market will prevent the continuous growth by dilution long before this limit has been reached: as Marris (1964, p. 27) indicates,

> when the expansion process occurs in steps, the market has time to learn, and to learn to discount, the fact that the firm is one which is liable to practise dilution.

In a similar manner, the discipline of the stock-market prevents the unlimited growth by retaining earnings. On the assumption that the price of the firm's shares reflects the discounted value of all expected earnings—dividends and capital gains—Marris demonstrates how the price of shares is affected by retained earnings. As in the case of a new issue, the effects on market price of shares is determined by the expected profitability of the investments for which the retained earnings are to be used. If the new investment is expected to generate future earnings large enough to compensate the dividends currently forgone, share prices will be maintained; if not they will decline.

Beyond the limits set by the managerial restraint profitability is negatively related to the rate of growth. Higher growth rates can only be achieved at the price of a declining rate of profit, and this in turn will negatively affect the price of shares. Ultimately, the market valuation of the firm will decline to a point where the position of the firm's managers is endangered; discontented shareholders may band together with the intention of displacing the present management team, or—and probably more often—the fall in share prices may attract the attention of potential 'raiders' increasing the risk of takeover.

In Marris' theory, managers are assumed to have the objective to maximize growth subject to a security restraint, expressed in terms of the minimum 'valuation ratio' or ratio of stock-market value to the book value of assets, that management is willing to accept. The market valuation ratio thus becomes an index of the market's assessment of the firm's prospects under its existing management. A potential 'raider' will strike when the actual valuation ratio falls below his subjective valuation ratio, which reflects the gain he expects to make following a successful takeover and an ensuing change in policy. In practice, of course, the minimum valuation ratio—the ratio at which the most dangerous 'raider' will strike—cannot be known with certainty:

> Evidently, the typical individual firm will in real life be most unsure of the potency of their most dangerous raider. They will not, therefore, be certain of the magnitude of their market valuation ratio at which the probability of takeover becomes unity. Rather they may visualise a functional relationship between the valuation ratio and the subjective risk of takeover (Marris, 1964, p. 45).

The minimum valuation ratio and the severity of the financial restraint depend on management's subjective assessment of the risks of takeover (and on the disutility attached to this risk).

Locational Restraints

The discussion so far has been based on the assumption that productive resources can always be acquired at rates sufficient to ensure the desired rate of expansion and that customers and clients can efficiently be served from existing establishments. To introduce the spatial dimension, a fourth class of restraints will now be added. These *locational restraints* include all factors and circumstances which make growth at existing establishments unfeasible or impossible. These restraints are important because at any one time the growth of the firm proceeds from a set of 'inherited' resources, most of which are tied to particular locations and cannot easily be transferred. Three types of locational restraints are distinguished. First, additional inputs may not be available at existing locations in amounts sufficient to sustain the desired rate of expansion: the *input access restraint*. Second, the costs of serving particular geographical markets may limit the volume of sales: *the market access restraint*. Third, the time and cost of transmitting information, people, and goods between establishments sometimes limits the efficient co-ordination of the firm's resources and may be an important impediment to profitability and expansion: *the intra-organizational access restraint*.

The maximum rate of growth of the firm obviously depends on its access to needed inputs and to its clients and customers, but also on an efficient flow of information and materials between the constituent parts of the organization. A high degree of accessibility will permit a higher rate of growth than where access needs to be increased by locational adjustments. To increase capacity at existing establishments requires less managerial attention than when growth necessitates the geographical dispersion of activities.

A MODEL OF CORPORATE GROWTH

Sustainable growth requires capacity, production, and sales to expand in balance. If capacity utilization remains constant, the rate of growth will be the same for these alternative measures of size. It will be assumed that the firm's only goal is to achieve a rate of growth which its managers consider desirable and attainable within the limits set by the financial restraint, that is the desired rate of growth must be equal or less than the rate of growth associated with the minimum valuation ratio that managers are prepared to accept.

At the beginning of the planning period the firm operates a number of establishments and produces a certain number of products which are sold on a given set of markets. Each product will be characterized by certain functional properties, which determine the range of needs which it is capable of satisfying and the manner in which these needs are satisfied. Different products—as opposed to varieties of the same product—are distinguished when their functional properties differ by some magnitude and when, therefore, the factors which determine the level of demand over time are substantially different (Rasmussen, 1955, p. 96). A 'market' will be defined as a set of (actual or potential) customers within a specified geographical region, who buy and use the product in order to satisfy the same class of need.

To increase its sales volume, the firm may pursue one or more of several possible strategies. Each form of expansion can be achieved internally or by external acquisition or merger. Following the classification suggested by Ansoff, four basic growth strategies may be defined:

(a) *Market penetration*: the firm seeks increased sales of its present products in its present markets.

(b) *Product development*: the firm seeks increased sales in its present markets by developing improved versions of its present products.

(c) *Market development:* the firm seeks increased sales by taking its present products into new markets.

(d) *Diversification*: the firm seeks increased sales by adding new products and markets, departing from its present product/market combinations (Figure 7.1).

According to the technological and market requirements of the new

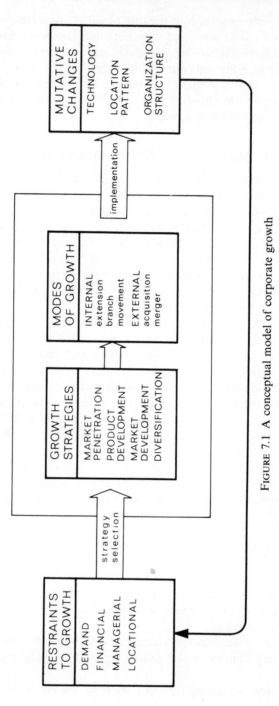

FIGURE 7.1 A conceptual model of corporate growth

product/market position, diversification strategies are divided into *horizontal, vertical, concentric,* and *conglomerate* (Ansoff, 1957, 1965, pp. 94–120). At any time, the mode and direction of growth selected depend on management's perception of the firm's 'productive opportunity' given the set of resources currently controlled. The number and types of possible growth strategies are determined by the combination of restraints to growth operating.

The firm's sales of a particular product in any given market represent some share of the total volume of demand for that product in the specific market. The development of total demand over time defines the 'life cycle' of the product in this market. For the single-product/single-market firm, the slope of this curve measures the rate of growth of demand and determines the limits to growth set by the demand restraint. For the multi-product/multi-market firm, the level of the demand restraint depends on the rate of growth of each product/market and on the relative share of each combination in total revenue. As long as the growth aspirations of management are kept within the boundaries of the demand restraint, no mutative changes are necessary and growth can continue within existing product/markets. In the early stages of the product life cycle, market penetration may be the relevant strategy, in the later stages product development becomes increasingly important. Capacity and production can be extended at existing establishments as long as inputs can be obtained at rates and prices which permit the firm to attain the desired rate of growth. However, at some point this may no longer be possible. The input access restraint comes into force when there is no adjacent land on which to accommodate extensions or when skilled labour cannot be obtained at existing locations.

Technological changes may be induced as the firm seeks to economize the use of the factor in short supply at the existing location. But such adjustments will not always be sufficient to sustain the desired rate of expansion: one solution is to acquire another firm (or part of another firm), and another is to set up a new establishment at a more suitable location. The form of growth actually selected will depend on the amount of managerial time that can be devoted to the planning and execution of these measures, and on the availability of a suitable firm for acquisition. In reality, the considerations governing such decisions may become quite complex. On the one hand, external expansion generally permits a faster rate of growth since its execution requires less managerial attention; on the other, internal expansion projects often create important career opportunities for lower and middle-management officers, who may thus prefer this mode of growth. With time, an increasing share of the firm's wares will reach the 'mature stage' of the product life cycle and unless the desired growth rate is accordingly reduced, the firm will not be able to attain the desired rate of growth within its contemporary product markets. Hence, it will be necessary to increase the relevant demand by entering previously unexploited markets (market development) or by adding new products (diversification).

Market development

Growth by market development allows the firm to raise sales while retaining existing products. Since less managerial capacity is absorbed this strategy tends to permit a faster rate of growth than diversification into new product lines. It will seem particularly favourable when new markets can be efficiently served from existing locations and when inputs can be obtained at rates which permit the extension of capacity at existing establishments. However, at some point the market access restraint may limit the rate of sales increase attainable in the new market. Locational adjustments are induced as the firm strives to overcome the restraints to sales expansion imposed by transport costs, customs barriers, or unfamiliar market conditions. Frequently, acquisitions represent the only feasible means to achieve the competence or production capacity required to maintain or increase market shares.

Diversification

Diversification generally reflects some 'imbalance' in the set of resources controlled by the firm. Finding itself with excess capacity at some stage of the production process, the firm may seek to develop or adopt new products to increase capacity utilization. To exploit its marketing competence, it may seek additional products which fit into the present sales mix. In the first case, the technological basis of production remains the same, but the marketing requirements of the new product may be quite unrelated to the firm's previous activities and experience. In the second case, diversification may take the firm into new technological areas. In either case, unless both technology and marketing are related, diversification is generally accomplished through acquisition or merger. As new products, markets, and establishments enter the activity matrix of the corporation, problems of co-ordination and control multiply. Periodically, problems of intra-organizational access may threaten management's ability to ensure an adequate return on investment and to prevent the valuation ratio falling below its minimum value. To overcome such restraints, changes in organizational structure and in the allocation of functions between establishments may be necessary, and will frequently alter the composition of employment at the establishments affected.

GROWTH AND LOCATION

Geographical Patterns of Corporate Growth

It is necessary to examine the spatial dimension of growth. This section defines a set of 'prior expectations'—evolving from the previous discussion—as to the geographical patterns of corporate development typically associated with the four basic strategies of growth. In the graphical representation of 'ideal' growth patterns, three geographical levels are distinguished in Figure 7.2. The innermost circle represents the 'core area' in which the firm was first founded, and in which, during the early stages of development, employment tends to be concentrated (McNee, 1974, p. 55). Typically, the head office of the corporation will be retained in this area long after the region has ceased to be the centre of the firm's activities and employment. Hence, for a considerable time, the home region will reap the benefits of the firm's expansion in terms of growing and diversified employment opportunities. The intermediate circle delineates the national market. The area between the national market and the outer circle, representing 'the rest of the world', is divided here into four sectors (I–IV) representing different foreign markets. Differential access to these areas—resulting from transportation costs, cultural differences, customs barriers, or other impediments to trade—is indicated by the broken line enclosing country IV.

Expansion without Diversification

The strategies of market penetration, market development, and product development form the basic growth vector in any corporation's development. Hence, the geographical pattern associated with these strategies is the basic framework of corporate growth generally. Diversification adds complexity, but the overall pattern remains the same. In the absence of diversification, the growth pattern of the firm is largely determined by the nature of its market, including the number, location, and buying behaviour of its actual and potential customers. The rate of growth and geographical distribution of demand determine the rate at which marketing activities are extended to new areas and the concomitant increase in production capacity. Sometimes, such as when the firm is operating as a contractor to a larger corporation, it may attain a sufficient volume of sales within its home region. Frequently, the owner/manager of the firm is content to let the fortunes of his firm be tied to those of his local customer(s). More often, the local market proves too small to sustain production at levels needed for

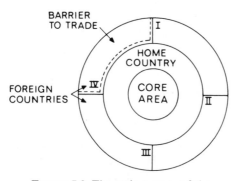

FIGURE 7.2 The action space of the corporation

profitable operations. A distribution system has to be organized to ensure efficient access to customers on a wider geographical scale. Having first developed a national market organization, activities will gradually be extended to foreign markets. In some cases, however, products are so specialized that to attain a sufficient volume of operations the firm is forced almost immediately to extend activities internationally. Consequently, the time absorbed in passing through the successive stages of the ideal model varies considerably between firms.

Stage 1   During the early life of a firm, its ties with the immediate surrounding environment are likely to be very close. Personal contacts with financiers, suppliers, and customers are often decisive factors for early survival and growth. Typically, new firms are located where their founders have previously lived and worked. The 'concept of business' of the new enterprise usually reflects the expertise and knowledge acquired by its founder while employed by other firms in the same or related industries. The choice of location (Figure 7.3) is made before, or is concomitant to, the decision to enter a particular line of business (Hamilton, 1974a, pp. 7ff). Initial expansion is usually on an incremental basis. Production capacity is increased by means of extensions as the need arises. Locational changes—in the form of branch establishments or as complete relocations—are usually impelled by shortage of factory space (or other input access restraints) and are generally confined to locations within the home region (Cameron and Clark, 1966, p. 143; North, 1974, p. 225). However, sometimes the firm may be induced to move over greater distances to gain the benefit of financial subsidies provided by state or local authorities or to get access to a pool of cheap labour (Luttrell, 1962, p. 48; Law, 1964; Cameron and Clark, 1966, p. 135; Linge, 1978a, p. 64).

Stage 2   The rate of growth of the local market is usually slower than that to

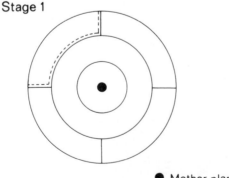

Stage 1

● Mother plant and head office

FIGURE 7.3 The single-plant firm

Stage 2

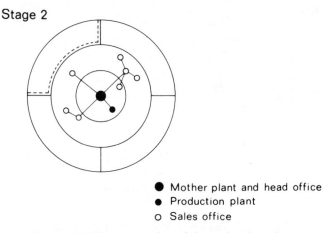

● Mother plant and head office
● Production plant
○ Sales office

FIGURE 7.4 The penetration of the national market

which the firm aspires. Marketing activities will soon be extended on a national scale. Concomitantly, managerial staff will be expanded to handle the increasing number of diverse tasks associated with a growing volume of operations. The choice of marketing channels and the design of physical distribution systems are complex decisions influenced by a wide range of considerations. At one extreme, the firm may rely entirely on merchant middlemen (wholesalers, retailers) to perform the various functions associated with the distribution of their products: transport, warehousing, or promotion. At the other extreme, the firm may develop a 'corporate vertical marketing system', combining the successive stages of distribution under its own ownership and authority. The latter mode of distribution tends to be preferred when products are bulky or perishable, or when they are unstandardized or require installation or maintenance services. The location of the corresponding physical facilities (retail outlets, sales offices, workshops, warehouses) is determined (North, 1974, p. 235) mainly by the need for proximity to customers and clients (Figure 7.4).

Stage 3   For some time, the growth rate of the firm will be limited by the financial resources and managerial planning capacity absorbed in the development of an efficient market organization. However, as market access is gradually improved, capacity for further expansion projects becomes available. At this stage—unless demand is growing faster than capacity can be expanded at existing locations—the firm will generally attempt to find foreign outlets for its products. Usually, the competence needed for the successful exploitation of foreign markets has to be acquired externally. As a first step, a network of sales agents (Figure 7.5) is adopted in a number of promising export markets (Hörnell et al., 1973).

Stage 3

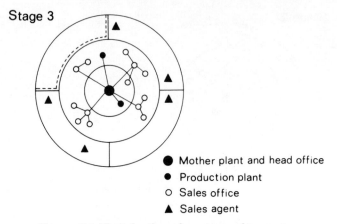

● Mother plant and head office
● Production plant
○ Sales office
▲ Sales agent

FIGURE 7.5 The adoption of overseas sales agents

Stage 4 The fixed costs of engaging a sales agency are generally lower than those of operating a wholly owned sales office, but total costs tend to rise more steeply with increasing volume. Thus when sales in foreign markets reach a certain volume, the establishment of selling subsidiaries is sometimes motivated by the concern to reduce costs per unit sold. More important, perhaps, is the possibility of expanding market shares by the development of an extended market organization, and to increase information and control of foreign operations. As in the case of the national market, the location of sales establishments is dominated by the need to be near customers. Frequently, foreign subsidiaries are established through the acquisition of former agents in which case their location (Figure 7.6) then determines the initial locus of foreign expansion (Groo, 1971).

Stage 4

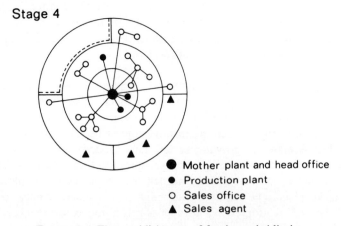

● Mother plant and head office
● Production plant
○ Sales office
▲ Sales agent

FIGURE 7.6 The establishment of foreign subsidiaries

Stage 5

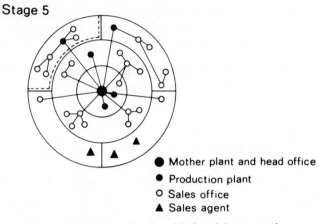

● Mother plant and head office
● Production plant
○ Sales office
▲ Sales agent

FIGURE 7.7 The multinational industrial corporation

Stage 5 Production capacity cannot be expanded indefinitely at the mother plant. At various points in the growth process locational restraints force the decentralization of production and the setting up or acquisition of branch plants. As the volume of exports grows, the market access restraints, such as custom barriers and transport costs, induce the firm to set up or acquire production or assembly plants in foreign markets. When possible, the acquisition of a foreign firm is often an attractive alternative because it allows a rapid increase in production capacity and immediate access to an established market organization (Figure 7.7). Similarly, the fastest way to increase capacity in the face of input access restraints (shortage of labour, factory space, or other inputs) is to acquire another firm. Conversely, to establish a branch plant is both time consuming and costly so that this strategy will be adopted only when demand is growing rapidly and there are prospects of considerable gain. In the former case, locational considerations tend to be subordinated to the search for a suitable company; in the latter, the firm faces the classical decision problem of finding the most suitable location for a given activity, and the complex task of optimizing market, input and intra-organizational access at a new location. In either case, the direction of search and the range of alternatives considered are related to the previous history of the corporation and to the geographical scale of its current operations. At an early stage of growth, search is limited to the home country or region, but the internationally operating firm often includes foreign locations among the set of feasible alternatives.

Diversification

Continued growth without diversification is impossible. To ensure high and stable growth rates for any longer period, the firm must intermittently enter new lines of activity. Diversification, which may be undertaken during any stage of the firm's development, is usually motivated by the existence of excess production, distribution, managerial or financial capacity, and its direction is determined by the amount and type of free capacity.

Horizontal diversification This is undertaken during the early stages of development (stages 1 and 2) to exploit the firm's production capacity and technological competence more efficiently. New products are developed or adopted which require only minor adaptations of equipment and technological skill; the technological basis of production remains the same. Since marketing capacity is less well developed, products are preferred which fit the needs of existing customers. At later stages of development (stages 3 and 4), horizontal diversification is a way of utilizing excess marketing capacity. Frequently, additional products and a larger volume of sales can be handled by the sales organization without proportional cost increases. Unless associated with excess production capacity and declining demand for the firm's existing products, horizontal diversification is generally carried out through acquisition or merger. External growth is particularly advantageous when the firm enters new technological areas of production. It may also increase market access by the incorporation of a developed market organization. However, the co-ordination of marketing activities of the enlarged firm usually requires some reorganization and relocation of physical facilities.

Vertical integration This may reduce uncertainty and stabilize capacity utilization; but it may also increase the firm's dependence on a particular segment of final demand, reducing overall flexibility. However, increasing capital investments in fixed and specialized productive facilities make results increasingly sensitive to fluctuations in throughput and output. Backward integration assures access to raw materials and semi-fabricated products while forward integration increases market control and may reduce fluctuations in demand. Vertical integration, by extending the firm's authority to adjacent sectors of the corporate environment, increases the scope for planning, co-ordination, and control and enhances the effectiveness of expansion strategies and the competitive strength of the corporation. Similarly, integration facilitates the handling of logistical problems associated with the procurement of raw materials, production, and the distribution of finished products. In the case of internal growth, the location of vertically integrated production plants is governed by the Weberian minimum-transport principle. However, when integration takes the firm into new technological areas, external growth—acquisitions of previous suppliers and customers—may be the only feasible mode of expansion.

Concentric and conglomerate diversification These are strategies accomplished almost exclusively through external growth and are generally pursued by large firms (stage 4 and 5). Their purpose is usually to increase stability of earnings by taking the firm into new final markets, but they may also be a means of finding new growth opportunities in the face of stagnating demand for existing products. With the addition of new production technologies and new market environments, the complexity and variety of managerial tasks rapidly increase. For this reason, and because the scope for 'positive synergy' is usually limited, organizational integration is kept to a minimum. Authority and responsibility for administrative and operative decisions are delegated to divisional and regional headquarters. The geographical decentralization of managerial functions is reflected in the employment structure of the firm's establishments. Yet strategic control of the allocation of investment funds is retained by the corporate head office. The discretion of subordinate managements—especially as related to growth—is accordingly reduced.

CONCLUSION: SOME REGIONAL IMPLICATIONS

Employment in a region will increase when firms located there grow by extending existing establishments or by setting up additional ones there, and when outside firms move in or locate branch plants there. Conversely, employment will decline when a region's establishments decrease in size, close, or emigrate. A theory of regional economic development must distinguish the way that such changes come about since they imply different types of behaviour.

Empirical evidence indicates that in many industries a large share of initial location decisions is made by individual entrepreneurs setting up a new business in their home town or village. However, our present knowledge of the sociological and economic determinants of entrepreneurial activity is rather fragmentary, especially in a historical and spatial perspective. This is the more unfortunate as the founding of new firms still seems to be a principal impetus to regional economic development, and since pronounced geographical variations in the incidence of new firms suggest that some regions tend to be much more favoured than others. The addition of new organizational units benefits the region by the expansion of employment opportunities and also because the addition of new work and the demand for new goods and services give further impetus to regional growth (Jacobs, 1969, pp. 49ff). If successful, the output of locally controlled firms will expand, increasing the scope for a more refined division of labour. The multiplicity of new managerial, technical, and research and development (R & D) work will add to the diversity of regional employment. Moreover, while too small to exploit fully internal economies, local medium-sized firms tend to maintain strong and diversified input linkages with the regional economy (Kipnis, 1977).

During the early phases in the development of an industry, entrepreneurial decisions may result in an apparently haphazard or 'random' geographical pattern of establishments (Hamilton, 1974a; White and Watts, 1977). In conditions of rapidly increasing demand, profit margins tend to be wide and efficiency and operating costs need not be crucial for short-term survival. In time, however, the rate of growth in demand will tend to decline and competition grow more fierce. Where economies of scale are important, industry concentration will increase through the takeover, diversification, or death of smaller and less efficient firms. Since assured market access is a prerequisite for the attainment of scale economies the surviving firms will sometimes be those that by virtue of their initial location have immediate access to large and growing urban markets. But a less central location can frequently be compensated for by the early development of an efficient and geographically widespread marketing organization. Most manufacturing firms have rather few customers, being subcontractors of other manufacturing companies or selling primarily to the wholesale departments of large retail chains.

The growth and geographical extension of the successful firms take place through mergers, acquisitions, and, but probably less often, the establishment of branch plants and offices. Advantages of specialization induce the concentration of tasks and functions to particular establishments: thus production plants become increasingly specialized in longer production runs and other economies of scale. R & D activities are concentrated at particular establishments and strategic decision-making centralized at the corporate head office. In general, the processes of corporate growth and industry concentration have tended to work in favour of large urban agglomerations (Ahnström, 1973, pp. 197ff; but see also Leigh and North, 1978). Because of large local markets, external economies, and other favourable conditions for corporate growth, big cities tend to have more large firms than small cities. As these corporations grow, administrative and managerial work at the head office expands, increasing the share of high-income, professional employment in the region. Conversely, less densely populated areas are frequently at a disadvantage since the firms there tend to be smaller and are more likely to be taken over or driven out of business. Loss of organizational independence usually involves the transfer of significant managerial tasks and functions to the corporate head office, while development potential is reduced by the concentration of R & D facilities and the need to consider the interests of the organization as a whole. The process usually entails the decentralization of routine production from the metropolitan home town of the big corporation to small and medium-sized towns with lower wages and more stable labour. However, specialization of production makes 'peripheral plants' more vulnerable to adverse changes in demand and in business strategies (Hamilton, 1978a).

The patterns and processes of growth, readjustment, or decline in individual capitalist corporations contribute collectively to the dynamics of the entire industrial system, at least in capitalist or mixed economies. While such change may originate partly in forces operating in the external environment, more important is that each stage in the evolution of a corporation transmits particular combinations of positive and negative effects into the environment of specific levels of the spatial hierarchy. As the corporation evolves, the balance and the scale of its advantageous and disadvantageous impacts upon the levels change.

Chapter 8

Industrial Development and Regional Interaction: the Case of Norrland

JAN-EVERT NILSSON

INTRODUCTION

Consider two regions at different stages of development. The chronological difference between them, were there no other considerations, suffices to ensure that their development would follow precisely similar paths. Region B does not reach—until say 1980—the equivalent point on its development path to that attained by region A in 1930. This means that their equivalent points are not really the same, because the environment facing B in 1980 is substantially different from the one which confronted A 50 years earlier.

The dynamics of regional development may be defined by both internal and external forces and the balance between them depends on how open or closed the region is. For the open region the external forces are the most relevant as are the internal forces in the closed region. Usually, it is assumed that the degree of openness or closure is correlated to the size, in one or several dimensions, of the region (Friedmann, 1966, p. 21): the smaller the region, the greater its dependence on external forces. Whole countries tend to have more closure than subnational areas; large regions tend to be more autonomous than single cities. But scarcely any region, independent of size, can achieve total closure so that every study of regional development paths must consider changes in environment.

These changes in the environment cause a revaluation of the regional resources, which in turn define the size and character of the interdependence between the region and the environment. Thus history never repeats itself. A certain change in one area is caused by forces or a network of forces which are unique for that area. If somebody wants to stimulate or create a similar change in another region at another time, he will have to use other means.

If social phenomena are changing continually, historical knowledge about a certain phenomenon will have only limited relevance for the present. With this insight as a starting point, this chapter interprets how industrialization has changed the character of interactions between regions and also the conditions of regional development using, as a case study, circumstances in northern Sweden after the middle of the last century. The purpose is not to present a detailed historical analysis, but a holistic perspective which can be used for a theoretical interpretation of structural changes in regional interactions.

139

NORRLAND—A BRIEF BACKGROUND

The analysis is focused on Norrland (the northern part of Sweden) which occupies about half of Sweden and contains about 11 per cent of the Swedish population. Figure 8.1 shows that the population of Norrland grew from 240,000

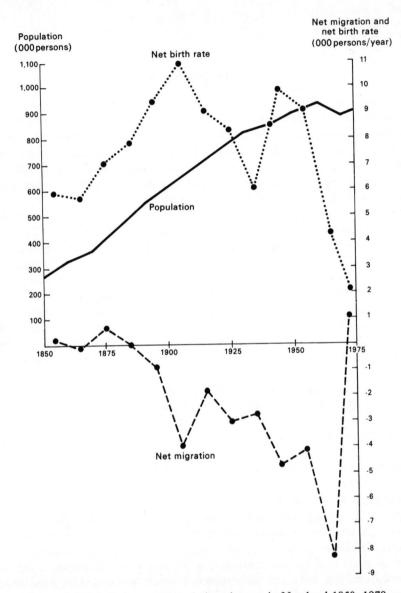

FIGURE 8.1 Population and population changes in Norrland 1850–1970

inhabitants in 1850 (7.5 per cent of the Swedish total) to 910,000 in 1960, but then declined to 900,000 in 1975. The growth in population was sustained mainly by a rate of natural increase that was high both absolutely and relatively; some net inward migration did occur but only for a few decades in the last century when Norrland was incorporated in the international economy. During this period, characterized by the establishment of sawmills and the cultivation of new land, Norrland was acting as a frontier in the national economy. However, this expansion levelled off at the turn of the century; and as a result of this and a high net birth rate, an increase in out-migration, which acted as a balancing factor between employment opportunities and the size of the population, was inevitable.

The economic structure of Norrland during the first half of this century was different in several essential ways from that of the rest of Sweden. The forest industry—sawmills and pulp factories—had been a base for a few industrial centres, but most of the workforce was occupied in forestry activities located in relatively sparsely populated areas. At that time production was still limited to winter and spring and thus furnished full-time employment for only a few people; nonetheless forestry work was essential to enable peasants to improve their economic conditions even though it only provided them with casual work. Under these conditions, it was in the interests of forestry operations to perpetuate a situation in which large numbers of peasants worked in small, or even less than viable, production units.

Until mid-century public policy toward agriculture also supported a structure dominated by small production units. But during the 1950s Sweden experienced stable economic expansion characterized by full employment at the national level which meant that some regions experienced excess demand for labour. This was the situation particularly in the industrial centres outside Norrland which were most affected by the economic expansion. Public policy toward agriculture was revised to free labour resources from farming activities and to increase their productivity. Many people in Norrland transferred from agriculture to manufacturing and this meant moving to industrial centres outside the region. At the end of the 1950s stimulation of interregional migration became an essential aspect of the successful Swedish policy for economic growth.

As can be seen from Figure 8.1, the reorientation in public policy was not the only explanation of the stagnation and decline in Norrland's population. The Second World War was followed by a short 'baby boom', but since then there has been a decline in the net birth rate: although this has been a national phenomenon, it has been more pronounced in Norrland because of the high initial values there.

This short sketch of Norrland gives a picture of a large continuous territory still characterized by high employment in agriculture and forestry and comparatively low employment in manufacturing. In 1970 agriculture and forestry occupied 12 per cent of the total workforce in Norrland (compared with 8 per cent for Sweden as a whole) while manufacturing absorbed another 24 per cent of total (compared with 31 per cent). Structural changes resulting in greatly decreased manpower requirements released labour resources which have not been reabsorbed within the area, and this has led to unemployment and a shift of surplus labour to the expanding regions in southern Sweden. Continuously, then, national development has redefined the possibilities and conditions for industrial progress in Norrland.

INDUSTRIAL DEVELOPMENT IN NORRLAND

The most characteristic feature of industrialization in Norrland has been its dependence on other regions. This section of the chapter outlines the interactions between Norrland and other nations and regions and the way these have affected development possibilities: the basic facts are not new, but the lesson to be derived from them is somewhat different from the usual concept.

The Rise of Sawmilling

The industrial revolution happened to originate in Britain which had a limited range of natural resources. Timber was needed for building houses and making furniture, and as a fuel for smelting iron, burning bricks, and warming dwellings. Much of this timber had to be imported. At first, trade policy favoured imports from Canada and other parts of the British Empire, but between 1842 and 1863 Britain switched to free trade because tariff protection no longer offered any advantages and a new policy was needed to sustain economic growth.

This radical change in tariff policy opened up possibilities for resource-rich regions. Norway, which had already been exporting timber to England, lacked adequate stocks of easy accessible forest resources to meet Britain's growing demand. This export market therefore provided the stimulus for a major expansion of the Swedish sawmill industry. In part this took place by logging in more remote areas, so that the line between exploited and non-exploited forest moved to the north and west, and in part by changes in the character of the industry.

Sawmill production in Sweden was protected by traditional laws which reduced competition and deterred potential new producers. As a result demand increased faster than productive capacity and it became clear that a change in public policy would be necessary if Sweden were to meet overseas orders for timber. Eventually, the laws were abolished and expansion in Norrland changed in character and increased in pace. The driving forces behind the exploitation of the timber resources were not the small local farmers but wealthy merchants from outside the region: capital flowed into Norrland from the south of Sweden and also from countries like England and Norway. In most of the sawmills founded at this time merchants played a dominant role for two reasons. First, their trade activities enabled them either to accumulate sufficient funds or to use their established business contacts as a bank to finance what, at the time, was a rather capital-intensive activity. Access to capital in one form or another was an essential condition during this period when there was no evidence of an organized capital market. Second, the merchants also had the ability, established through their trade activities, to sell goods on the unstable export market. Because of the simple processing technology which characterized the sawmill industry, the ability to sell was as important as experience of, and knowledge about, production. Finance was mainly needed as working capital: investment capital was less important.

The possibilities for the existing population of Norrland to exploit the local resources were restricted primarily for two reasons. First, the pre-industrial society simply produced for its own needs and hence the regional market was too small to foster a rich merchant class. Second, Norrland's peripheral location and unfavourable weather conditions made it difficult for the local inhabitants to keep in contact with England. Thus merchants mainly from Stockholm and Göteborg became intermediate agents, and later—because they had or could attain the economic resources necessary—decided to exploit the perceived opportunity themselves.

Apart from some small-scale ironworks, Norrland was without any form of industrial production at the beginning of the sawmill era. Thus the serious shortage of qualified labour had to be overcome by recruiting experienced timber workers from Norway and, to some extent, from other parts of Sweden which had earlier experienced expansion in sawmill production. Norrland's interrelationship with other regions and countries is illustrated in Figure 8.2. The sawmill industry held a central position in Norrland and all hopes for future industrial development were based on it. In fact, however, the expansionary phase was short-lived: by about 1900, Norrland's timber exports, which had quadrupled during the previous three decades, stagnated. Although it remained important internationally, the timber trade was no longer the expansive and driving force in the region's development. Moreover, the prospects for a new expansionary phase seemed dim. The turn of the century also marked the apogee of the agglomerations that had developed on the basis of the sawmill industry (and whose total population was about twice that of all the cities in Norrland).

Sawmilling Replaced by Pulp and Paper-making

During the latter part of the nineteenth century textile production and some other consumer-goods industries were growing importance in Sweden; there were signs, too, of an emerging independent engineering industry. Unlike sawmilling, these activities were stimulated by the expansion of the internal market. Furthermore, these new industries were urban rather than rural-based so that by the beginning of the First World War a quarter of Sweden's population

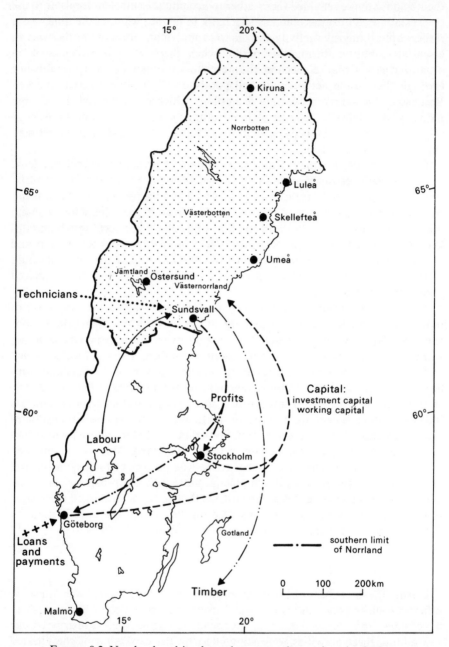

FIGURE 8.2 Norrland and its dependence on other regions in the late nineteenth century

was living in cities. These changes in the national industrial structure were not reflected in Norrland where centres of production based on different types of industries were still the exception. Timber working absorbed nearly all entrepreneurial activity and there was no room for industries constituting a base for growing cities. This fact, combined with a continued expansion of the area under the plough, explain why urban centres in Norrland at the beginning of the First World War remained simply commercial towns housing only 9 per cent of the regional population.

Timber production stagnated at the turn of the century, but forest products attained increasing importance as the raw material for pulp and paper; again, the development process started in the south and the new industry moved to the north. The rise and expansion of the pulp industry enabled better use to be made of forest resources and especially of the smaller trees. The close financial relationships between the sawmill and pulp industries explain why the expansion of the pulp industry resulted in hardly any new firms. Pulp production in Norrland increased rapidly, but because of its capital-intensive character and its quickly changing technology this industry did not become as important in employment terms as the sawmills had been at the turn of the century. Initially, the two industries were complementary since the pulp industry made it possible to utilize wood resources more efficiently, but in due course they began to compete for wood resources and this harmony was disrupted. The demand for pulp increased faster than demand for timber: since price changes were about the same for the two industries the strength of the competition depended on their ability to rationalize their activities. The pulp industry was the more successful, partly as a result of a less mature production technology, and during the 1930s in particular many sawmills went out of business. Although the demand for paper increased rapidly after the First World War, this had only a small effect on Norrland because the pulp industry was largely controlled by capital from other regions. Hence, location decisions were based strictly on short-term economic criteria: good access to a big port was regarded as more important than having the wood resources and/or the pulp industries within easy reach.

The Emergence of Capital-goods Industries

The first stage of industrialization in Sweden was dominated by resource-based industries and consumer-goods industries. In a later second stage, which began at the end of the nineteenth century, a market for capital goods grew up and led to a rapid expansion of this kind of manufacturing. At least two types of ventures can be identified. First, there were some rather large firms, based on Swedish innovations, which in many cases supplied the international market: today some of these enterprises form the core of large national systems of production. Second, there were also many small firms, most of which manufactured only for the regional markets in Sweden. Both types of firms experienced rapid growth after the First World War and Norrland shared in this expansion. Thus between 1913 and 1940 employment in the engineering industry in Norrland increased by 270 per cent, compared with 222 per cent nationally, although this imposing expansion had only a small effect in absolute terms because the initial base was small. For instance, apart from a few rare exceptions among industries based on the small but expanding regional market, the number of new firms established in Norrland was insignificant.

The low rate of establishment of new ventures may be explained by the bad starting point of the region and by the cumulative character of enterprise: new firms not only educated engineers, salesmen, and specialized workers, but also many future founders of firms. From the beginning of the twentieth century technicians and workers became an even more important group of entrepreneurs, and after the First World War often became founders of new firms. This may partly be explained by the creation of a more efficient capital market, but more important was the appearance of a new type of firm—the subcontractor. As technology progressed, there was a greater specialization of manufacturing functions that often dictated locational proximity of successive stages of production and by-product industries. This increasing interdependence was characterized by a mounting complexity of inputs both of raw materials and semi-finished products, and by a growing tendency for multiplier effects of large manufacturing units to be localized rather than geographically diffuse. From this time can be identified the emergence of local systems of production centred around one large firm; the growing complexity of manufacturing made it seem profitable to draw on the resources of subcontractors. Technological changes, including better machines and new materials, made it possible for small firms to produce a wider variety of components. The increased number of subcontractors was one essential factor behind the appearance of new types of founders of firms: technicians and workers replaced the merchants in the capital-goods industries, and the expansion of these activities also multiplied the number of potential entrepreneurs. This cumulative effect, which concentrated future growth in the capital-goods industries, gave an advantage to regions that already had large production units on which further industrial development could be based. In this respect the inhabitants of Norrland were at a disadvantage because of their initial lack of experience in this type of manufacturing.

Mining and Metallurgical Industries

Iron ore deposits in northern Norrland have been mined on a small scale since the eighteenth century. The building of the railway from Kiruna to Narvik in 1903 stimulated production of iron ore, all of which was exported in an unprocessed form until 1940 when a blast furnace was built at Luleå. This publicly owned plant was a policy response to try to reduce the effects of the widespread closure of the sawmills. The big Västerbotten ore deposits—containing gold, silver, copper, arsenic, and pyrites—were not opened up until 1926. At first, this ore was exported without being processed, but soon afterwards AB Bolidan built a smelting works at Skellefteå. Together, these two industries, mining and mineral processing, represented the greatest innovations in the Swedish industry since the First World War, and parts of Norrland became the most rapidly expanding districts in the nation. Neither mining nor processing could rely very much on known technology, so that every expansion in production became a challenge because it depended on the solution of several technical problems which, in turn, provided opportunities for local entrepreneurs and innovators. New firms were established to secure technological economies. In this way technical restrictions acted as a challenge for industrial production, resulting in increased orders for existing firms and providing an incentive for the establishment of new ones. During the 1950s many of these firms began to sell their products on national and international markets and, as a result, expanded their linkages with subcontractors. During the 1960s some of the most successful firms were bought by large Swedish companies. The expansion in the Skellefteå region was imposing (between 1920 and 1940 the population increased from 3000 to 8500) and resulted in the emergence of a dynamic local system of production which even today is considered an exception in Norrland. In most other parts of the region growth was externally initiated and based on well-known technology which did not give rise to dynamic local systems of production. The need to reduce unemployment in this part of Norrland was again used as an argument when an expansion of the capacity of the Luleå plant—the 'Steelworks '80' concept—was discussed during the 1970s, and references were made to the local spread effects that had been produced by the smelting plant at Skellefteå. The proposed 'Steelworks '80' project—now abandoned because of the high investment cost involved and the poor market outlook for steel—would have fallen into this second category since there would have been few local supplier linkages.

Industries in Search of Labour

A new phase in industrial development commenced after the Second World War when the conditions for industrial expansion were extremely good. The destruction of a considerable part of the productive capacity of Europe outside Sweden seemed to provide a good opportunity for that country to increase its exports. During the war Swedish industry had largely concentrated on the production of munitions so that domestic demand for consumer goods had been only partly satisfied. Thus the immediate post-war years were characterized by high demand, rapid economic growth, and full employment. During the 1950s, despite a slowing down in the rate of expansion, full employment was sustained. But then followed a period characterized by drastic changes in the industrial structure: during the 1960s both the number of takeovers and amalgamations and the number of closures increased, with the result that the importance of the larger firms in the economy was enhanced. This coincided with a change in public policy toward agriculture which was now concerned to bring about increased productivity, a policy that implied concentration of production in bigger and more efficient production units. At this time agriculture still played an important role in Norrland: 35 per cent of the total workforce in 1950 was employed in agriculture and forestry. Employment in manufacturing was of minor importance and was largely located in small coastal centres. The small urban centres situated in the more sparsely populated areas were almost entirely based on agriculture and forestry in which conditions were changing rapidly; hence if they were to maintain even their existing populations these settlements would have required a significant increase in manufacturing activity. In fact, however, regional productive capacity in manufacturing—much of which was concentrated in the engineering industry—barely matched the national rate of expansion.

During the 1950s there emerged the first signs of a new development pattern in Norrland. The expansion in manufacturing can to a large extent be explained by an increase in the number of factories that were integral parts of larger enterprises. In other words, some local systems were transformed into national and even, in some cases, into international systems of production. This new pattern, explained by an increasing shortage of labour in the traditional industrial agglomerations in the south of Sweden, may be considered as a welcome opportunity for increasing employment in peripheral regions like Norrland.

Industrial development in Norrland after the Second World War has some similarities to the expansion during the second half of the nineteenth century and the beginning of the present one (Figure 8.3). Capital and know-how are supplied by large manufacturing firms instead of rich merchants located in the south of Sweden; investment capital is mostly directed to the coastal agglomerations; and labour is recruited both locally and also from the sparsely populated areas of the region. But there are also important differences. During the last century growth resulted from the exploitation of natural resources unique to the region: nowadays the expansion is dictated by conditions outside it. The location of production units in a region having surplus labour arises both because of the shortage of employment opportunities in peripheral regions and also because of labour shortages in industrial centres. In this sense the relocation of productive activities is an act of coercion imposed mainly on firms having difficulties in satisfying their labour needs. Recent expansion in Norrland has been based to a great extent on activities of firms (such as those in textile, clothing, and footwear manufacturing, as well as some engineering activities) which are no longer able to recruit sufficient labour in areas where there is an excess of demand over supply. In such industries the labour input is high even though the manufacturing plants are often small and, for the most part the workforce consists of unskilled female

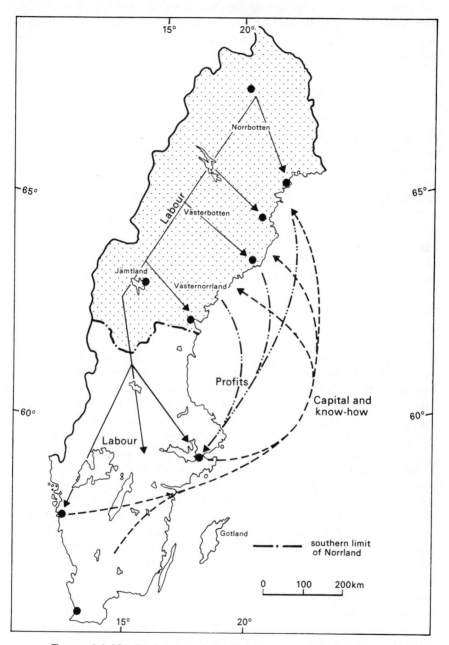

FIGURE 8.3 Norrland and its dependence on other regions after the
Second World War

labour requiring only a minimum of skill to operate relatively uncomplicated machinery. Any expansion in Norrland that was based on activities of this kind would imply a dependence on activities which, in established industrial agglomerations elsewhere, already belong to the past.

INDUSTRIAL DEVELOPMENT AND REGIONAL DYNAMICS

Historical comparisons suggest that the combination of regional convergence and high levels of national growth require a shift from development based on natural resources to that based on human resources. An economy that continues to grow will sooner or later arrive at the point where further growth requires drastic structural changes. During the period considered in this chapter the Swedish economy did in fact shift from the one form of development to the other, and this in turn changed the bases for regional development in Norrland. Yet behind this superficial picture can be identified a more stable basic structure which can be expressed in terms of centre/periphery linkages. Central to the national economy is the great heartland concentration of industry and the national market: spread over the national landscape are units which, in one way or another, are linked to industries in the heartland.

The Norrland region is still, and always has been, a part of the periphery or hinterland. In the first stages of industrialization Norrland depended directly on demand from Britain and on capital from the national heartland. Initially, the abundant timber resources were of particular advantage to Norrland and, later, ore deposits also became a valuable asset; between them these two natural resources were for a long period essential determinants of the regional growth potential. But, even so, it was not these resources that shifted Norrland from a natural resource-based development to one based on human resources: instead it was demand for labour, in the period after the Second World War, which replaced natural resources as the determinant of a new regional growth potential. The conclusion is simple. Norrland has never had the opportunity to develop by processes controlled *within* the region: rather it has always been dominated by *outside* forces. This domination effect is evident when, in one or more dimensions, a region exercises an irreversible or almost irreversible influence on another region (Perroux, 1950, p. 188). In the early stages of growth this dependence on another region may lead to faster economic development (North, 1955, 1959). In such a case, of course, the region is economically and perhaps even politically tied to another, but should income and population growth continue—primarily as a result of growth in exports—the linkage may begin to change. For instance, thresholds for the production of goods and the provision of services may be reached within the region itself, thus enabling a substitution to be made from production for export to production for the regional market. In Norrland, however, the expansion of the resource-based industry failed to change the character of regional interrelationships since it was insufficient to facilitate internally generated development in the form of local and /or regional systems of production. It is true that a few local systems of production came into existence, but these were too small to make an impression on the structure and the development of the regional economy. This circumstance cannot be explained only by the fact that important market thresholds were never attained; another more basic reason was that the expansion of natural resource-based industries did not stimulate sufficient new enterprise to reduce the dependence of peripheral regions on the human resources of the heartland. This stable dependence on outside human resources is a superficial sign of the position of a region which is dominated.

To create an internally generated process of development a region has to be transformed from its role as a dominated region to that of a leading region. This can be achieved by taking initiatives to make sectors with high potential productivity even more efficient, a task that can be undertaken by firms controlled in, or by persons living in, the region concerned through innovations to both production methods and products. The creation of something new brings the possibility for reassessing established relationships. The emerging industrial centre may modify not only its immediate geographical environment but, in some cases, the entire structure of relationships in the national economy (Perroux, 1955). As a new dynamic centre of agglomeration and accumulation of capital and of human resources, its linkages with other similar centres change in such a way that it starts to bring about innovations and alterations: a dominated region may thus begin to change into a dominating region.

The opportunity for a dominated region to become a dominating one is also subject to the conditions in the latter areas. In times of economic expansion, dominating regions can control development elsewhere, whereas during periods of economic turbulence—which, in effect, are crises of established systems of production—their capacity to control other regions is considerably reduced. Such a situation may not only increase incentives for regionally based initatives but may also foster regional self-reliance, both of which may threaten established regional linkages (as occurred during the development of mining in Norrland in the early 1930s).

Until the beginning of this decade the stability which has characterized the Swedish economy after the Second World War has helped to make existing dominating relationships stronger; it found expression in the rapid expansion in dominating regions. Initial locational advantages at a certain stage of change became magnified during the course of development: in other words, it seems that geographical differences start out as a mild concentration and end up as a system of massive localization based on internal and external economies of scale (Ullman, 1958). One essential force behind this pattern of development is the enlarged systems of production which during the last two decades have been combined with increasing financial concentration.

Since the Second World War in particular, industry has been characterized by concentration and emergence of large multi-regional systems of production. The big firms, usually also controlling the systems of production, have become more dominant in the economy, and multi-regional, multi-product enterprises have increased in number. These firms traditionally function according to a centre/periphery model: strategic decisions made by head office policy-makers are transformed into plans which are then transferred to the actual production units. The growing number of multi-regional firms has resulted in an increased concentration of policy-makers and, since the principal management functions of the largest firms are located in metropolitan areas, the dominance of these regions over others is enhanced. The geographical concentration of policy-makers implies a corresponding concentration in the possibilities for economic initiatives and this, in turn, results in increased stability in established interregional linkages. One observable feature of this concentration is the geographical pattern which follows the development of an idea to a standardized product (Pred, 1973). When a multi-regional and multi-product firm begins to manufacture a new item, it frequently does so in the region where its principal management functions are located. However, as production becomes standardized and competition becomes more pronounced, it often happens that the original plant is replaced by factories in dominated regions where labour and cost savings are available. Meanwhile, the administrative functions expand in their original area and take new initiatives; they finance innovations made inside the company or bought from others and commence the manufacture of new products in the same region. Industrial development, accompanied by enlarged systems of production which transform dominated regions, creates a spatial structure in which the peripheral regions can be likened to the arms and legs of a body which has its head in the dominant metropolis.

The structural changes will also alter the premises for the growth centre (or growth pole) policy favoured by the Swedish and other governments in Western Europe. The theoretical foundation of this policy has lost its relevance with the claim that firms need proximate locations in order to secure technological external economies and to gain from being close to other firms in related industries. This was true in the early stages of industrial development when transport costs were high and the production process was split between separate specialized companies, but now transport costs have become much less important and many companies have production facilities in several regions. In later stages of industrial development it is still possible to find small firms clustered around a plant owned by a multi-regional firm in spatially concentrated complexes, but these are less the result of the external economies offered by such locations than the fact that multi-regional firms have chosen to build up a spatially concentrated network of subcontractors. They survive, not as a result of the collective strength secured from a shared production process with other firms of the same size, but because of the success and support from multi-regional firms. A successful growth pole policy thus requires a large firm to locate major plants in a growth centre and to build up a network of local subcontractors. The disadvantage of such a strategy in advanced industrial societies is that the established centre becomes dependent on what is happening at the key plant. Hence, a local system of production in the growth centre is more vulnerable than one based on technological external economies which secures collective strength from sharing the production process with similar-sized firms.

INDUSTRIAL DEVELOPMENT AND GEOGRAPHICAL ENVIRONMENT

It was indicated earlier how the adjustment of the economic structure—primarily in the form of the rise and expansion of multi-regional systems of production—has changed the premises for development in Norrland. This change is not only an economic phenomenon but also a change which influences, and at the same time is influenced by, the policy-makers' perspective of reality. In the pre-industrial society the spatial dimension was the natural base for each identifiable group, as exemplified by Norrland in the middle of last century. The central position of the spatial dimension reflected the emphasis placed on producing one's own needs. Each family, having a great deal of independence and largely producing its own requirements, was occupied with much the same activities as others. Poor communications limited the area within which goods and services could be bought, sold, or exchanged. The fact that the spatial dimension determined a group of persons with common identity thus made regional development a goal rather than an outcome.

Economic development has been based on an increasing division of labour and has been accompanied by the continuous breaking down of territorial identity groups. These have been replaced by functional identity groups in which individuals tend to relate more closely with other people specializing in the same activities. For example, a manager in a multi-regional, multi-product firm has a tendency to identify himself with other managers of large firms instead of with a particular region. In that way space becomes a restriction only insofar as it makes it more difficult for him to keep contact with other members of his peer group. This basic change in the dimension of identity increases the problem of maintaining special regional interests, especially in regions dominated by others. The effects are most easily identified in public policy-making. Regional governments are usually not active in the traditional sense of pushing for institutional reforms, and their decision-making is restricted to defined sectors and to some types of overall planning within the institutional framework established by the national organs. Essentially, regional decision-makers are mainly engaged in the task of modifying, adapting, and implementing given national policies in ways that meet special local needs. The concentration of policy-makers seems to have resulted in a new stable order of specialization in which subservient regions have to support the dominating region with commodity goods, semi-finished goods, and standardized products. The only way in which a subservient region can achieve an internally generated development, in contrast to the growth without development offered by the dominating regions, is to free itself from the linkages with those dominating regions. It must construct its own institutions and organizations because internally generated regional development only becomes possible by increasing regional independence. But to achieve this it is also necessary to change the structure of the multi-regional systems of production and to replace their centre/periphery organization by a more equal arrangement in which each region has the same opportunity to take initiatives. This is a hard task.

The present leaders of business, labour, and government naturally attempt to use the past in order to present the image of the future, conserving the perspectives which made the present institutions and organizations successful. These perspectives decide to what extent the present regional changes can be viewed as a normal evolution. The resulting problem, as seen through the eyes of policy-makers, is to find remedies to counteract the regional imbalances and stimulate existing institutions. As the overall aim to provide a balance between change and stability, their approach is to seek remedies that intensify or weaken various operative forces, and to make present institutional formats work with minimum change. This conservative view guarantees that the future will preserve to the maximum extent the shape of the perspectives which guaranteed success in the past. In Norrland this means continued growth without development. But the past is different from the present, and the present is different from the future: there is a need, therefore, for changes in institutional formats.

Chapter 9

From Firms to Systems of Firms: A Study of Interregional Dependence in a Dynamic Society

CARL G. FREDRIKSSON AND LEIF G. LINDMARK

TOWARDS A NEW LOCATION THEORY

In classical and neo-classical economic theory it is assumed that firms are small, profit-maximizing, and independent of each other in the markets where they operate. These assumptions are in themselves conditions that must be fulfilled if the mechanisms of price formation and other instruments of allocation are to develop the effects predicted by the theory. Traditional research into the location of industry has been based on these theoretical foundations. There are, however, many indications that most of the firms that are responsible for production in a modern industrialized society are confronted by highly imperfect market mechanisms (Galbraith, 1973, 1974). Thus while the basic theoretical assumptions may once have been a relevant description of many industrial sectors, they now cover only a small proportion of all markets. Furthermore, though they may have been good descriptive models during the initial stage of the industrial era, the theories have proved to be bad predictive instruments in our attempts to understand long-term changes in industry.

It is thus important to develop further the basic theoretical assumptions in order to see today's regional problems in their correct perspective and to understand the intrinsic dynamics of industrial evolution. To go on treating firms as 'black boxes' thus seems impracticable; a necessary change would be to provide a more diversified picture of firms which are traditionally seen as carrying on business with a single and one-dimensional end in view, based on the postulate of economic rationality. In other words, the picture of firms aspiring to obtain maximum profits within a cost-revenue analytic framework must be replaced by a discussion in terms of behavioural science of the processes that underlie and govern their actions (cf. Argyris, 1973a, b; Simon, 1973).

It is equally important to construct the analysis on a conceptual basis in which power and dependence relationships—*within* as well as *between* firms—are at least implicitly included in the discussion. The multinational concern versus the small family business, or the head office versus the branch plant, may be viewed as examples of concepts that can add to our knowledge of the causes and consequences of structural change and also of regional development. It is suggested, then, that a theory should be formulated in which information about

155

the behaviour of micro-units is integrated into a conceptual framework in order to generate new knowlege of the structure of the macro-system and of the processes that produce this structure (cf. Myrdal, 1973).

Accordingly, the following discussion is conducted in terms of a national economy segmented into a limited number of systems of firms having a considerable geographical distribution and competing with each other. However, the market mechanisms within each system of firms are strongly suppressed. This situation, in which the productive units of society are interwoven with each other through flows of materials, capital, information, and values without being involved in decisive competition, can be conceptualized as 'integration'. Thus here it is argued that modern industry is highly integrated and that there is a clearly discernible spatial pattern to the structure and development of these systems of firms.

Clearly, the concept of integration may refer to a state as well as to a process. In this chapter no distinction is made at the conceptual level between these two interpretations, since the present structure of industry can be regarded both as the result of earlier historical processes and as a regulator of potential future changes. In order to express a well-founded opinion about the development of industry both structure and processes must be discussed in detail.

FRAMEWORK FOR UNDERSTANDING INDUSTRIAL LINKAGES: CONCEPTUALIZATION OF A STRUCTURE

Firms as Transformers of Resources and Decision-units

The basic principle of the following analysis is that firms—independently of the national economy—fulfil two fundamentally different functions in any economic system. On the one hand, firms undertake the necessary transformation of resources in society. By bringing together labour, capital, energy, and other inputs in a process of production, they endeavour to supply an output consisting of various goods or services. These in turn may serve as the input of the resource transformation of the next firm or be consumed by the public. It is the result of this process of transforming resources that gives the industrial firm its revenue.

On the other hand, to a greater or lesser extent—depending on the national economy—society has delegated to firms the responsibility as well as the authority for the planning and management of their own work. At the one extreme the activities of firms are greatly curtailed in this respect and they are only allowed to be in charge of the purely 'operative' work. In such cases society, other firms, or other organizations are responsible for the administrative as well as the overall strategic planning. In other instances firms are given considerable freedom to devise plans of their own, sometimes to the extent of them being directly contrary to the intentions of official national economic policies.

According to Thompson's (1967) integrating conceptual framework of organizational theory, these three different planning activities may be associated with different levels within the firm: the technical, the administrative, and the institutional level.

When considering the activities of firms, location theorists usually refer to the first dimension—the aspect of transforming resources. What must be stressed, on the basis of this discussion of principles, is that the transformation of resources is an integral part of a planning and controlling system. This distinction allows discussion of the first dimension primarily in terms of flows of material (or money) while in the latter dimension there seems to be more justification for analysing events in terms of flows of information (or values). These ideas are summarized in Figure 9.1. This distinction has been made even though it is recognized that flows of material are always closely related to flows of information. Measured in terms of their share of the total costs of flows, it should thus be possible to distinguish a wide spectrum of flows from 'material-intensive' to 'information-intensive' (cf. Pred, 1973, Törnqvist, 1973). This point is taken up again in the concluding section of the chapter which interprets the findings in a regional perspective of development.

Organizational Domains

Earlier organizational research concentrated on describing processes and norms within firms. In recent years, however, importance has been attached to environmental matters and their implications for (among other things) the organizational structure of firms and the possibilities of their making economic progress. The series of studies of the organization of firms and their strategic planning that has followed the pioneering works of Chandler (1962) and Ansoff (1965), emanates from this partially new outlook. Firms are not exclusively mechanical phenomena; rather they are organisms which, through adaptation and strategic planning, can handle interference from their environment.

The extent to which firms can carry out their activities satisfactorily from the point of view of business economics as transformers of resources and decision-making units is thus not entirely an internal problem but is largely regulated by

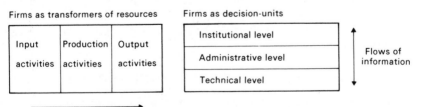

FIGURE 9.1 The two-dimensional picture of the firm

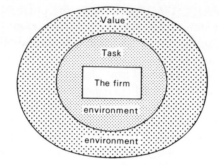

FIGURE 9.2. The firm and its environment

the environment of the firm. Analogous with the ideas which were expressed fairly early (e.g. by Dill, 1958), a distinction may be made between task environment and value environment. The task environment includes not only the external components with which firms are in direct contact, such as customers, suppliers, and banks, but also political groups and trade unions. The value environment, on the other hand, consists of the superstructure in which the firm is supposed to operate: it may also include potential customers and suppliers who may indirectly affect the firm's chance of continued existence such as by opening new markets or developing new materials and products. This view of the firm is summarized in Figure 9.2.

Returning to the distinction between flows of material and flows of information, it can be argued that the flows of material which primarily affect the firm in its capacity as a transformer of resources are exchanged between the firm and its task environment. The same is true of large parts of its flows of information. To a great degree the exchange of information concerns the firm's strategic planning and thus it can be claimed that there are important relations with the value environment. In fact an important element in such strategic planning is the attempt by firms to identify their own 'place'—and that of the task environment—within the all-embracing value environment. Conversely, by studying flows of material some conclusions can be drawn about parts—very significant parts nevertheless—of the task environment of firms, but little can be said about the value environment in which they operate except in terms of implicit conclusions. This claim is essential to an understanding of the concept of production systems and the analyses of the long-term changes of industry which will be discussed later.

THE CONCEPT OF PRODUCTION SYSTEMS

The concept of a production system has been used in various contexts and at various descriptive levels. If, initially, the concept of a production system is interpreted at a highly descriptive level, it can be observed that in many cases it is synonymous with the industry of a country in general. At the other extreme some organizational studies use the concept to denote various forms of interdependence between sections of a firm. In yet another dimension it may be said that firms in the same line of business constitute a production system. A common denominator of all the levels of amplification is, however, the strong position of the concept in system theory, in which the relationships *within* the defined system are stronger than the relationships *between* the system and its environment.

By analogy, seen from the viewpoint of firms, every company with more than one plant constitutes a production system according to corporate law. From the fiscal point of view such production systems are clearly defined at least within the borders of each nation. These multi-plant companies may also make up fairly well-defined production systems as far as the transformation of resources is concerned since the output of one plant may serve as the input of the next. It may be assumed that between the units within these systems of 'firms' the market mechanisms have been heavily suppressed, even if they try to create an artificial market climate through internal pricing. However it cannot be assumed—even in the case of those multi-plant companies in which the units do not enter into any mutual customer–supplier relationship—that this is tantamount to suppressing the demands for co-ordination and control within these production systems. On the contrary, it is relevant to assume that various executive organs will demand integration through information channels other than the primary price and market mechanisms (Lawrence and Lorsch, 1967).

In this connection, then, integration does not refer solely to the co-ordination of various activities brought about by production engineering (the problem of materials handling) but may also include the co-ordination of decisions at various levels—the problem of controlling and planning. According to this approach, systems of production are multidimensional. One possible way of describing this structure is in terms of different systems superimposed on each other, where the co-ordination through productive engineering constitutes the 'lowest', most obvious and most easily identifiable structure. Yet it must be said at once that the co-ordination of production engineering activities—reflected in mechanization and automation—seems at present to have been carried considerably further than the co-ordination of decision activities.

What is interesting here is that there seems to be general agreement about discussing production systems—in the sense of materials handling—which comprise considerably more firms than those belonging to one particular enterprise. This is true even if the approach to systems or the concept of production systems is not explicitly treated. There are a number of Swedish studies, and even more in English, dealing from various angles with subcontractor relationships and 'make or buy' problems in which emphasis is put on the potential advantages of co-operation to both buyers and sellers. Considerably less attention has been focused on the conditions and consequences of co-ordinating decisions outside the scope of market mechanisms between firms which are legally 'independent'. This is perhaps natural since such an approach is basically a powerful attack on the philosophy of market economics.

Nevertheless both large and small firms have now 'realized' that considerable advantages in the form of increased efficiency may be gained through the co-ordination of decisions—at a formal as well as an informal level—between firms belonging to different legal entities. Even in making the simplest items large numbers of firms/production units are involved in various stages of turning the raw materials into the final product. Here, as in several other recent studies, the concept of a production system has been reserved to show how production units, without apparent organizational or legal connections, are linked through flows of material. These associations constitute only one dimension—but as will be made clear later a central one—of the relationships of firms with their environment. These relationships, if they can be identified, express both the potentialities and the restrictions to be found in the development situations encountered by firms.

Transformation of Resources and Efficiency

According to most experts the specialization and division of labour that takes place between firms in a production system results in a more efficient utilization of resources in industry from the viewpoint of both the firms and the nation. They argue that specialization and large-scale production lead to increased efficiency. But why this should be the case is seldom explained except in terms of highly fragmentary and simplified basic assumptions. Yet studies of the behaviour of organizations may help widen the understanding of what is included in the concept of business efficiency.

A starting-point is that the essential goal of all organizations and firms is their own continued existence. They fight against every threat to their survival and try to eliminate the uncertainty that the future holds in store. One of the basic elements of market economics is that continued existence is guaranteed by high profitability. In order to survive in competition with others, firms are forced to prove their profitability even on a relatively short view. As Thompson (1967) argued, the primary means of achieving this 'increased efficiency' is the endeavour to isolate the operative (resource-transforming) activities from environmental interference. Whether this is done by firms trying to gain power or influence over parts of their environment or by adapting in a flexible manner to the changes of the environment, the aim is the same: to try to neutralize or, if possible, to eliminate environmental interference by such means as stock policy, negotiations, and planning, or by establishing points of contact in the environment—'boundary-spanning units'.

This approach is in contrast to the 'school' in organizational theory that has seriously questioned the picture of firms as apparently rational organisms. Its most extreme advocates claim that decisions sometimes serve as excuses for solving entirely different problems (like the personal difficulties of the decision-makers) and/or that problems are created in order to serve as 'alibis' for applying already available solutions (March, 1971; Cohen *et al.*, 1972). In the latter case the decision-making process is the opposite of that postulated in the economically rational model, in which the starting-point is a problem to which the best possible of all conceivable solutions is chosen; instead there is a solution to which a problem is sought.

In other cases attacks are made on the myths formed in traditional research (such as the myth of the good long-term planning view, or of shaping the decision-making processes, or of the organizable organization) without directly suggesting any alternative approaches. Still others present sketches of firms acting on the principle of survival by maintaining a high degree of flexibility and a quick response to the environmental changes (Hedberg *et al.*, 1976). However, in these descriptive models it is difficult to find any tenable arguments explaining why, in spite of this 'anarchy', firms manage to maintain their activities and to produce reasonably similar articles over a long period. It is fairly obvious, though, that various writers refer to at least two different types of efficiency criteria.

In principle a differentiation can be made between the internal and the external efficiency of firms (and by analogy, of production systems) (Thompson, 1967; Lawrence and Lorsch, 1967). Internal efficiency may be rather vaguely defined as the ability of the firm 'to carry out certain specific tasks with a given consumption of resources' and is directly associated with its role as transformer of resources. This criterion of efficiency can be divided into two different parts. For a sawmill to produce boards of a given dimension and quality is a result of technical efficiency. If, however, the sawmill wastes half the timber, production is not economically justifiable: the economic efficiency is low. Good economic efficiency in combination with low technical efficiency will hardly be identified in other than extremely generous environments.

Irrespective of whether or not at a given time a firm has a smoothly functioning organization (high internal efficiency) it is by no means certain that the firm will be able to survive. The reason may be that the firm is unable to handle its dependence on the environment—the external or organizational efficiency is low. The sawmill may have to face a shortage of raw materials, or the demand for the products may cease because of structural changes in the economy. This is especially interesting when external demands undergo rapid changes. The introduction of new laws, import restrictions affecting trade with other countries, new products appearing on the market, or a sudden and drastic decrease in demand are all examples of changes that may (and do) occur in centrally unplanned and 'open' economies. For firms and production systems to be successful in the external sense of the concept of efficiency, they have to be able to make rapid predictions and take steps to counteract this environmental interference.

A Tentative Conclusion

Before trying to analyse the existence of production systems in the Swedish economy, attention must again be drawn to the fact that satisfactory internal efficiency in production systems is not tantamount to having achieved acceptable external efficiency. Examples like Rolls Royce Ltd in England and Facit AB in Sweden indicate that this is not always the case. When such a large-scale company fails to predict the future and take the necessary adaptive measures, the effects are all the worse on the national economy and on the particular regions affected by its failure. Some aspects of regional problems and the dynamics of development are considered again later.

PRODUCTION SYSTEMS IN THE SWEDISH ECONOMY: THE FUNCTIONAL DIMENSION

In Sweden in the early 1970s there were about 13,000 industrial firms with 5 or more employees and roughly the same number below that size. About 95 per cent of all industrial firms had fewer than 100 employees. The predominance of small-sized companies may seem to be conspicuous but in fact is not unique compared with other Western industrial countries. The United States—often thought to be dominated by big business—has a slightly higher proportion of small and medium-sized firms (International Labour Office, 1961; Committee of Inquiry on Small Firms, 1971). However, the firms with fewer than 100 employees account for only about one-fourth of all industrial employees in Sweden. Moreover the handful of manufacturing companies that employ more than 500 people account for no less than three-quarters of Sweden's industrial production.

Co-operation Between Small and Large Firms

The data for this study were collected by means of a postal questionnaire sent to all companies with manufacturing plants employing more than 10 workers in 8 of the 70 so-called 'A-regions' of Sweden (see Figure 9.3). The information sought included purchases from suppliers, sales to customers, the age and capacity of machinery, and staff training arrangements. Data were also obtained about the employment trends of the companies and their economic development during the 1967–72 period. The complete coverage of the study region embraced 724 firms—nearly one-tenth of all those in Sweden with more than 10 manufacturing workers. In addition 10 case studies were carried out to obtain a better understanding of the decision-processes and market conditions of small firms, the details of which have been reported elsewhere (Fredriksson and Lindmark, 1976).

This survey showed that a very extensive network of materials transactions exists between Swedish manufacturing firms within which a division of roles can be discerned. Of the 724 firms studied, 100 are part of some large manufacturing

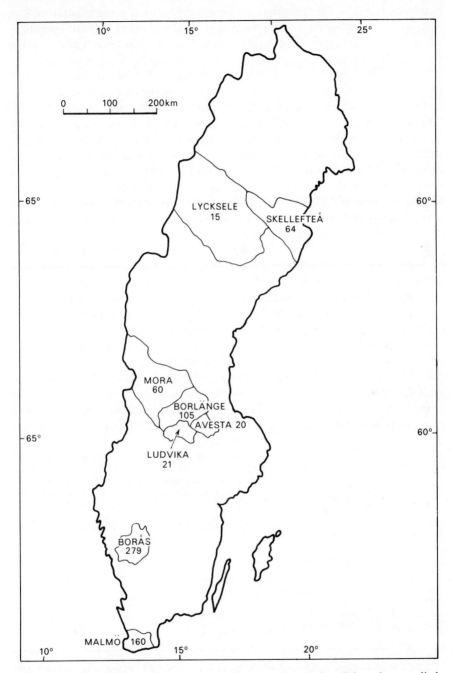

FIGURE 9.3 The number of firms surveyed in each of the 8 Swedish regions studied

enterprise (large in the sense that the parent company is a manufacturing firm with more than 500 employees); even though these embraced only one-seventh of all businesses surveyed (the majority of which were small branch plants rather than the main plants), they accounted for five-sevenths of the total inputs.

The picture of large-scale companies as 'bearers' of large national systems of production corresponds well both with earlier studies and the authors' own analyses of the orientation of small and medium-sized firms towards different functional markets. To a considerable extent small firms function as subcontractors, a role particularly characteristic of those in the metal and engineering industries, in which no fewer than 2 out of 3 small and medium-sized firms operate as subcontractors (see Figure 9.4). Half of these sell at least 20 per cent of their output to the 30 largest manufacturing companies of the country. Moreover, for 1 in 8 of the legally independent subcontractors such sales make up the dominant element since more than half their output is supplied to the 30 largest manufacturing companies.

In Hamilton (1974c) there are several papers in which these notions of 'industrial systems' make up the recurrent theme, and the functional distribution of labour between large and small firms forms the (implicit) undertone of the analyses. Earlier, and from other starting-points, Baumback et al. (1973, p. 8) have argued that 'it is the manufacture of producers' goods (products made for other manufacturers) wherein most of the opportunities exist for the small independent enterprise. As big business grows, so does small business'. Further, other studies (Staley and Morse, 1965; Yoshino, 1968; Committee of Inquiry on Small Firms, 1971) have shown that, for example, 89 per cent of General Motors' 26,000 contractors had fewer than 500 employees, 90 per cent of Renault's had fewer than 300 employees, and 88 per cent of the contractors of the big Japanese companies owned capital of less than U.S. $28,000. The picture of large motor

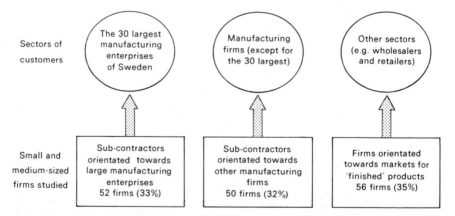

FIGURE 9.4 Small and medium-sized firms in the metal and engineering industry and their orientation towards various kinds of customers (158 firms)

companies as buyers and the small and medium-sized firms as subcontractors is thus strongly supported by the available empirical data.

It is argued here that the increasing domination of large-scale companies combined with the continued existence of small firms can be explained by the fact that large and small firms do not compete primarily with each other in a highly industrialized economy. Rather, they complement each other, and the relative competence of big firms lies in their being able to handle their dependence on the environment, that is to be efficient in the external sense of this concept. In this respect small firms have to rely on their own flexibility and adaptability to environmental change and hence may complement big companies by exploiting markets that are small in volume or geographical extent. New 'non-institutionalized' markets may also for shorter or longer periods constitute 'niches' within which small firms are 'allowed' to operate. In a dynamic and non-centralized national economy there will always be scope for a considerable stock of small firms of this character (cf. Penrose, 1959).

It is suggested, too, that the majority of small firms play the role of complementing large-scale companies in an entirely different dimension. Despite the much-talked of 'economies of scale', the unique competence of small firms is their high internal efficiency. Economies of scale in production are synonymous with large-scale business only in exceptional cases. In many—but not of course all—branches of trade and manufacturing processes, acceptable internal efficiency is achieved even with small volumes of activity. This is true not only of the manufacture that is based on the technology of unit and small series production, but also of considerable sections of the technology of large series and mass production. The general exception to this claim would be industries based on process technologies. In cases where production is also exposed to frequent and rapid changes, the purely economic criteria of evaluation lose a great deal of their relevance, which provides further arguments in favour of small, flexible firms.

In summary, the knowledge we possess of industrialized economies and of the behaviour of firms within them indicates that a kind of complementarity has developed between firms of various sizes. Small firms constitute the base on which the large market-orientated companies have to rely in order to satisfy their demand for input goods. The existence of a number of 'stable' and 'efficient' production systems under the umbrella of the planned activities of large-scale companies would lend further support not only to the notion of the competence of small firms from the viewpoint of internal efficiency, but also to the view of large firms as being generally better equipped to face the demands for external efficiency stipulated in a modern industrial state.

On Stability and Efficiency in Production Systems

For a discussion of production systems to be relevant one prerequisite must be fulfilled: the flows of material must have some degree of stability. The validity of this condition has been called into question by several authors who try to prove that the situation of subcontractors is very unsafe by persistently claiming that buying companies often change their sources of supply. They argue that this is largely a consequence of the changes that always take place in a well-developed economic system. Logically the notion of stable systems is contradictory to the theoretical postulate of rationality which forms the basis of much of the discussion and research.

One argument brought forward, for example, is that during slack periods the

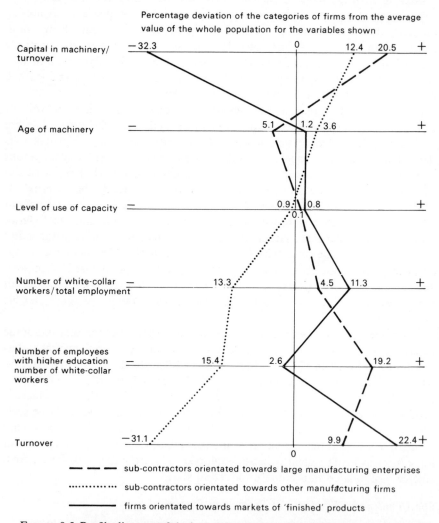

FIGURE 9.5 Profile diagram of the internal structure of the independent small and medium-sized firms manufacturing metal products and machinery

buying company will find it necessary to transfer to itself the production of items placed with subcontractors. The motive for this is supposed to be the wish to keep up their own employment in order to increase efficiency. As a consequence, small subcontractor firms are often considered not only less efficient in the internal sense of the concept, but also as one-sidedly dependent on the buying companies, which are often larger. Thus many authors maintain that the diminutive role of the subcontractor has been chosen in the absence of alternative activities. The production systems that can be identified would, in these circumstances, be temporary phenomena in a changing world.

The analysis of the indicators of the degree of internal efficiency exhibited by the firms studied here lends no support, however, to such conclusions, and this is particularly so in the case of the subcontractors incorporated in production systems of large-scale companies. The results do not support the idea that subcontractors, either in terms of facilities or personnel, are less well equipped than firms that operate in the markets of finished products. For example, the metal products and machinery subcontractors which orientate themselves towards large concerns show a capital intensity that is clearly above the average for all small and medium-sized firms in that sector. Likewise, the workforce of these firms has a higher educational level than the average firm (Figure 9.5). Furthermore, subcontractors, regarded as a group, seem to be in an equally good or even better financial position than other small and medium-sized firms judging from an average assessment of their position during the 6 years through 1972. However, as indicated in Figure 9.6, the 'other subcontractors' category shows the most favourable values.

This diagram also suggests that the subcontractors involved in the production systems of the largest manufacturing concerns have to pay a price. Possibly this is because demands within large companies for high internal efficiency have restraining effects on the economic 'elbow room' while, at the same time, making safe and expansive development possible. Thus subcontractors of large companies display a very favourable trend as measured in terms of turnover per employee during the period studied. Moreover, recessions do not seem to hit subcontractors harder than other small and medium-sized firms.

These results provide indications of a high stability within the production systems; this is confirmed by the firms studied here, most of which had engaged the same subcontractors for many years. The majority of contractors had cooperated with the buying companies during the major part of their lives—amounting in many cases to more than 30 years. Contractors are replaced only to a very small extent, since the firms considered that well-established contacts were of great value and outweighed the somewhat higher prime costs they sometimes had to pay to an established contractor compared with the offers received from new would-be contractors. The results clearly seem to point to a more pragmatic interpretation on the part of manufacturers of the postulate of economic rationality than economists usually assume.

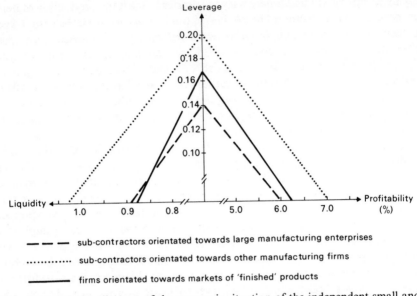

FIGURE 9.6 Profile diagram of the economic situation of the independent small and medium-sized firms manufacturing metal products and machinery. Liquidity (acid test) is defined as 'current assests-inventory/current liabilities'; leverage (debt ratio) as 'total debt/total assets'; and profitability (return on turnover) as 'profit before taxes/turnover' (cf. Weston and Brigham, 1975, pp. 19–53)

In the majority of cases the transactions between buying companies and contractors were designed so that the volumes of the flows of material were largely regulated by the turnover of the buying companies. Production was not 'taken home' to any great extent even during recessions, since the buying company was anxious to remain in contact with its contractors pending the expected subsequent economic upswing. In other cases such a step was not possible in any case since the product or process placed with a contractors was outside the actual production potential of the buying company. Similar conclusions are also presented by Håkansson and Wootz (1975) in a doctoral dissertation on the purchasing behaviour of firms: they suggest that the relationships between buyers and sellers in industrial markets are usually very stable, and that stability tends to increase in relation to the extent of previous contacts.

In the light of these empirical data the conclusion can be drawn that subcontractor relationships, and consequently also production systems, are considerably more solid than is usually stated by economists. Accordingly, it can also be observed that subcontractors orientated towards the large-scale companies in this study, on average sell more than 36 per cent of their output to their major customer, which means that the strength of the customer–supplier relationship in the industrial market appears considerably greater than for firms orientated towards other markets.

PRODUCTION SYSTEMS IN THE SWEDISH ECONOMY: THE SPATIAL DIMENSION

Local Production Systems

This functional division of labour between large and small firms stands out in a even more interesting light when the results are interpreted in the spatial dimension. Thus the networks of materials transactions extend over large areas, though with noticeable concentrations on certain regional clusters of firms, in spite of the fact that, in an international perspective, the study is concerned with small and sparsely populated regions. (Five of the 'A'-regions surveyed have between 45,000 and 82,000 inhabitants, and the 3 largest have from 140,000 to 440,000 inhabitants; excluding Malmö the population density averages 16 persons per km^2—or 6 persons per sq. mile.) In relation to the total volume of industry the local neighbourhood market is thus strongly over-represented although, on average, firms obtain only a little more than a tenth of all their purchases from other local industrial firms. If goods and services bought from local wholesalers and retailers are also included, local purchases make up nearly a third of the total. These results are also largely valid for firms in the regions examined in which the industrial environment is poorly developed.

If the flows of material are studied from the viewpoint of contractors, an even more interesting pattern emerges. The small and medium-sized firms orientated towards supplying other manufacturing companies with input goods, such as parts and components, sell no less than a third of their output to local customers. For roughly one-tenth of the subcontractors, local manufacturing industry is the wholly predominant market in cases when more than half of their output is sold locally (Table 9.1). There are considerable differences between the branches of industry. More than others, the metal and engineering industries are strongly represented among the subcontractors that sell large parts of their output locally. The textile and clothing industries show an interesting if somewhat different pattern because the Boras region—the centre of those activities in Sweden—is included in the study. The course of development here has resulted in the growth of several rather large companies which operate as suppliers to a great number of small firms undertaking the next stage of production. Thus in these industries there is an 'inverted hierarchical' structure of production in which a small number of contractors deliver highly standardized input articles to a great number of buying firms. But in the case of the metal and engineering companies, it is almost without exception the small firms that account for the supplies, and in most cases it is the plants belonging to the largest manufacturing enterprises of the country that constitute the nodes to which the supplies are directed.

TABLE 9.1 The sales of small and medium-sized subcontractors to local manufacturing industries. [Source: fieldwork]

Share of sales (per cent)	Number of firms	Share (per cent)
Nil	68	32.6
0.1– 5.0	36	17.2
5.1–10.0	21	10.0
10.1–20.0	25	12.0
20.1–50.0	38	18.2
More than 50.0	21	10.0
Total number of firms	209	100.0

A closer study of these local concentrations of flows of material reveals that in the majority of cases they consist of not very extensive transactions in financial terms (although for the small locally orientated subcontractor firms they are proportionally very significant) covering part of the demands of the large buying companies for special supplies. They form a contrast to the financially important (but for a smaller number of comparatively large contractors proportionally less significant) flows of material consisting of more standardized products and processes conveyed across long distances. In other words, standard supplies are chiefly provided by large companies (sometimes via wholesalers) which, through their relative insensitivity to distance, form national or international patterns, whereas the more distance-sensitive special supplies are largely taken from small and medium-sized firms in the local market.

In Figure 9.7 there is a visual impression that these customer-specific supplies across short distances over time may be important. This example is of an old multi-plant company in the forest and mining industries with some 10 plants in the 4 regions of the county of Kopparberg included in the inquiry or in adjacent regions. The purchases made can largely be described as industrial service, that is they consist of special supplies. Of the total of 166 'independent' small and medium-sized firms located in the county of Kopparberg no fewer than 38 are subcontractors to this particular large enterprise. In addition there are a further 4 subcontractors in a couple of the other more remote regions.

Special Supply and Local Production Systems

By analogy with Perroux's (1955) theory of growth poles, it can be claimed that large firms—through their own capacity for development and/or by virtue of economic assets—control or channel the conditions of economic development in other sectors of industry. Or, like Hirschman (1958) and Myrdal (1957), it can be stated that the growth of some firm somewhere at some time (perhaps initiated through some unique innovation) has, through a cumulative growth process, now come to encompass whole systems of production and consequently several regions of the country. Moreover, most experts seem to agree that the existence of a favourable industrial neigbourhood environment will have been an

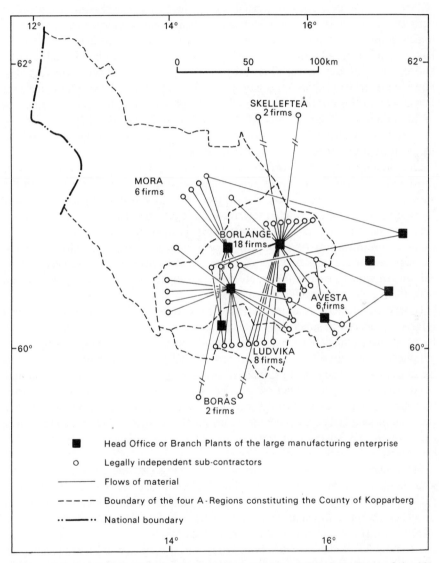

FIGURE 9.7 A regionally delimited subcontractor system belonging to one of the 30 largest manufacturing enterprises in Sweden. Only subcontractors in the 8 regions studied are depicted

important prerequisite for the growth and further development of the production systems of these firms.

If the previous discussion of flows of material and information is linked with an analysis of the spatial dimension of the environmental concept, it can be suggested that, along with the diminishing importance of transport costs, the relevance of the concept of external economies will be increasingly associated with the information exchanged between firms and their environment. As a logical consequence of this it is primarily firms as decision-making units, and to a lesser extent firms as transformers of resources, that need to be located in large and dense agglomerations. This categorization must not obscure the fact that flows of material are always more or less closely linked with flows of information. It is chiefly in this interplay between flows of information and material, and less in unidimensional discussions of transport costs, that determinants of the existence of local production systems within the external frameworks of the national or international system should be sought.

One starting-point for further discussion is that the more standardized a product is, the less information may generally be said to be associated with the supply in question. Conversely, the supplies that are customer-specific in one or more respects are often characterized by extensive technical co-operation between the buying and selling firms. This co-operation requires reliable and rapid communication of information, which is at present usually conveyed through personal contacts. These distance-sensitive contacts limit the geographical area in which possible contractors should be located, if placing production with them is to be considered profitable.

It may therefore be assumed that the production of non-standardized articles is largely placed with subcontractors located in the same geographical area as the buying firm. In the case of even more specific purchases there may be only a few suppliers available so the buyer is forced to look further afield despite this need for close co-operation. The problem of conveying information affects the choice of co-operators in yet another respect. For special supplies, the factor of distance may be at least of equal importance in establishing and maintaining contacts between buying firms and subcontractors, partly because of the limited searching capacity of the buyer, and partly because of the difficulties sellers have in establishing themselves in the market.

Since firms have limited resources for spotting suitable co-operators, their knowledge of remote, potential special suppliers is usually limited. In addition, the evaluation of potential co-operators in distant places is likely to be more uncertain than the judgement of those nearer to hand. This state of affairs is also affected by the complexity of purchasing decisions and their organizational positioning (cf. Webster, 1965; Hill, 1973). The greater the influence wielded by the production department of the buying firm on the purchasing process, the fewer the potential contractors that may come within the range of vision of the firm. This is because the production department curtails the chances of the purchasing department putting its know-how into practice, while at the same time the production department itself may possess only a limited knowledge of the market. This will be particularly conspicuous when the time element is of decisive importance in the choice of contractor.

Nor is it difficult to find examples of economic criteria of evaluation being pushed into the background by factors such as terms of delivery, quality, and personal contacts in these and similar situations. It would be tempting to believe, however, that such situations constitute an exception rather than the rule. This objection may be justified, inasmuch as their monetary value in relation to all purchasing decisions is small. It does not mean that they are unimportant to the continued existence of the firm: indeed the possibility of rapidly solving problems emerging outside the range of standardized norms is vitally necessary to the development of firms.

This dichotomization of flows of material into standard and special supplies on the basis of the amount of information associated with them is, it appears, essential to the understanding of the spatial structures of production systems. Standard supplies (and certain unique special supplies) seem to constitute the base of the national and international pattern of transactions, while local systems rest on special supplies. Exhaustive case studies indicate that the proportion of standard supplies in the metal and engineering industries in many cases is high—up to 80 per cent of all input goods. As a consequence, even in regions which have a good industrial structure, local production systems merely form small parts of larger national and international systems. This analysis of the connection between national and local production systems can be further examined by an analysis of the relationships between firms in the regions studied and the biggest manufacturing company in Sweden—AB Volvo.

LINKS BETWEEN NATIONAL AND LOCAL PRODUCTION SYSTEMS: THE VOLVO CASE

The Car Industry as Growth Generator and Focus of Production Systems

The industrial evolution has been paved with numerous technical innovations of revolutionary importance but few have brought about such vast changes as the steam engine, the railway, and the car. It is no exaggeration to suggest that the car industry has developed into the 'motor' of the Western economy through its effects on other sectors. As a tangible example, these spread effects are often indicated in calculations by including employment among the systems of subcontractors supplying the motor vehicle companies. The considerable exchange within these systems is indicated by the fact that a car is made up of a large number of components: on average about 55 per cent of the production value of European passenger cars consists of components and semi-manufactured goods bought from subcontractors (DAFSA, 1973). For AB Volvo in 1970 the corresponding figure was 64 per cent, which implies that the phrase 'to build a car the Volvo way'—that is, with considerable production placed in the hands of subcontractors—has some relevance.

These 'subcontractor-intensive' motor vehicle companies also have a very unbalanced subcontractor structure; in terms of value they rely heavily on a small number of very large component manufacturers. In some cases complete engines or electrical systems are supplied by a few world-wide companies. In addition, as indicated already, in the cases of General Motors and Renault there are very many small and medium-sized subcontractors. No directly comparable figure is available for AB Volvo, but it is known that Volvo's passenger car division used over 1300 subcontractors, more than 700 of which were Swedish.

Volvo as the Focus of Supplies in Swedish Manufacturing Industry

The survey indicated that a few large manufacturing concerns dominate the markets for input goods. For the small and medium-sized subcontractors (excluding subcontractors in the textile and clothing industries) the supplies to the 30 largest manufacturing concerns in the country correspond roughly to one-third on average of the entire output of the subcontractors. More than half this amount is produced by sales to 5 large Swedish enterprises, namely, AB Volvo, Stora Kopparbergs Bergslags AB, ASEA, AB Cementa, and SAAB-Scania AB.

Not unexpectedly, perhaps, Volvo heads this list. A closer examination of this enterprise's purchases in the 8 regions studied shows that it had 31 suppliers which, in turn, drew parts and components from 60 other firms. In other words, one firm in every twenty in the study area is directly involved in Volvo's subcontractor system and, in addition, approximately one firm in every twelve is indirectly affected. If textile, clothing, and some other firms are excluded along with factories owned by other multi-plant companies, the ratios alter considerably. Of the 'independent' small and medium-sized metal and engineering firms studied, roughly one in ten is a direct supplier to Volvo; if the indirect suppliers are also included, as many as one in every five may be directly or indirectly related to Volvo's system of handling materials.

Regional Imbalance in the Flows of Supplies

The remarkable aspect of these findings is that Volvo itself does not have *one* industrial plant in the regions studied. Given the general conclusion drawn earlier about the local character of the production systems, there is a strong probability that in regions where Volvo has large industrial plants, it would be an even more conspicuous focus of the output of many small subcontractors.

If the analysis is applied to the lower level of individual suppliers and industrial plants within the Volvo enterprise there is a strong support for the idea that the proximity between buyers and sellers appears to be an important determinant for the existence of subcontractor relationships. Most of the suppliers are in the two southernmost regions studied and these are nearest to Volvo's plants. But it must be pointed out that several of the flows that make up large quantities of the supplier's turnover are conveyed across long distances. Thus two suppliers from the Skellefteå and Malmö regions send substantial quantities more than 600 km (370 miles) to Volvo's plant at Eskilstuna, two suppliers in the Borlänge region concentrate on the Göteburg unit (more than 400 km—250 miles—away), and a supplier in one of the other 3 regions in Central Sweden delivers large quantities of its products to both Eskilstuna and Göteburg (see Figure 9.8). Although these results may be due to chance, it is much more likely that the shape of contact areas, the volume and character of supplies, the design of the policy-making system of firms, and other variables which have not been fully explored in this study have had a modifying effect on the importance of the factor of the distance in the structure of subcontractor systems.

Imbalance of Supplies in Terms of Volume

The total value of the goods supplied by these 31 subcontractors in 1970 amounted to only 4 per cent of Volvo's total purchases from all sources and little more than 8 per cent of those bought in Sweden. This is, of course, to be expected since the study has been restricted to firms in only 8 of the 70 Swedish A-regions. Nine plants belonging to other large-scale Swedish companies account for a large proportion, by value, of these supplies but in most of these cases the Volvo contract does not account for even 10 per cent of the output so that it is by no means the most important customer. From what can be gleaned about the production policies of the subcontractors, these flows of materials may be classified as supplies of standardized products. Without probing deeper into these parts of Volvo's supply system, these buyer—seller relationships appear to be characterized by a relatively high degree of mutual independence.

This is probably not true, however, of the majority of the 18 legally 'independent' small and medium-sized metal and engineering firms included in this group of 31 subcontractors since, on average, these sell about one-third of their output to Volvo. In short, Volvo is a rather important customer of every fourteenth metal and engineering firm in the regions examined; Volvo is by far the biggest customer of every twenty-fifth firm, buying on average half their outputs. If the indirect suppliers are taken into consideration, even more small and medium-sized firms may be said to be very strongly attached to Volvo. Although this study was based on sampling data that were not primarily designed for an analysis of the whole scope of Volvo's national production system, it indicates that in Sweden about one metal and engineering firm out of fifteen with fewer than 500 employees depends on supplying the prime producers of motor vehicles, trucks, and tractors. For the country as a whole this may well be an underestimate.

A Further Tentative Conclusion

Available data suggest that these Volvo suppliers employ an average of about 60 people and that they have a smaller than usual administrative superstructure.

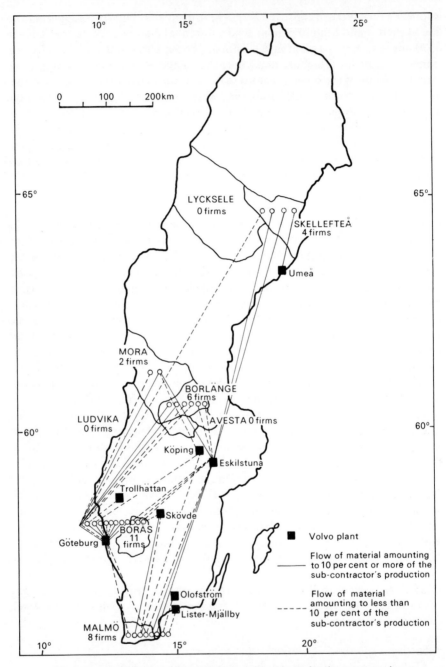

FIGURE 9.8 Links between national and local production systems in Sweden—the Volvo case

It seems that this study has found here an asymmetrical position of dependence: a large part of Swedish small-scale industry is entirely in the hands of the large-scale company of Volvo. Yet this may be a too hasty conclusion. The suppliers seem to possess a well-equipped assembly of machinery, be in a good financial situation, and to have enjoyed a favourable development during the 6-year period studied: in short Volvo's suppliers appear to be in a better position than most other small and medium-sized firms. Like other large-scale companies, Volvo is highly dependent on the contributions of many subcontractors, an assertion supported by the fact that the supplies from the small and medium-sized firms are modest in terms of value and involve relatively high administrative and other overhead costs. Moreover in the majority of cases the supplies are of a non-standardized character which means that the large company would find it difficult to manufacture them itself. In many instances positions of dependence may well be the reverse of the usual way of looking at things.

The tentative conclusion is that not only have large sections of industry been integrated at the technical level, but also that the whole production system seems to benefit by this integration when measured in terms of growth and short-run internal efficiency. For these groups of firms to be successful over a longer period, it will hardly be sufficient simply to co-ordinate their production activities. Toughening international competition will probably also make it necessary for them to co-ordinate their entire control and planning structures to enable them to meet changes in market positions in a flexible way. Innumerable examples can be found of the most important subcontractors accepting the purchase agreements of the large-scale company and adopting its methods of production engineering, accounting, and costing. Recent innovations in the field of information technology will improve the prospects of rendering the exchange of information between the various parts of production systems more effective.

As Thorngren (1977) suggests, complex systems of information supply are being developed which will be able to handle pictures, text, data and sounds, and to control both flows of material and information within whole systems of firms. The technology already exists; for economic reasons its implementation is not yet fully motivated, and for psychological reasons the dynamic conservatism of social structures may still be strong enough to resist these changes. The fact that more or less experimentally new organizational solutions have been found, based on new achievements in the field of information technology, may perhaps be regarded as the first step towards breaking the resistance to these changes (cf. Sayles and Chandler, 1971).

TECHNICAL RENEWAL AND SOCIAL CHANGE: PRODUCTION SYSTEMS IN A DYNAMIC PERSPECTIVE

To judge from the above analyses, the chief forces of change in the industrial sector are to be found in a limited number of hierarchical production systems, at the peak of which are the country's large companies. In a spatial perspective this means that, in analysing the development of regions, more importance ought to be attached (at least in the short run) to the development within units of large production systems than to the relocation/new location of small independent companies. In this connection it may also be worth pointing out that by describing industry in hierarchical terms there is no intention to give a normative conception of how industry should be organized; it is only meant to be an analytical concept used to reflect 'reality'. Earlier in this chapter this reality was described in terms of stability and instability, and this may have caused some readers to conclude that production systems in this descriptive model are not exposed to change. In fact, of course, changes do occur, and they are probably more the result of changes in the environment of firms/production systems than of internal changes.

A Note on Structural Change

Many of the changes that affect individual production systems as well as industry as a whole are of a temporary nature. They may not only consist of business cycles, but may also be due to temporarily emerging competition in certain markets. Other changes are of a more permanent nature, even though they may be regarded as a result of pure chance, at least if the development is seen from the viewpoint of the production systems: examples are transfers of ownership and replacement of management. Also included here are many decisions made at a higher political level, such as those affecting transport policy and restrictions on trade where the decision-makers do not primarily pay regard to potential effects on the pattern of transactions between industrial companies. In other words, it seems that many changes that affect the structure of production systems are difficult to predict since they are situation-specific rather than related to any structural phenomenon.

Yet other changes are of a more permanent nature and may more predictably be said to alter the conditions of the activities of production systems. Here the fundamental force of change seems to be the continuously increasing economic concentration. Firms endeavour to grow in order to 'guarantee' their own continued existence, since stagnation is a breeding ground for economic and organizational problems that are difficult to overcome. Manifest features of this process of growth and economic concentration are the increasing numbers of mergers and transfers of ownership that can be observed in all the industrial countries of Western Europe. In recent years mergers in Sweden have not always consisted of large firms buying up small ones. Not long ago there were reports that AB Volvo and SAAB-Scania AB—Sweden's two car manufacturers—were carrying on far-reaching negotiations (subsequently shelved) about merging. If the merger were to be carried through, about 10 per cent of all the employees in

Swedish manufacturing industry would be incorporated into one and the same organization. The projected new company—with its existing large production systems—would make up a new production system without comparison in Swedish industry. It is difficult to predict how this amalgamation of the two production systems into one would affect the large numbers of small and medium-sized subcontractor firms, but it would hardly be surprising if in the long run many of them became redundant, with ensuing regional unemployment.

The process of economic concentration forms the framework within which other basic changes take place. The constant need for technical innovation is perhaps the essential driving force behind the changes in firms/production systems that take place in the course of time. In a world in which the concept of prosperity has a materialistic foundation, technical innovation is the most important feature of structural change and the main condition of the continued existence of production systems in the long run. By maintaining a high technical standard a firm can gain the lead over its competitors. The willingness of consumers to pay a relatively higher price for a technically more advanced product makes increasing future profits possible, despite the additional cost of technical development.

Another structural force of change that may be found in a market economy is the necessity to try to identify and/or create new markets for the finished product. New earnings may be generated not only by developing new geographical markets, but also by finding new categories of customers in existing well-covered markets. In one respect this force of change counteracts the demand for technical innovation. The life cycles of products are lengthened by finding new market segments, which leads to a growing body of older production activities on which business is based; this naturally promotes growth but at the same time reduces the chances of flexibility and adaptation.

Thus the results of technical research and development work will—at least in a short-term view—affect only marginal sections of the activities of the production system. For instance, even during a 5-year period British Leyland would be unable to switch entirely from producing cars to manufacturing space shuttles or any other totally different product if at the same time it intended to maintain the total level of production in the company and its subsidiary production systems of subcontractor firms.

The last of the major driving forces that can be identified is commonly referred to as 'the cost hunt'. Competition can be met and markets expanded or safeguarded by increasing internal efficiency. It is obvious that demands for changes within this dimension are expressed during period of economic recession (cf. Cyert and March, 1963). In production systems these economy drives and waves of rationalization manifest themselves in such forms as standardized production engineering and decision-making which, in turn, lead to increasing opportunities for mechanization and automation. Thus the ultimate effects of this cost hunt are a growing stabilization of the production systems with diminishing possibilities for flexibility and adjustment to further structural changes.

Evidently the mechanisms of technical innovation, market expansion, and cost hunting always operate within production systems, even though attention is focused on only symptoms or parts of one of them at a given time. It is also probable that the focal point of attention on the part of decision-makers—if they take any interest at all in structural changes—will depend on what sort of environment the production system is located in. A generous environment (such as where business is based on patented products or is protected by customs duties or other State subsidies) is likely to have a dampening effect on interest in innovation.

Implications at the Level of Production Systems

For production systems to survive it is necessary to match their structure continuously against environmental changes. Some decisions, made at a superior strategic level within the management of the large-scale company that supports a hierarchy of smaller subcontractor firms, will have a decisive influence on the future structure of the whole production system. Good examples of this are decisions about new products and markets that are to be commercialized. Other decisions—often made at some lower level of the company's hierarchy—affect only individual processes of production in certain plants.

It is appropriate here to refer to studies of the structure of decision-making in organizations and of the demand for data on which different decisions are based. Following Ramström (1967), information can be differentiated according to various degrees of structure, and it can be argued that decisions at the institutional level are associated with highly unstructured information. On the other hand, decisions at the technical level are based on highly structured and standardized information in the traditionally hierarchic decision procedure characteristic of firms. This fundamental difference between the flows of information has usually been discussed at the intra-organizational level, but will be directly applicable to the inter-organizational networks that production systems form in the descriptive model discussed here.

Also should be mentioned the arguments advanced by Thorngren (1970), who states that different flows of information between an organization and its environment are related to each other temporally in different ways (cf. Goddard, 1968). Thus like Thorngren, a distinction can be made between *programme* processes which, referring to routine activities, are likely to contain the most well-structured information, *planning* processes referring to changes in these routine activities, and *orientation* processes designed to give changes their proper direction. Thus in a production system can be found simultaneously flows associated with programme processes as well as flows linked with the planning and orientation processes of firms.

In the light of the empirical data already presented it is possible to conclude that in the former type of flows—programme processes—should be found the majority of the standard supplies that are exchanged within the framework of the system. The same will apply to the flows that could be called special supplies, even though it can be assumed that a considerable part of these are concerned with planning processes. What appears relevant to this discussion of production systems is that the material portion of flows will be substantially larger in programme processes than in planning processes. Further it can be assumed that the material portion of orientation processes is almost non-existent, and that these flows appear only to a limited extent in the production systems that have been here defined and discussed. The flows that have been the chief subject of discussion so far and have the widest demonstrable scope in terms of money, will thus be those which are attributable to the routine activities of firms. This conclusion has some bearing on the understanding of the dynamics of the development.

On Functional Changes in Production Systems

The picture of the flows exchanged within the framework of production can be elucidated by arguing that there is usually very little reason to replace suppliers that take part in programme processes. On the contrary, any replacement made by a firm will have repercussions on its own organization and on its own production unit. Another way of stating this is that, through their very low internal efficiency, the suppliers that are replaced will as a rule have already caused more disturbance than that which is likely to follow their dismissal. Thus in the short-term view taken here, instability is judged to be a waste of resources.

On the other hand, it cannot be assumed *a priori* that stable relations should be equally desirable in the flows of material associated with the planning and orientation processes of production systems. On the contrary, a high degree of openness in these relations will make it easier to find new materials, new products, or new processes of production. The conflicting demands, on the one hand for long-term organized change in order to be able to reorganize programme processes in time and, on the other, for 'anarchic openness' to new alternatives, place the firms within production systems in a dilemma. Large companies usually refer this dilemma to separate research and development units located in information-intensive environments, but similar strategies are not feasible for small firms which, instead, have to rely on their flexibility in routine activities. To some extent they also have to play the 'anarchic' role which large-scale companies may utilize. Statistics of mergers and transfers of ownership indicate that large companies tend to buy potential new markets and technology rather than new production capacity (Rydén, 1971).

Earlier the importance of product and market development and rationalization, as driving forces of the evolution of production systems was emphasized.

Now it can be added that the incorporation of these changes into an organizational framework is at least of equal importance; in other words, changes must be organized. Unlike rationalization measures, changes in product and market development require increased resources and this, in turn, means that the changes lead to a relatively larger growth of employment at the top of production systems. We can also find the same tendencies in the new systems that form like new shoots sprouting from the branches of a tree: such new lines of business tend to have a markedly larger proportion of employment in orientation and planning functions than older ones.

On Spatial Changes in Production Systems

An attempt should be made to see the outlined development in a spatial perspective in the light of the clearly discernible priority given to the local market at the present time. It can be speculated that local production systems discussed earlier which are basically composed of programme flows are likely to disintegrate. Together, standardization, large-scale production, and well-planned activities may be assumed to intensify competition—perhaps previously geographically restricted—between suppliers of input goods, and lead to a reduction in the number of supply points. The result would be a more global network of material-intensive flows between well-informed buyers and sellers. Hong Kong, Taiwan, Brazil, and other countries are tending to appear more frequently in the supplier lists of buying firms. It may be assumed, however, that personal local contacts have the effect of making the disintegration of complexes a slow process. Yet changes in the structure of decision-making brought about by more extensive staff participation in management/bureaucracy and computer processing may contribute effectively to depersonalizing these flows (cf. Thorngren, 1977). This in turn may cause economic and technical factors to feature as the principal mechanisms of evaluation, and this may accelerate the process of change.

However, the flows of planning and orientation are in a radically different situation. Since there is a great demand for unstructured information, it is especially advantageous to locate these units in large information-intensive regions. The last few years have seen several large Swedish companies locating development units close to their market, that is in the more central parts of Europe. Further it can be noted that in production systems where programme, planning and orientation processes have been spatially separated, the planning and orientation flow may have widely different effects on various sections of the firm. Findings in Great Britain indicate that a deliberate location of the research and development (R & D) units of firms in certain regions, and transfers of ownership to companies whose head office is located in a remote region, will have significant long-run repercussions on the location of routine activities. Production units close to the head office or R & D units seem to be better off in comparison with other more distant branch plants.

In summary, the local concentrations of flows of material that have been recorded in this study will in many respects reflect the unstructured demand for information that accompanies many transactions related to materials. Thus the local neighbourhood market, particularly for firms in certain lines of business and in certain regions, seems to offer great possibilities for embracing the demand for flows of material linked not only with routine activities but also with planning and orientation processes. However, the bulk of flows in the local market will still consist of movements of material connected with the programme processes of firms. But in the light of the structural changes identified here, and the development of communications technology, it is argued that programme flows in particular are likely to become spatially foot-loose far more rapidly than would otherwise have been the case.

PRODUCTION SYSTEMS AND REGIONAL DEVELOPMENT

During the 1960s there was considerable debate about the possibilities offered by forward and backward linkages for stimulating self-generating development in industrially backward regions. The discussion was carried on far outside scientific circles and led to political action in many places. Findings about the present industrial structure and the concept of what forces will form the future structure may now be combined into a regional perspective of development. The knowledge that the world is always changing is the most important key to understanding regional processes of development; the historical aspect is interesting only insofar as it can be argued that the forces behind the present structure will also exist tomorrow.

A Picture from the Past

Earlier in this chapter a brief account was given of a local production system in central Sweden, centred upon a multi-plant company engaged in forestry and mining, which reflects the result of a 100-year development (see Figure 9.7). It is not a unique case; in the two northernmost regions studied an almost identical local production system was found which had been built up round AB Boliden—a large metallurgical company—which is something of an industrial base in that part of Sweden. Industrial expansion in the region started in the 1920s and was orginally based on the exploitation by AB Boliden of the non-ferrous ore deposits in the Skellefteå field and on harnessing waterfalls on the Skellefte river. The ore was exported in its crude state but, because of its particular chemical composition, foreign smelting plants could only use small quantities. A mainly new process was invented and formed the basis for a big smelting plant built in the late 1920s at Skellefteå because of the availability of electricity and transport facilities. After the first decade AB Boliden branched out in various directions by exploiting new mines and enlarging the smelting plant. Nowadays the company employs more than 3000 of the 11,000 industrial workers in the Skellefteå region.

In retrospect can thus be discerned the historically important role that AB Boliden has played in the development of the region, not only through its direct employment but also indirectly through the supplier transactions to which it has given rise. AB Boliden's machine servicing needs caused it to initiate other firms in the region that took up the manufacture of transport and mining equipment. A new phase in the development of the region started in the 1950s when AB Boliden's subcontractors began to launch their own products but, even so, this company remains very important in the region through its extensive purchases from small and medium-sized metal and engineering firms. However, no firms have been established in the region to refine or otherwise utilize AB Boliden's products so that the development through forward linkages has thus been weak or non-existent (Hirschman, 1958).

A Picture of the Future

It is useful to consider the extent to which similar processes of development may be repeated in other regions in other countries and at other times. The prediction must be based on the fact that today's industrial structure is fundamentally different from that of the 1920s. Fifty years ago the Skellefteå region was part of an industrial world in which the basic industries accounted for nearly all employment; the cost of transportation was a decisive location factor and the activities of firms were focused almost exclusively on achieving technical efficiency. Nature provided 'free riches' which guaranteed economic progress to those that succeeded in mastering the problems of production. If the existence and extraction of rich local mining deposits is disregarded, there is in almost every respect a different situation today—a simplification justified by the fact that the key firms in large production systems are output- rather than input-orientated in their spatial organization.

When it is recognized that the overall complexity of the social organization has increased, and that the concentration of economic activity will significantly influence future regional development processes, it can be realized that the bases of regional growth are no longer likely to be situation-specific phenomena. Power and dependence in the existing industrial structure are important regulators for the future. In an industry with hierarchical production systems where orientation, planning and programme processes have been spatially separated (or are at least separable), a step-wise analysis must be made of the concept of regional development.

Considering first the flows that are associated with routine activities, it was observed earlier that the prospects of long-distance conveyance will probably become greater in the future. Thus individual regions may be expected to retain a decreasing share of intraregional flows or, in other words, they will be exposed to growing leakages from the regional system. The theory of the increasing insensitivity of programme flows to distance does not, however, contradict the opposite interpretation: it can be expected that in various places extremely specialized industrial complexes will emerge. What is interesting here, and also in line with the discussion of the desirable present and future stability of programme flows, is that there is a good chance of controlling these flows at the regional level. From the viewpoint of regional policy it seems that it may be possible to create and maintain a stable regional structure of industry by deliberately controlling the bulk of material-intensive programme flows. Traditional measures, such as public investment to aid firms and regions hit by crises and the location of new production units in areas with a weak industrial structure, may have to be supplemented by measures designed to affect the flows of material that are related to routine activities within different production systems. The latter may consist of direct measures such as negotiations to find 'packet solutions' like those used in the United States for purposes of regional planning and those related to the sale of the Swedish Viggen military aircraft to certain West European countries. In the latter case, the Swedish Aircraft Company—SAAB Scania AB—offered potential buying countries valuable subcontracts for this plane. Furthermore the company, through negotiations in which the Swedish Government played active role, offered to promote the expansion of subsidiaries of other big Swedish firms already operating in these countries. As another alternative, transportation subsidies or other general measures of support may be linked with purchases of input goods in certain regions.

However, the major problem of regional development is likely to arise in connecting these programme flows with planning or orientation flows. In a stable regional structure of industry there is an obvious risk that peripheral regions will tend to lag behind at one level of planning and orientation: hence a stable structure may easily develop into a conservative structure. A regional dispersal of planning and orientation processes ought to become, therefore, at least as important as a widespread network of material-intensive flows. These prospects are considerably hampered by the fact that the flows contain substantial portions of unstructured information. To bring about regional development, it is not sufficient to try to raise the industrial structure of regions from one level to a quantitatively higher level merely by active measures designed to affect routine activities. Such a change will at best serve to break down existing regional hierarchies and to initiate a short-lived process of adaptation until the new level has been reached. In order to encourage a self-generating process of development of a qualitative nature, it is more necessary to find some means of promoting the growth of information-intensive environments, such as by improving communications and by controlling the locations of research and development work. It is doubtful, however, whether political measures of this kind will ever become extensive enough to change the pattern of development in any decisive way. In an historical perspective, new technologies have constantly succeeded each other and have been dispersed in waves that, in due course, have resulted in pressure for economic rationalization. Through the exploitation of economies of scale in production and transportation this led to rapidly increasing economic concentration. As the European countries then constituted the world centre of industrial development, their national borders served as important frames and restrictions in defining the geographic dimension of intra-European allocation of resources, and their colonial relations defined the frame of under-development in the rest of the world.

In the current world economic order, made up by dominating transnational companies, bilateral trade agreements and supranational free trade (and/or restricted) areas, the former centres have much less influence. The conditions for regional development have not really changed, even though assuming new forms. Situated at the bottom of an increasingly closely structured and well-organized hierarchy of global, continental, and national monopoly-satellite constellations, individual regions are forced to react at the second or third remove like puppets on a string pulled by the controlling units. For instance, it is difficult to see ways in which the Swedish steel industry, even though strongly export-orientated since the nineteenth century, can 'survive' the attempts of North American and West European countries to save their own—in many respects less efficient—steel industries. The small firms and regions affected by these measures are finding themselves in the front line facing the consequences of decisions taken far above their heads. The conclusion is that it will be increasingly difficult to bring about a self-generating development in regions which are outside the limited circle of power and decision centres of the global economy.

Chapter 10

Enterprises in Trouble: the Geography of Wholesaling in the Australian Agricultural Machinery Industry, 1967–72

David A. Wadley

PROGRESS IN THE GEOGRAPHY OF ENTERPRISE

A useful synthesis of progress in the nascent geography of enterprise has been provided in Hamilton (1974c) who reiterates the questioning of traditional location theory:

> fundamentally, until recently, the [location] problem was still cast largely in the mould of the nineteenth-century or early twentieth-century 'free-market' economy. That is, the main lines of . . . analysis were appropriate to the time when, and to the regions where, small firms with one, usually single-product, plant were economically (and not only numerically) dominant, technologies and business organization were small-scale and simple, and location decisions were made essentially in response to relatively simple economic, social, political and spatial environments external to the manufacturer. It is the developments of the past thirty years that have made traditional industrial locational analysis lose some of its utility—certainly its claim to universality—and indeed that demand our re-interpretation . . . of the location of modern industry (Hamilton, 1974a, p. 5).

Given these developments, Hamilton (1974a, p. 6) outlines the current tasks of spatial enquiry. One is the long-recognized problem of understanding the initial investment process. Others more novel are to concentrate on the forms and implications of the growth and organization of the enterprise, to investigate motivations for locational initiatives, and to study adaptation to the environment in both an absolute and comparative (i.e. cross-cultural, cross-sectoral) sense. Such a brief is a broad one for a behavioural approach, which, while founded in the work of Alchian (1950), Tiebout (1957), and Simon (1957, 1959), did not really crystallize until the end of the 1960s (e.g. Krumme, 1969; Dicken, 1971). Writers in *Spatial Perspectives* broach these objectives and hence spotlight emerging but neglected trends in the industry sector of advanced and developing nations.

There are, however, differing opinions about the universality of the findings and the way ahead. One view doubts whether 'pleas . . . for *more* case studies are really justified' (Hamilton, 1974a, p. 14); an opposite position is taken by McNee (1974, p. 50) and Beyers and Krumme (1974, p. 102), who are concerned to establish the wider applicability of their results by means of other examples.

Despite the desirability of progress toward nomothetic ends, Hamilton's injunction may be premature: there are at least three grounds for further empirical investigations of corporations. First, the behavioural analysis has focused on a limited number of industries, foremost of which is the petrochemical group (McNee, 1958, 1961, 1964; Rees, 1972, 1974; Chapman, 1974); electronics, plastics, and pulp have occupied other writers (respectively, Krumme, 1970; North, 1973, 1974; Barr and Fairbairn, 1974), while Steed (1968, 1971a, 1974) has considered the problems of shipbuilding and linen production. Yet, even admitting additions as diverse as steel (Warren, 1973; Heal, 1974) and sugar-beet (Watts, 1974), there is scope to cast the net wider, not only in manufacturing but also in the primary and tertiary sectors. Varying market structures might well influence corporate activities.

Second, interest by geographers in the spatial policy of large undertakings is almost exclusively a transatlantic phenomenon. The impact in Britain's established industrial areas has received detailed scrutiny (e.g. Townroe, 1971, 1972; Parsons, 1972). Aspects of the continental European situation have been charted by Fleming and Krumme (1968) and Krumme (1970), while developments in North America, the home of the corporation, are of perennial interest (e.g. Ray, 1971). Elsewhere, work has most often been set in the context of multinationalism: in Australia, for example, study either of enterprises *per se* or of international concerns has been minimal and usually the preserve of economists (Brash, 1966; Parry, 1974).

Third, since corporations are clearly a 'going thing' in the commercial environment, they are more likely to be found in growth industries. Yet if geographic enquiries were to dwell too much on expanding types of production, they might transmit a biased view of the problem. In this sense, there are two important gaps in our understanding of the major enterprise: the relationship of its development to the business cycle and locational repercussions which ensue when corporations meet economic distress. The rationale of the following examination of Australian agricultural machinery wholesaling rests on these issues. It concerns a previously unexplored industry in a country which, for corporate geography, is *terra incognita*; it differs from prior contributions in its strongly systematic framework; and its interest is solely with the behaviour of selected firms rather than with regional implications of their adaptation to the altered environment. Further, the enquiry deals with only one aspect of vertical integration (wholesaling), thus departing from nearly all previous longitudinal and cross-sectional studies.

THE PROBLEM INDUSTRY: AGRICULTURAL MACHINERY

From 1945 to the late 1960s, the Australian economy enjoyed a long secular upswing. The expansionism of agricultural policy was nowhere better demonstrated than in the doubling of sown wheat area between 1959–60 and

1966–67. Despite warnings in 1964–65 about the coming saturation of world markets, the area under wheat and indeed the total of all cropping continued to climb. By 1968 wheat growers and those in several other industries were facing economic turbulence, variable seasons, storage problems, falling prices, rising costs, and an increasing dependence on uncertain exports. In 1970–71 aggregate farm income reached a (deflated) post-war low while, simultaneously, rural debt spiralled.

Manufacturers supplying the farming industries were, of course, affected by such trends. But for machinery producers these immediate depressants of domestic sales formed only part of a much broader and longer-term problem. Since the Second World War there has been vast technological improvement in their product but, while quality and size have been upgraded, price relative to other agricultural inputs has fallen (Heady and Tweeten, 1963, pp. 265–7). The demand function still appears very complex. Economic theory sees purchases predicated not solely upon the level of technology and relative costs in the factor input mix but also upon farm income and the prevailing interest rate (because many sales are made on credit). At any time there is an inventory situation which the farmer holds to be optimal, and shifts in any of these independent variables might necessitate a change to reinstitute equilibrium. Since econometric models stress that demand elasticities are geared more to the farmer's income than to the price of equipment (cf. Griliches, 1960; Rayner and Cowling, 1967, 1968), a recession in the rural sector should markedly prejudice suppliers for, unless a complete breakdown of services ensues, machinery buying simply stops until prospects improve. Other factors which affect landholders—seasonality, drought, fire, flood, and commodity surpluses—are all periodically capable of eroding willingness to invest and so leave the equipment trade among the riskier lines of business.

During the 1960s farmers in Western countries began rationalizing their land-holdings and using contractors who could run machines at near-optimal efficiency. These factors became superimposed upon all the industry's 'normal' operating uncertainities to reduce demand. Scant compensation emanated from the developing nations where, despite great need, purchasing power remained low. As a result, by the end of the decade, the production and export of equipment outside the communist bloc became all but static, frustrating manufacturers' hopes of achieving economies of scale which were potentially significant in all areas of supply. Had the available scale economies been used, it is estimated that only 9 plants would have been required to produce the 809,500 tractors sold in non-communist countries in 1966 (Barber, 1971, pp. 132 and 144). In fact, supply was fragmented oligopolistically with 16 brands emanating from an even greater number of factories sharing 80 per cent of the market. A chief strategy adopted by producers to tackle the dilemma was geographic expansion and this tactic, catalyst of corporate multinationalism found a fertile reception in Australia where foreign investment was generally welcome. Beyond this, if a firm chose to commence domestic machinery manufacture, the avoidance of tariff barriers acted as yet another incentive. All these concerns prompted greater European and American participation in the Australian market between 1955 and 1965 and predisposed chronic excess capacity by the time of the rural recession. In 1967 companies with varying degrees of vertical integration established in Australia for less than 15 years accounted for well over a quarter of the tractor sales and enjoyed comparable success in other lines of equipment. The 17,900 tractors sold that year were divided among 13 imported and 2 locally manufactured brands, and 9 overseas and 3 domestic makes vied for the 4400 harvesters despatched. Then, through the combination of global and national over-capacity and the major downturn in demand which has already been discussed, a precipitous situation arose since during the next 4 years deliveries of the main types of machinery were almost halved. It now remains to be seen how such a crisis affected the behaviour of the leading enterprises in the industry.

THE METHODOLOGY

Selecting the Firms

The first problem to be tackled was that of selecting the firms to be studied intensively. At the onset of the recession in 1967, there were 725 farm-equipment manufacturing and repairing establishments in Australia but many were very small operations wholly occupied in maintenance. A mere 3 per cent of producers engaged 56 per cent of the industry's 15,400 employees and delivered 59 per cent of the total value of output (this total being $A127 million). The existence of a situation of corporate oligopoly is confirmed by an official statistical series which shows that in 1968–69 the first twenty enterprise groups (defined as the unit comprising all operations in Australia of a group of legal entities— enterprises—under common ownership or control) accounted for 78 per cent of the turnover and 26 per cent of the workforce of the entire machinery trade: virtually half this contribution came from the first four alone.

Little information is available in Australia from either government or private sources about the operations of individual companies. The impasse was partly overcome by approaching the Melbourne-based Tractor and Machinery Association of Australia which suggested the names of 19 suppliers that it thought would account for about three-quarters of total turnover and employ- ment. These organizations, more than representing the core of the oligopoly, were found to be suitable for the purposes of the study in that they (a) acted in a number of locations within a recognizable corporate structure of holding and operating companies, and (b) ran the risk of being affected in some way by the rural recession. Each undertaking was visited for 2–10 days depending on its size and the extent of its co-operation. Amongst the information sought was access to annual reports, price books, marketing agreements, product literature, and internal studies as well as detailed statistics on employment, stocks, selling patterns, and product volumes. This data gathering was supported by formal interviews with senior management.

Classifying the Firms

The data obtained were a necessary prerequisite for the next stage in the research, that of classifying the firms. All 19 operated in at least the three mainland southeastern States of New South Wales, Victoria, and South Australia (thus permitting spatial comparisons to be made at the subnational and national levels), and each had average annual machinery sales exceeding $A0.5 million during 1967–72. But on a number of key issues—head-office location, origin, longevity, and type of production—the companies showed marked differences (Table 10.1; Figure 10.1). In addition, every individual's equipment range was of different composition and extent and appeared among an unique array of other horizontally linked corporate functions.

To counter the diversity, to align the sample at the start of the recession and to accord with hypotheses of the wider project (Wadley, 1974), a computer-based classification was used to differentiate the organizations on the basis of their relative participation in the equipment industry in 1967. The programmes employed are derived from a battery of grouping and diagnostic routines first designed by ecologists (Lance and Williams, 1966; Williams *et al.*, 1966). The same or related approaches have since been used in general geographic situations (Stimson, 1970; Scott and Austin, 1971) and, more specifically, in industrial research (Rimmer, 1969). The mainstay is MULTBET which, through a centroid strategy, produces a polythetic, agglomerative, hierarchical classification with similarity measures advanced in the form of non-factorial information statistics: essentially, the procedure involves scanning and assessing both qualitative and quantitative attributes of a set of enterprises and progressively fusing most similar individuals to form a hierarchy. Then GROUPER dissects the relationships between the groups generated by MULTBET and states for each comparison the variable means and contributions to the similarity measure.

Hence, the MULTBET sorting was applied to the 1967 data for the 19 firms using 17 variables which reflected corporate size, structure, and function (Table 10.2). The outcome was a major distinction between 4 *large* and 15 *small* organizations based on relative sales of tractors, the single most important product category of Australian demand (Bernasek and Kubinski, 1963, p. 460). Large competitors not only dominated this field but also enjoyed prominence in a number of other machinery markets such that their annual sales, which averaged $A22 million during the period 1967–72, were at least five times that of their opposition. They were longer established (averaging 53 as against 40 years) and employed six times as many workers in agricultural operations as their small counterparts. Yet this focus represented only one-quarter of their aggregate

TABLE 10.1   Attributes of the selected firms, agricultural machinery industry, Australia, 1967. [Source: fieldwork]

Operating firm	Head office location	Origin	Longevity in 1967[a] (years)	Importer and/or manufacturer	Farm equipment product range	Other corporate lines
Alfarm Distributors Pty Ltd	Albury (N.S.W.)	Aust.	12	I	Harvesting equipment	
Allis Chalmers Australia Pty Ltd	Sydney	U.S.A.	21	I	Tractors, tillage, and harvesting equipment	Heavy engineering, industrial equipment
Australian Motor Industries Ltd	Melbourne	Aust.	1	I	Tractors	Automobiles
J.I. Case (Australia) Pty Ltd	Sydney	U.S.A.	67	I/M	Tractors	Construction equipment
Chamberlain Industries Pty Ltd	Perth	Aust.	20	I/M	Tractors, all major equipment	Construction equipment
Connor Shea and Co. Pty Ltd	Melbourne	Aust.	15	M	Tillage, seeding equipment	Industrial equipment
Fiat of Australia Pty Ltd	Sydney	Italy	22	I	Tractors	Automobiles
Ford Motor Company of Australia Ltd	Melbourne	U.S.A.	42	I	Tractors, selected equipment	Automobiles
Horwood Bagshaw Ltd	Adelaide	Aust.	130	M	Fiat tractors (S.A. only), major equipment	Industrial equipment
Howard Rotavator Pty Ltd	Sydney	U.K.	17	I/M	Tillage, seeding, and haymaking equipment	Horticultural equipment
International Harvester Co. of Australia Pty Ltd	Melbourne	U.S.A.	65	I/M	Tractors and all lines of equipment	Automobiles, construction equipment
Leyland of Australia Ltd	Sydney	U.K.	17	I	Tractors	Automobiles
Ralph McKay Ltd	Melbourne	Aust.	35	M	Tillage, seeding, specialized equipment components	Small industrial engineering goods
Massey Ferguson (Australia) Ltd	Melbourne	Canada	82	I/M	Tractors and all lines of equipment	Construction equipment
Mobilco Ltd	Melbourne	Aust.	22	I/M	Tractors, general, and haymaking equipment	Horticultural equipment
New Holland Division of Sperry Rand Australia Ltd	Melbourne	U.S.A.	22	I/M	Haymaking, harvesting equipment	
David Shearer Ltd	Mannum (S.A.)	Aust.	90	M	Tillage, harvesting equipment	Minor structural engineering
John Shearer Ltd	Adelaide	Aust.	90	M	Tillage, seeding equipment	
Thiess Equipment Distributors Pty Ltd	Sydney	Aust.	1	I	Tractors, harvesting equipment	Automobiles, mining

[a] Longevity of agricultural machinery distribution in Australia.

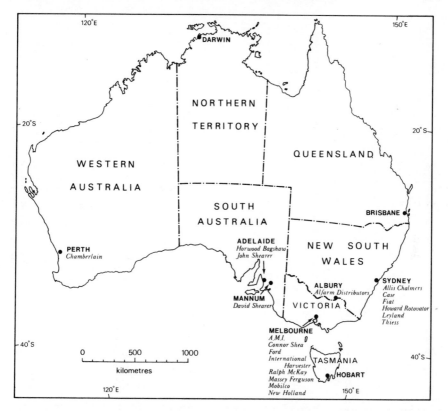

FIGURE 10.1 Location of head offices and principal factories of selected firms in the Australian agricultural machinery industry, 1967. [Source: fieldwork]

activity as measured by sales whereas farm equipment constituted half the business of the more specialized and therefore more exposed small supplier.

Within each main category, two other points were thrown up by the grouping routines. In the large category, they segregated 2 full-line from 2 long-line enterprises, the former being not only the stronger tractor sellers but also participating in the full array of equipment markets while the latter confined their involvement mainly to tractors, tillage, and seeding machinery. Similarly, in the small category, the classification sorted 7 tractor from 8 implement companies. The first were relatively young firms which imported and assembled tractors from their overseas principals; by contrast, the latter were predominantly Australian owned and integrated through all levels of manufacture to produce tillage and harvesting lines. Notwithstanding the many diverse characteristics of the selected companies, an overall impression can be offered of their corporate spatial organization at the break of the recession as a preface to discussion of change in the marketing networks.

TABLE 10.2 Parameters included in classification of selected firms, agricultural machinery industry, Australia, 1967. [Source: fieldwork]

Variable	Variable number	Type	Measure	Possible conditions	Criterion
Sales aggregate corporate total agricultural machinery agricultural tractor tillage equipment seeding equipment haymaking equipment harvesting machinery general equipment specialized equipment components spare parts	1 2 3 4 5 6 7 8 9 10 11	Quantitative	Actual (or estimated) $A value	Absolute numerical	Size, structure Function, size, structure
Longevity of company's machinery distribution in Australia	12		Years to 1967		Size
(Proportional) employment in agricultural machinery operation	13		From the 30 June 1967 head-count statistics		
Degree of manufacturing integration	14			Fully integrated/fabricator/ assembler	Size, structure
Head-office location	15		Ordered multi-state	Sydney/Melbourne/Adelaide/ Perth/other	Structure
Country of ownership	16	Qualitative		Australia/Britain/United States/Italy/other	
Total corporate product line (functional diversification)	17		Disordered multi-state	Agricultural machinery (wholesaling)/industrial equipment/construction machinery/trucks/automobiles/engines/engineering/ agricultural machinery (retailing)	Function, size, structure

RESULTS: PATTERNS OF ADAPTATION

To appreciate modifications in the wholesaling of Australian agricultural equipment merchants between 1967 and 1972, the operation must be seen first against a demand small by world standards and spread over vast, sparsely populated distances. There is not the fairly intensive regional administration common in North America nor the quaint parochiality of distribution in parts of Europe. Rather, marketing is an uncomplicated process designed to cover large areas as efficiently as possible.

In 1967, the manufacturing operations of the nineteen corporations were concentrated at a single, often-diversified plant invariably located in one of the State capitals (Figure 10.1). Here also was the head office so that management closely controlled processing and/or fabrication. Products for the particular State market were wholesaled direct from the factory. For inter-State orders, the four large organizations shipped to vertically integrated branches whereas the average small competitor used a mixture of his own depots and those of independent middlemen. But every wholesaler's function was similar—light assembly to save transport costs, collection of marketing information, advertising, and all the normal sales responsibilities. Finally, the ultimate intra-State retail distribution was performed by franchised dealers: the nineteen firms had no financial commitment in this arena and hence were not always able to intervene directly. Wholesaling thus occupied a central place in a simple, closely knit system. Owing to the extent of its vertical integration, the sector experienced spatial adjustments partly as a function of those in the production/administration sphere. These events must be therefore traced at the outset.

Changes in Production and Administration

A corporation's manufacturing and control is the heart of its operation and hence any locational change forced upon these activities represents a severe repercussion of prevailing economic conditions. Lloyd and Dicken (1972, pp. 146–8) have pinpointed the frequent reluctance of managers to effect geographic alteration anywhere in an organization, and nowhere would such reticence be more pronounced than in production and administration because of the appreciable risk involved. There was relatively little variation in the manufacturing operations of the four large undertakings. Only one took action by jettisoning a branch plant in Bendigo, a Victorian provincial centre, and some industrial land in the State capital, Melbourne. The small organizations, in contrast, exhibited greater locational instability; two ceased machinery manufacturing at branch factories and concentrated all operations at head-office sites, thus maintaining workloads but reducing financial exposure. More important were three withdrawals: two corporations sold off their equipment entirely, quit the industry and pursued their other interests; the other became insolvent and sold its assets to a small competitor. Together, these withdrawals caused the closure of two factories and the takeover of a third and their effects spilled over into the wholesale area where, as will be seen, they prompted further significant spatial change.

Spatial Change in Wholesaling

The machinery industry's wholesaling between 1967 and 1972 is of particular geographical interest because a confluence of both long- and short-term forces necessitated drastic revision of marketing patterns. The 1960s saw considerable advances in communications in Australia with the introduction of internal jet travel and subscriber trunk dialling—both innovations of critical importance to hard-pressed distribution executives attempting to overcome 'the tyranny of distance' in a vast continent. Moreover, as in the automobile industry (Stubbs, 1972, p. 28), models and options of equipment had been proliferating to the extent that it was becoming unfeasible to maintain assembly and inventory-holding in all States. These long-run influences dovetailed strongly with the effects of diminished demand to signal contraction of wholesale facilities as an appropriate *modus vivendi*. The greatest pressure was on firms purveying tractors or sophisticated machinery rather than simple products like tillage tooling, and on those with large numbers of corporately controlled branches since much less immediate financial risk was involved in maintaining non-aligned distributors who effectively carried their own overheads. Finally, contraction was a better proposition for the higher-volume operators who could fill in the gaps between States with good dealer networks, than for smaller concerns where a lack of representation might have signified no market presence at all.

Yet before the spatial impact of these considerations can be gauged, two further points must be made. First, a wholesaling environment differs from those of production and administration. Whereas the discussion so far has centred upon an easily manageable complement of 19 main and 7 branch factories, the 19 enterprises serviced the nation through no fewer than 101 wholesale establishments, some of which were corporately owned and others were non-aligned. Since the milieu is more complicated than that of manufacturing, wider generalizations must necessarily be applied. Second, an appropriate terminology for describing the various planned and unplanned spatial strategies effected in companies' sales organizations during the recession has not developed. Since there is a need for a taxonomy of changes in the networks of firms in circumstances both of retreat and of expansion, it has received surprisingly little attention in the geography of enterprise (cf. Steed, 1971b, p. 324). The terms suggested here—rationalization, stability, retraction (integrative and terminal), reorientation, and forward integration—represent no more than a first attempt to name the various situations which arose.

Thus *rationalization*, a partial, selective, and controlled contraction, became the key spatial tactic adopted by 3 of the 4 large organizations during the recession. All had corporate outlets in at least 5 of the 6 States (Table 10.3) but this overwhelming reliance on vertically integrated distribution proved to be a double-edged sword. In buoyant economic conditions, it might indeed signify comprehensive market control but during a downswing it could indicate over-exposure. A programme of rationalization was facilitated by an essential stability in the production sector and an ability (derived from relatively high sales levels and the fact of exclusive contracts) to apply a strong hand with franchisees. Initially, the strategy was possible only for the 3 Melbourne-based concerns which enjoyed high degrees of network authority from a centre offering superior accessibility. In fact, as shown in Figure 10.2, no other State capital afforded such concentrated rural demand within a relatively confined area well served by transport connections. When International Harvester and Ford completed a withdrawal from their Sydney and Adelaide branches by 1968 they were left on the Australian mainland with only a Perth–Melbourne–Brisbane network, thus clearly showing rationalization as a tactic for coping with the long-term forces of the 1960s. It was only in 1970–72 that Massey Ferguson made indentical cutbacks and adopted the same simple configuration. This lag is explicable because contraction for Massey Ferguson (the least aggregately diversified major corporation) meant the sale of premises rather than their use for other company purposes; moreover, since this firm was the industry's leading seller, it may have taken longer for turnover at the branches to drop below economic thresholds. Undoubtedly the processes of oligopolistic imitation mentioned by both Alchian (1950, pp. 217–9) and Hamilton (1974a, p. 26) had a hand in this sequence of events but, equally, the new pattern accommodated the potentials and limitations of the emergent market more adequately.

TABLE 10.3 Wholesale representation, large firms, agricultural machinery industry, Australia, 1967. [Source: fieldwork]

Class	Firm	Wholesale representation by State[a]						Total Australia
		N.S.W.	Vic.	Qld.	S.A.	W.A.	Tas.	
Full-line	International Harvester	B	F	B	B	B	I	6
	Massey Ferguson	B	F	B	B	B	B	6
Long-line	Chamberlain	B	B	B	B	F	—	5
	Ford	B	F	B	I	B	—	5

[a] B = corporate branch distribution; F = corporate factory distribution; I = independent distributor.

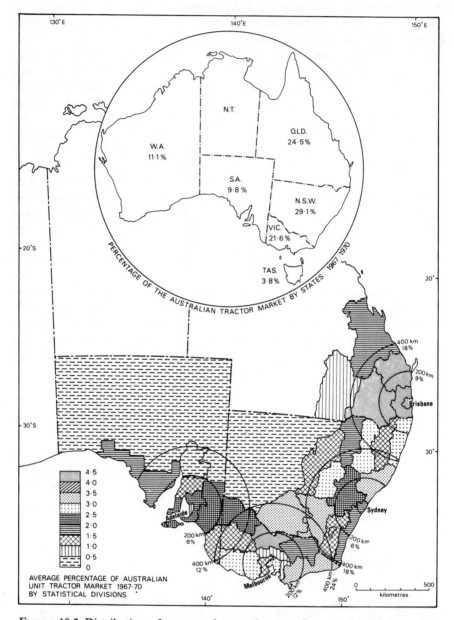

FIGURE 10.2 Distribution of tractor sales, southeastern States and total Australia: average for the period 1967 to 1970. [Source: Wadley, 1974, p. 128]

The fourth large producer, Chamberlain based in Perth, at first maintained *stability* and made no significant change during the recession but then in 1973 closed its Sydney branch. Reasons for hesitation included the firm's greater than usual need for control in eastern Australian markets (2000 km—1240 miles—away), its attempt to move strongly into industrial and construction equipment for which capital city display was essential, and the fact that its existing metropolitan branches (see Table 10.3) were all relatively new, well situated and amply suited for farm-machinery marketing. A final factor was Chamberlain's merger with an American competitor late in 1970 which necessitated the winding up of its partner's Australian network before rearranging its own. The case of this producer demonstrates the interdependence of non-spatial and spatial strategy in the corporate sphere.

Rationalization stands apart from other courses in its suggestion of management discretion and control. One could point beyond the delays in the implementation of the policy to the pricing, field representation, and sourcing strategies planned to ease in the new arrangements (Wadley, 1974, pp. 132–6). Indeed, many executives regarded the move as sanguine for it allowed better warehousing and handling techniques to be applied to a reduced amount of merchandise. All 3 Melbourne suppliers referred to the greater efficiency of the post-rationalization pattern on a cost–service basis (Figure 10.3) and, if a distinction can be drawn between network contraction and atrophy, it was not apparent among the 4 large enterprises.

The same cannot be said unequivocally for the wholesaling arrangements of the 15 small companies where the situation is clouded by the mix of corporate and independent outlets—numbering, respectively, 16 and 20 for the 7 small tractor concerns and 26 and 17 for the 8 implement companies (Table 10.4). This variation contributed to a great heterogeneity in action. Generally, the tractor organizations remained static or collapsed into forms of forward integration involving bulk or direct retail selling whereas in contrast, the implement enterprises, with their more extensive vertical commitment, displayed different reactions—rationalization and reorientation for sounder members, stability or retraction for the smaller or weaker ones. To tease out the trends, the two classes of firms can be considered separately.

While the overall dependence of tractor marketers on independent middlemen may have reduced financial exposure, it also restricted choices open to management. Thus *stability* was the course of a group of 3 corporations whose integration was limited (Table 10.5); this policy was assisted by weighty overseas backing and interests in machinery lines less affected by recession. Moreover one of these 3 firms was involved in centralizing its manufacturing and this, too, probably promoted quiescence. *Retraction* was experienced by the other 4 tractor enterprises which, despite sizeable corporate stature, were of limited importance in the machinery industry. Inflows of finance could certainly have alleviated their difficulties but, apart from a distinct lack of incentive, uncertainty about the

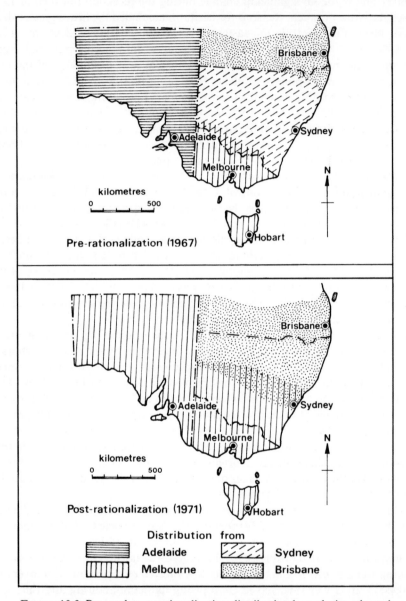

FIGURE 10.3 Pre- and post-rationalization distribution boundaries adopted by large Melbourne agricultural machinery firms in southeastern Australia during the period 1967 to 1972. [Source: Wadley, 1974, p. 134]

TABLE 10.4 Wholesale representation, small firms, agricultural machinery industry, Australia, 1967. [Source: fieldwork]

Class	Firm	Wholesale representation by State[a]						Total Australia
		N.S.W.	Vic.	Qld.	S.A.	W.A.	Tas.	
Small tractor	Allis Chalmers	F	—	—	—	I	—	2
	A.M.I.	I	F	I	I	I	I	6
	Case	F	B	B	B	I	I	6
	Fiat	F	B	I	I	I	I	6
	Howard	F	I	B	I	I	I	6
	Leyland	F	I	B	I	I	—	5
	Thiess	F	B	B	I	B	—	5
Small implement	Alfarm	F	—	—	B	—	—	2
	Connor Shea	B	F	I	I	I	I	6
	Horwood Bagshaw	B	B	B	F	I	B	6
	Ralph McKay	B	F	I	B	I	—	5
	Mobilco	B	F	I	I	I	B	6
	New Holland	B	F	B	B	B	I	6
	David Shearer	B	I	I	F	I	I	6
	John Shearer	B	B	B	F	I	I	6

[a] B = corporate branch distribution; F = corporate factory distribution; I = independent distributor.

profitability of parent companies led executives to cut costs, concentrate on other lines and curtail deficits. Integrative retraction—the approach of 2 firms (Australian Motor Industries and Leyland) operating within automobile enterprises—saw tractor distribution merged with that of vehicles. Terminal retraction was an even less palatable approach: Allis Chalmers and Thiess Equipment Distributors negotiated huge bulk sales to former dealers who afterwards assumed direct importation of the brands involved. As can be seen from Table 10.5, a number of wholesale facilities was lost in these moves. Clearly, the structural adjustments of terminal retraction required a fundamental change in wholesaling practice: the integrative version possibly did so too.

Whereas tractor firms had been selling in the Australian agricultural machinery market for an average of only 24 years, the 8 small-implement enterprises had been operating for 56 years which no doubt had assisted them to build greater vertical integration into their wholesaling. The majority ran depots in all 3 southeastern States and only one had not yet expanded nationwide (Table 10.4). These relatively high levels of exposure, combined with corporate functional specialization, stimulated a significant amount of adjustment in policies variously named rationalization, reorientation, stability, and forward integration (Table 10.6).

TABLE 10.5 Wholesale representation strategies, small tractor firms, agricultural machinery industry, Australia, 1967–72. [Source: fieldwork]

Wholesale strategy	Participants	Locational repercussions	Impact on total distribution network	Year
Stability	Case	Change of Hobart independent distributor	Minor	1968
		Replacement of Perth independent distributor with wholesale branch	Major	1971
Stability	Fiat	Intrametropolitan relocation of Sydney head office and wholesale branch	Minor	1968
Stability	Howard Rotovator	Establishment of Melbourne wholesale/retail store	Major	1968
		Closure of Melbourne wholesale/retail store	Major	1971
		Intrametropolitan relocation of Brisbane wholesale branch	Minor	1971
Retraction, integrative	Australian Motor Industries	Change of Brisbane independent distributor	Minor	1970
		Cancellation of Brisbane distributor	Major	1971
		Cancellation of Sydney distributor	Major	1971
Retraction, integrative	Leyland	Replacement of independent distributors with wholesale branches in:		
		Melbourne	Major	1971
		Perth	Major	1971
Retraction, terminal	Allis Chalmers	Closure of Newcastle (N.S.W.) warehouse	Major	1971
		Cancellation of Perth independent distributor	Major	1971
Retraction, terminal	Thiess Equipment Distributors	Closure of wholesale branches in:		
		Sydney	Major	1972
		Melbourne	Major	1972
		Brisbane	Major	1972
		Perth	Major	1972

From the outset, economic standing appeared a chief factor in prescribing choice of tactics. The *rationalization* of 3 of the small implement group was generally less thoroughgoing than that of the large concerns but occurred in similar circumstances. The trio—of which 2 were Melbourne based—were fairly robust marketers with machinery volumes significantly above the small-firm average. Closure of inter-State office reduced costs but did not require any fundamental adjustments of their wholesaling arrangements. A rather indistinct course, best termed *reorientation*, was undertaken by 2 South Australian organizations which balanced the downgrading of representation in Victoria by expansion in Western Australia (Table 10.6). This sortie into Perth, representing an unusual instance of wholesale investment during the recession, was entertained only because suitable replacement agencies were unavailable when an existing wholesaler withdrew. Such a strategy might almost be seen as a variant of stability since its chief effect was a relative shift in spatial emphasis (or asset distribution).

Stability, the approach of 2 fairly minor firms, was founded on the restricted use of corporate branches and a greater dependence on non-aligned distributors. Compared to the reorientating firms, both these suppliers were fortunate that no upheavals occurred among their independent middlemen—a risk always inherent in this method of wholesaling. Finally, the smallest implement firm was forced into *forward integration*—an action differentiated from the terminal retraction of the tractor companies only in that it did not run to excessive bulk selling or failure. Because of inadequate sales and the unwillingness of either wholesalers or dealers to accept costly harvesting lines, the firm employed its own staff in a combined wholesale/retail capacity to assist remaining franchisees and to canvass field orders like the nineteenth-century North American entrepreneurs. In the process, the Adelaide branch was lost and the predictability of pre-recession wholesaling arrangements went overboard.

This, then, was the diversity of experience at the wholesale level in the machinery industry during the rural setback. All large sellers and the biggest implement ones rationalized in response to either a long- or short-term economic stimulus; the more viable tractor competitors and the average-sized implement organizations opted for stability; and, finally, the smaller companies were forced into making structural alterations in retraction or forward integration which changed the whole nature of product distribution. It is now appropriate to probe deeper into factors associated with these various policies.

SOME DETERMINANTS OF CORPORATE SPATIAL POLICY

The downswing in farm activity did not cause cataclysmic change in either wholesaling practice or patterns in the Australian agricultural machinery industry: in fact most companies retained their existing arrangements and simply adjusted the extent of their representation. Yet the theme of contraction

TABLE 10.6   Wholesale representation strategies, small implement firms, agricultural machinery industry, Australia, 1967–72. [Source: fieldwork]

Wholesale strategy	Participants	Locational repercussions	Impact on total distribution network	Year
Rationalization	Horwood Bagshaw	Closure of Melbourne wholesale branch	Major	1971
		Intrametropolitan relocation of Sydney wholesale branch	Minor	1972
Rationalization	Ralph McKay	Closure of Melbourne wholesaling subsidiary	Major	1970
		Change in Toowoomba (Qld.) independent distributor	Minor	1970
Rationalization	New Holland	Closure of wholesale branches in:		
		Sydney	Major	1970
		Adelaide	Major	1970
Reorientation	David Shearer	Replacement of Melbourne independent distributor with wholesale branch	Major	1969
		Closure of Melbourne wholesale branch	Major	1970
		Closure of Adelaide parts depot	Minor	1970
		Change in Perth independent distributor	Minor	1971
		Replacement of Perth independent distributor with wholesale branch	Major	1972
Reorientation	John Shearer	Intrametropolitan relocation of wholesale branches in:		
		Melbourne	Minor	1970
		Sydney	Minor	1972
		Replacement of Perth independent distributor with wholesale branch	Major	1972
Stability	Connor Shea			
Stability	Mobilco	Replacement of Sydney wholesale branch with wholesale/retail store	Major	1970
		Change in Brisbane independent distributor	Minor	1971
Forward integration	Alfarm Distributors	Closure of Hobart wholesale branch	Major	1971
		Closure of Adelaide wholesale branch	Major	1967
		Establishment of wholesale/retail store in Toowoomba (Qld.)	Major	1970

was pervasive and was expressed in subtly different ways. Effects among the small companies were also highly significant: the volumes necessary to support the more formal wholesaling methods disappeared and the networks atrophied. An explanation lies in the pre-conditions and correlates of individual strategies.

Pre-conditions to Wholesale Action

A corporation's choice among five main geographical manoeuvres— rationalization, stability, reorientation, retraction, and forward integration—which characterized Australian farm-equipment wholesaling between 1967 and 1972 can be related in part to its overall financial conditions before and towards the end of the recession. While direct cause–effect relationships should not be posited between *aggregate* accounting data and policy in what might be only *one* of a large enterprise's fields, the trend of this enquiry is productive. Rationalization, the distinctive option which offered prospects of reducing costs without necessarily sacrificing market control, was entertained exclusively by businesses in a sounder position during the downswing. Proof is available in financial ratios relating to liquidity and income (Table 10.7). Liquidity, the degree to which assets represent or can be converted to ready money without appreciable loss of value, denotes the extent of producers' short-term solvency throughout the crisis. As a gross indicator, the current ratio (current assets/current liabilities) shows ability to meet immediate commitments. A proportion of 2:1 has been classically regarded as 'safe' but a healthier position is widely favoured (Graham *et al.*, 1962, p. 218). In any event rationalizing enterprises, unlike their competitors, did not breach this limit.

The current ratio has recently drawn criticism for its failure to acknowledge the relative convertability of holdings. A finer tool, the 'quick' ratio (current

TABLE 10.7 Relative corporate economic condition, selected firms by wholesale strategy, agricultural machinery industry, Australia, 1967–71. [Source: fieldwork]

Wholesale strategy	Financial condition				Trading condition	
	current ratio		quick ratio		net return on sales	
	average 1967–68	average 1969–71	average 1967–68	average 1969–71	average 1967–68	average 1969–71
Rationalization	2.38	2.11	0.85	0.64	0.05	0.00
Reorientation	2.33	1.83	0.81	0.60	0.05	− 0.15
Stability	1.90	1.99	0.57	0.53	0.04	− 0.01
Retraction	1.96	1.52	0.54	0.50	0.02	− 0.03
Forward integration	1.07	1.03	0.48	0.45	[a]	[a]

[a] Withheld for confidentiality.

assets less stock/current liabilities), compares direct monetary equivalents against existing obligations (Graham *et al.*, 1962, p. 219). Ordinarily, a firm's current assets less inventory should equal its imminent debts, but in the agricultural machinery trade, with its rather slow-moving products, ratios of less than unity are not uncommon. Here again, however, the rationalizing corporations exhibited the more favourable condition both before and near the end of the depression. Further examination of Table 10.7 reveals only too clearly the financial problems promoting courses of retraction and forward integration.

The same picture is apparent using an income ratio—net return on consolidated net sales—which relates directly to trading activities and is applicable to analyses over short periods (Sheridan, 1974, p. 83). While on average none of the 19 corporations performed well in the years 1967–71, the rationalizing ones remained among the strongest. Income ratios decrease between the stabilizing and retracting firms as might now be expected though the very poor result of the reorientating group reflects the onset of failure in one of its members. Thus from the above analysis, choice of wholesale action can be identified from both balance sheet and profit and loss accounts, and the investigation can be amplified by considering other correlates of the various spatial tactics, such as a corporation's sales volume, objectives, financial exposure, longevity, and head-office location.

Correlates of Spatial Action

Rationalizing organizations exhibited the more satisfactory corporate finances throughout the downturn and, as suggested, they enjoyed the largest volumes of farm-machinery *sales*. Table 10.8 indicates that a turnover gradient differentiated groups of enterprises. Stability and reorientation were the

TABLE 10.8   Wholesale representation strategy by equipment sales size, selected firms, agricultural machinery industry, Australia, 1967–71 ($A million). [Source: fieldwork]

Wholesale strategy	Equipment sales of participant firms	
	five-year average	approximate range[a]
Rationalization	15.71	5.00–35.00
Stability	5.79	2.00–12.00
Reorientation	3.76	2.00– 5.00
Retraction and forward integration[b]	0.96	0.50– 2.00

[a] Generalized for confidentiality.
[b] For reasons of confidentiality, results from polices of retraction and forward integration have been combined.

approaches of moderately sized companies, whereas retraction and forward integration characterized the smallest contestants—the very ones which, from a distribution viewpoint, could least afford such action.

Here can be added to the emerging relationship of financial standing and wholesale strategy the element of *corporate goals*, following McNee (1972, p. 203). Because, as suggested in Massey Ferguson's 1969 annual report, 'it was not possible to predict the extent and dramatic suddenness of the market contraction', a producer's initial economic status was an important influence on its ambitions and capacities over the next 6 years. Interviews among the economically advantaged large merchants revealed that apparently they recognized from the start their ability to weather a crisis. Shielded by size and prosperity, their problem was to anticipate its severity and act accordingly. Concern developed upon the question of penetration in the realization that market share could fall almost overnight and that the road to recovery would be long and arduous as lost sales of machinery exacted retribution in future spare parts and service markets. Spatial policy was therefore predicated on the criterion that if the major supplier's representation was to be restricted for economic reasons it should not jeopardize its share of total industry sales. Thus rather than changing wholesaling mode or practice, the number of corporate outlets was reduced. The outlook in 1967 for smaller firms was less provident with a significant percentage entering the recession in a stressed condition. As circumstances worsened in 1969–70, initial disadvantage and lack of resources forced minor competitors to preserve liquidity by all available means, as is testified by withdrawals and failures. Often, then, tactics were selected from few alternatives: it is scarcely conceivable that any supplier would have willingly chosen the rigours of retraction or forward integration.

In the shrunken markets, the larger concerns found themselves *over-extended*. The data in Table 10.9 indicate that while rationalization issued from high levels of integration, its effect was not necessarily to reduce the corporate component of the network but rather to whittle down the absolute numbers of outlets on which

TABLE 10.9 Wholesale representation strategy by extent of corporate distribution, selected firms, agricultural machinery industry, Australia, 1967–72. [Source: derived from data in Tables 10.3 and 10.4]

Wholesale strategy	Number of outlets in 1967		'Corporate' as a percentage of total outlets
	corporate	independent	
Rationalization	28	6	82
Reorientation	7	5	58
Stability	18	17	51
Retraction	8	10	44
Forward integration	2	0	100

it was based. There seems little difference in the extent of exposure associated with reorientation or stability, again hinting that these two tactics were of the same genre. In the cases of retraction or forward integration, either or both the relative and absolute extent of corporate distribution was often low and this factor probably augured poorly for the maintenance of wholesale patterns. In sum, exposure did bear on the choice of spatial policy and it would be interesting to determine what might have constituted an 'ideal' level in relation to sales given that a certain spatial tactic was deemed desirable.

Complementing this parameter in affecting an organization's locational initiatives was its *age in the market* for agricultural equipment. Table 10.10 demonstrates that rationalization and reorientation, more than any other courses, were associated with significantly older companies, thus reinforcing the view that over the years representation had become more than adequate. The organizations whose tactics led to the structural and spatial dissolution of wholesaling were the youngest in the sample: seemingly they had failed to clear specific barriers to entry in the industry during their limited lifespans. Lastly, aside from noting that a Melbourne base seemed favourable to rationalization, little is gained from relating *head-office location* to choice of strategy (Table 10.10).

Thus two syndromes, largely economic in nature, explain spatial behaviour in wholesaling. In the depressed conditions expansion of facilities was negligible. On the one hand, for older organizations, with initial advantage, relatively large sales and high-level exposure, contraction required a shift to a new, trimmed equilibrium even though practices and, wherever possible, quality of service to retailers, were maintained. On the other, for newer concerns with low sales volumes and proportionately less vertical integration, stability was the best hope

TABLE 10.10 Wholesale representation strategy by longevity and head-office location, selected firms, agricultural machinery industry, Australia, 1967–72. [Source: fieldwork]

Wholesale strategy	Average (1967) age of participant firms (years)	Head-office location					Total
		Sydney	Melbourne	Adelaide	Perth	other	
Reorientation	90			1		1	2
Rationalization	65		5	1			6
Stability	27	3	2		1		6
Forward integration	12					1	1
Retraction	10	3	1				4
Average (or total)	41	6	8	2	1	2	19

since contraction in this situation held substantial risks—in some cases, the demise of wholesaling practice as it had existed prior to the setback.

ENTERPRISES IN TROUBLE: SOME CONCLUSIONS

It now remains to establish the relevance of the findings to ongoing work in the geography of corporations. Notwithstanding the initiatives of Steed (1968, 1971a, 1974), Krumme (1970), and Chapman (1974), this present study belongs among the more specific accounts of the spatial behaviour of enterprises. It has concentrated on the adjustment of a particular function in a lesser-known industry to extraordinary circumstances. This conclusion has two purposes: to interpret the results and to speculate on their capacity for generalization.

Interpretation of Results

In view of the current situation in several advanced economies, it is remarkable that more attention has not been directed to the geography of recession. Themes abound—the effects of oil prices on regions or nations, impacts on the more susceptible industries, spatial repercussions of planning and political measures (e.g. reconstruction schemes, regional development), the distribution of unemployment, and so forth. This enquiry shows that the operations of even global corporations are by no means immune from downswings particularly when, as in the case cited, they have more than just local or short-term components. But despite evidence of fairly terse correspondence between directorships, it is unlikely that the boards of giant overseas conglomerates would long recollect the Australian machinery debacle of 1967–72, whereas the ramifications on the employees of their subsidiary firms, the domestic industry, and the host nation were far more memorable.

There can be little doubt that when difficulties emerge, larger enterprises are better insulated—at least for the timespan with which this project was concerned. The first gain ensues from diversification since assets and personnel can be transferred in ways suggested by Steed (1971c, pp. 91–4) to other divisions which are operating satisfactorily. Second, benefits apply in terms of participation in the affected market. It is reasonable to accept from the theoretical underpinnings of urban geography that there must exist some threshold of operation for any corporate function to be conducted in a given way. In this instance of wholesaling action, these levels—the influence of which became apparent throughout this study—could be presumably measured in annual dollar turnover. Below about $A8–10 million sales throughput per annum, distribution on a predominantly corporate basis disappeared; below $A3 million, the upkeep of functionally specialized practices was impossible. Such economic determinants clearly exact spatial repercussions. More generally, it is not too simplistic to remark from this threshold notion that, while the larger corporation has indeed more to lose, if it sheds its facilities individually and does not collapse outright, it must stand to survive longer. This advantage (portrayed in the size/longevity relationships) promotes a living geography rather than a spatial legacy.

As indicated early in this chapter, the effects of business cycles upon enterprise behaviour must be questioned (cf. Sant, 1973). From the amount of adjustment observed here, economic conditions seem to have at least a localized effect on their activities. However, whether the results could be extrapolated to correspond with the chronology of corporate growth proposed by Chandler (1962, pp. 383–96) and later taken up by Steed (1971d, p. 55) is debatable. These authors agree that large undertakings characteristically exhibit four main stages of development: initial accumulation of resources, subsequent rationalization of their use, continued growth and, lastly, reconstruction to allow rapid mobilization of assets to meet changing situations. But this paradigm is based on over 150 years of American experience and, considering that in 1967 the oldest national and international companies had been in the Australian farm-equipment market for 130 and 82 years respectively, it is dubious whether the majority would have proceeded much beyond Chandler's second phase. Intangibles in the comparison of relative timescales in manufacturing development between different countries and the bearing of firms' participation in linked industries must leave the issue open but later examination could show that the 1960s and early 1970s represented a phase of rationalization—if only for the older firms. More historical investigation of the Australian equipment trade is required to settle the matter since available sources are scarce (cf. Homs, 1918; McLean, 1973a, b).

Generalizing the Findings

The experiences in wholesaling of agricultural machinery suppliers cannot be widened without some caution since there are divergences between the settings of a continental, long-distance economy and the marketing environment of a smaller, more pluralistic region. Due recognition must be accorded the context of high-level commercial development: the same patterns might not have applied in a less advanced country. Moreover, the enquiry concerned a producer-durables industry in what is essentially a consumer marketing milieu. Unlike other depressions the economic setback was short-lived, sectorally localized, and induced basically by factors within the demand function (rather than supply shortages). Perhaps the closest replication would occur in the motor vehicle, truck, and construction-equipment trades and, strictly, extension of the findings should be limited to these areas. Movement beyond the contingencies arrayed here should centre initially on the type of marketing environment and duration of the recession since attendant reactions of firms to differences in these parameters would probably vary little from that observed in farm equipment distribution. In fact, a longer, wider or more severe upset would probably only emphasize the advantages of the bigger concern. Thus similar corporate behaviour could be expected in such arenas as oil, automobiles, and specialized household appliances in a major business downturn—whether the depression of 1929, the Australian 'credit squeeze' of 1961, or the current malaise of 1974–77. The field is open and further contributions will advance not only industrial location analysis but also its neglected offspring, marketing geography.

Chapter 11

Market-Area Analysis and Product Differentiation: A Case Study of the West German Truck Industry

Neil M. M. Dorward

INTRODUCTION

Market-area theory is very much a theory of spatial oligopoly. Neo-classical analysis explains the firm's sales potential by its location in the conditions of a geographically dispersed body of consumers, an f.o.b. system of pricing, and homogeneous products. Insofar as a seller is not closely surrounded by competitors, he will have a delivered-price advantage in his local area. The greater the degree of locational dispersion, the greater will be the size of this monopolized local market area. Development of this theory has been attributed to economists such as Fetter (1924), Hotelling (1929), Lerner and Singer (1937), Smithies (1941), Lewis (1945), Chamberlin (1946), and Lösch (1954). In recent years some attempts have been made to incorporate product differentiation and uncertainty into the analysis. Both cause the sales territories of suppliers to overlap, leaving each supplier to struggle for a share of the overall market, not for a total dominance of an area within the market. Beckmann (1971), Lovell (1970), and Gannon (1973) have attempted to extend market-area theory to cover the special case of product differentiation—the practice whereby each firm sells a distinctly different variant of the generic product. Unfortunately, these extensions have left the theory relatively underdeveloped as their detailed analyses either constrain the differentiation parameter to zero, except where it contains a distance element (Beckmann and Lovell), or give it fixed value (Gannon). Some economists (especially Devletoglou, 1965; Greenhut, 1970; Webber, 1972) have tried to extend the theory of spatial oligopoly to incorporate uncertainty. Apart from that of Devletoglou, this work has had little impact on market-area theory. Yet even Devletoglou's model offers a rather limited treatment of uncertainty in that it dervies only from the indifference of buyers between small delivered-price variations.

This chapter seeks to question three of the implicit assumptions which appear to underlie recent investigations of the effect of product differentiation on the nature and intensity of spatial competition. First, while the usual approach to product differentiation acknowledges that buyers have different demand

213

schedules, it still assumes that these schedules are scattered in a random manner over the market plane. This precludes any spatial grouping of individuals with similar brand preferences. In addition, it depends upon the spatial homogeneity of the decision variables. However, different product requirements between buyers must directly result from their facing different environments, one of which is spatial. Consequently, it is preferable to assume that those buyers with similar product preferences and demand schedules are likely to be concentrated in those parts of the market where the environmental opportunities and constraints are similar. Second, the implicit assumption of a lack of association between product differentiation and local contact advantages between buyers and seller suggests a failure to understand the formulation of a product policy. In practice, a firm is more likely to specialize in that product variant which is closest to the consensus requirement of local buyers. Given the frequently observed distance decay in information, the local firm has the best chance of knowing local requirements (Goddard, 1971). The third assumption in need of revision is that which excludes local behavioural contagion between buyers, so denying generally perceived purchasing behaviour (Marris, 1964).

Such reconsideration of the place of product differentiation in market-area theory is prompted by frequent observations of large inter-area differences in market shares and the sales rankings of suppliers, and by the dispersed pattern of their plant locations in product-differentiated markets. Consequently, the primary aim is to investigate the possibility of subdividing the overlapping sales territories of such markets into market areas using criteria relating to the variable pattern and intensity of competition between suppliers. Thus a market area is being defined as an areally bounded competitive process which embodies a distinct set of behavioural relations governing the interaction between buyers, between sellers, and between buyers and sellers. In treating market areas as competitive processes, the analysis concentrates on the fundamental dynamics of competition in space. This includes the effects of product differentiation on the brand preferences of buyers and the same brand-preference effects on the future market structure, the expectation being that both effects will vary over the market plane. Therefore, when all sellers offer their product variants over the whole market, the market areas will represent the spatial environmental adaptations (or subsystems) of the overall competitive system.

The chapter develops the conceptual framework underlying the analysis and then presents the basic forces of competition operating to create market areas in the 8–16 tonne gross vehicle weight (g.v.w.) segment of the West German domestic truck market. Firm-orientated and market-structure approaches are both employed and their limitations are outlined. Finally a novel analytical approach, employing a Markov chain model of brand-switching behaviour, is explored which attempts to estimate and to classify the competitive processes into market areas.

PRODUCT DIFFERENTIATION AND MARKET-AREA
ANALYSIS IN THEORY

Product Differentiation and the Concept of Product

A product is a set of characteristics (Telser, 1964; Jenner, 1966; Lancaster, 1966) which in combination fulfil a function, or several functions in the case of complex products. Differentiation of a product results from manufacturers engaging in competition by varying both the number of characteristics and the emphasis given to each of those selected, subject to the criterion that the competing products fulfil the same basic need. In the long run, the existence of a number of differentiated products depends on the heterogeneity of buyer requirements in product characteristics, otherwise there would be a convergence of one optimum product (Jenner, 1966).

In formulating a product policy, the manufacturer selects that combination of characteristics by which he expects to attract a positive preference by a large enough body of customers to ensure the product's viability. This is essentially a procedure of product definition which, under product differentiation, means that several definitions are possible at any one time. Given a changing market environment, the products offered have to be periodically redefined and updated. The faster the rate of environmental change the greater is the tendency for products to reflect only partially the actual buyer requirements, so enlarging the opportunity for product differentiation. New characteristics have to be added and old ones dropped. Firms compete by looking for newly emerged market niches. Thus a product policy becomes a dynamic process of differentiation by which firms periodically (or, in extreme cases, continually) probe out the changing buyer requirements.

Product Differentiation and Overlapping Market Areas

With product differentiation, the price elasticity of demand is lower at any given price than with homogeneous products. Each firm is more of a monopolist, having a greater discretion over the price charged (Chamberlin, 1946). The inclusion of freight costs progressively raises the delivered price that buyers have to pay with increasing distance from the factory. This is equivalent to moving up the demand curve when price equals delivered price. For the linear demand curve, demand will be more elastic for the more distant buyer. Therefore, product differentiation by making the demand curve less elastic at any price will also reduce demand elasticity at any distant point. All buyers with a preference for a given brand of product, wherever they are located, may now be prepared to pay a slightly higher delivered price for that brand. Some potential buyers who were formerly so distant that the delivered price exceeded their notion of value under product homogeneity, may now consider the value sufficiently increased by product differentiation that they will enter the market as purchasers. The resultant extension of the sales territories will lead to the overlapping of the market areas of the individual firms.

The distance transcendence of product differentiation results in changes to the spatial structure of purchase probabilities. The substantial reduction in buyers' indifference between brands brings about an increase in buyers' spatial indifference towards their preferred brands. As a result, the general lowering of purchasing probabilities with increasing distance is likely to be lessened, or even reversed in certain cases. The spatial variation in the probabilities of purchasing from any one manufacturer depends upon the geographic distribution of the reference group, or market segment, of that manufacturer. The reference group consists of all those buyers and potential buyers who have very similar requirements from the product in question, as a result of similar socio-economic status or location (Marris, 1964). The spatial effect is more easily understood if it is assumed that the reference group served by each manufacturer is situated within his own locality, so recognizing the importance of spatial proximity in social and business contact. The seller experiences an increase in the local probabilities of purchasing his product as he continues to exploit his product's orientation towards the specific needs of that local market, an advantage reinforced by savings in distance cost. Outside this area buyers remain largely indifferent to his product, making any purchases on a random basis.

In the local areas of other manufacturers who likewise tailor their products to the specific needs of similarly concentrated local buyer populations, outside suppliers experience very low purchasing probabilities (Figure 11.1a). Product differentiation in this special case has considerably strengthened the quasi-monopoly positions of A and B. Their market areas remain in three parts, with a different level of spatial purchasing probability in each part. The zone of maximum advantage in the duopoly case would have $p_A > 0.5$, the transition zone $p_A \approx 0.5$, and the competitive fringe $p_A < 0.5$. Note that the $p_{A,B}$ are most unlikely to reach 1.0 or fall to 0. Even if none of B's or any other manufacturer's reference group are located within A's area of advantage, it is most unlikely that product differentiation can overcome all the competitive uncertainty and so $0 < p_{A,B} < 1.0$. (Each buyer within his reference group has his own unique set of specifications so that some buyers are always less satisfied than others with any product aimed at the whole group and as such tend to experiment by buying the products of more distant manufacturers.)

A more typical spatial structure is shown in Figure 11.1b. The reference group of buyers served by A is assumed to be scattered irregularly over the whole market with concentrations in certain regions and local pockets. A's sales territory now divides into two parts: a quasi-monopolistic local area and the remainder. The local area of advantage remains intact, buttressed by the joint supports of short distance and close contact. However, the majority of A's sales territory becomes one of considerable spatial variation in the p_A. The uneven

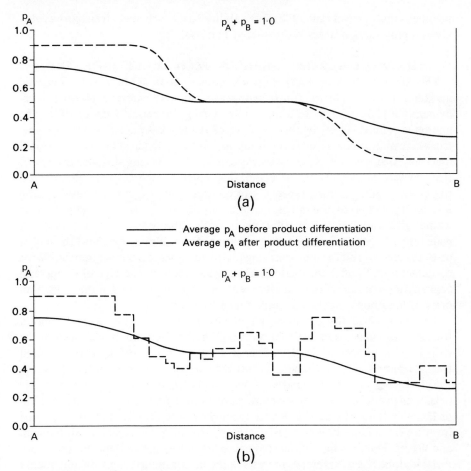

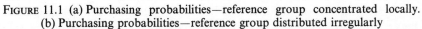

FIGURE 11.1 (a) Purchasing probabilities—reference group concentrated locally. (b) Purchasing probabilities—reference group distributed irregularly

distribution of the different buyer reference groups over the total market combined with products orientated to their respective requirements has considerably reduced the effect of distance as seen in the cross-section of Figure 11.1b. In markets with proportionately heavy distance costs, the irregular spatial pattern of purchasing probabilities would remain, though as distance from the plant increased, the peaks and the troughs of p^A would progressively fall in value at a rate directly proportional to the ratio of transport costs to factory-gate price. A dispersal of reference groups on scales greater than purely local concentrations makes the concept of a local plant monopoly quite unrealistic for the single-product firm. Local, regional, national, and even world markets tend to be shared, subject to the constraints imposed by transport costs and disposable incomes (the determinant of buyers' ability to absorb high transport costs). Overlapping market areas mean shared markets.

THE WEST GERMAN MEDIUM-SIZED TRUCK INDUSTRY

The sector of the West German truck industry analysed here is the domestic market for rigid vehicles (those with cab and load-carrying platform permanently attached) of 8–16 tonne g.v.w. during the period 1958 to 1971. The market is defined largely by the use to which the truck is put: 8–16 tonne g.v.w. trucks are mainly employed in distributing 4–9 tonne loads in local and regional markets. Although 12–16 tonne trucks can be used for long-distance transport, they operate mainly within a region. The chief purchasers of medium-sized trucks are manufacturers, especially of consumer goods, and wholesalers; the former delivering to the other manufacturers, their own local depots, and wholesalers, and the latter distributing to retailers. Since such trucks carry a very wide range of goods, each purchaser has specific requirements about the make-up of the chassis and the load-carrying platform. Since it is almost impossible for manufacturers to offer the medium-sized truck operator the type of design and engineering standardization that is acceptable at the lighter end of the short-haul market, final body-building is undertaken by specialists.

The market is almost totally dominated by the domestic producers. Imported trucks have made very little impression on the German buyer despite the reduction in import duties levied since 1958 on other E.E.C.-manufactured trucks. Imports of 8–16 tonne g.v.w. trucks fell from 3 per cent of the market in 1958 to 1.8 per cent in 1971 (*Verband Der Automobilindustrie*). The market shares of leading producers in the truck market are given in Figure 11.2. The production of Daimler-Benz, the market leader throughout the decade studied, has come from several plants in southwest Germany, including Gaggenau, Mannheim, and Worth. Daimler-Benz differs from its competitors in two important respects. First, it alone has widespread interests in the motor industry, producing quality cars, light commercials, medium- and heavy-goods vehicles, special-purpose vehicles, and diesel engines. Second, it is primarily a motor-industry specialist whereas its main competitors are subsidiaries or divisions of major industrial conglomerates closely involved also in heavy engineering and steel. MAN became the second largest competitor in 1960 with 16.6 per cent of the market when it edged ahead of K.H.D. Controlled by Gütehoffnungshütte, a coal and steel producer with interests in shipbuilding, its production was formerly concentrated at Nürnberg but in 1957 it moved to a new plant at Munich which allowed a substantial increase in output. Klockner Humboldt Deutz (K.H.D.) located at Ulm in southern Germany, was a wholly owned subsidiary of a large engineering group of the same name until Fiat acquired an 80 per cent holding in 1974. Apart from the two fringe firms, Faun and Kaeble, which specialize in heavy trucks, no other West German firms survived the period as independent producers. Henschel, which produces medium and heavy trucks at Kassel in

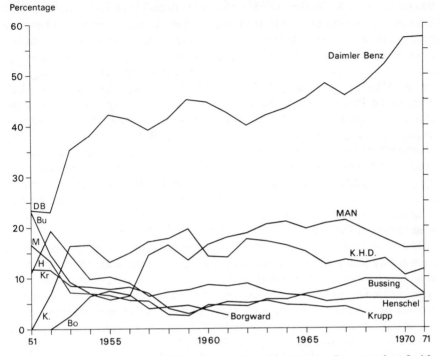

Percentage

FIGURE 11.2 Market shares of West German brands of truck of greater than 8–16 tonne g.v.w.—new registrations

central Germany, was acquired in 1965 by the Rheinstahl group. By the end of 1968 Daimler-Benz had gained a 51 per cent holding in Rheinstahl and this was increased to 100 per cent in 1970. Until 1966, Bussing's production came largely from Braunschweig. In the early 1960s, it came under the control of Salzgitter, the state-owned steel and general-engineering group and moved its operations to a new plant at nearby Salzgitter-Watenstedt. MAN acquired 50 per cent of the firm in 1968, which became total control in 1971, in part to prevent Daimler-Benz's further consolidation of the truck market.

All the remaining firms failed either to establish their trucks successfully in the market, notably Ford and International Harvester, or to sustain a long-term position (Borgward and Krupp). Of these, only Borgward was not financially backed by a major transnational corporation.

PRODUCT DIFFERENTIATION AND COMPETITION IN TRUCKS

Product Differentiation

Truck-manufacturers' product differentiation strategies are of three kinds. The first embraces those elements contributing to pulling performance: engines, transmissions, axles, power/weight ratios, and brakes. At one stage all main West German manufacturers made their own range of diesel engines and offered buyers a distinctive power-unit (K.H.D. remains the only European manufacturer of trucks with air-cooled engines). However, rising research and development costs during the 1970s have led manufacturers to co-operate, as instanced by the Daimler-Benz and MAN joint engine development and production programme. Pulling performance can be improved by redesigning gearboxes and rear axles: manufacturers compete, for example, by offering different systems of increasing the number of speeds in the gearing. But not all innovations are acceptable to buyers: the market-entry failure of International Harvester in 1965–66 can largely be explained by the fact that purchasers were not impressed by some aspects of its engineering, particularly that associated with its transmission system. Market-share success appears to require that the product be in line with current technological convention: any excessive variation from the mainstream of the market can harm commercial viability.

The second category of differentiation comprises the range of options varying from highly technical items (alternators, automatic lubrication, and turbochargers, which will either lower maintenance costs or increase performance) to the type of cab, size of fuel tank, route recorder, and axle position. These options provide manufacturers with a wide range of competitive opportunities.

The third strategy concerns price and cost. Price is not regarded as a key selling feature for trucks over 6 tonne g.v.w. The *autobahn* network, which places high stress on the power unit and the load-bearing mechanics, encourages buyers to put a premium on quality and reliability. Given that lower operating costs may compensate for a higher initial price, manufacturers largely compete on the strength of technical features while attempting to achieve cost controls sufficient to keep prices broadly in line with those of opposing firms. However, there is some competition in the provision of discounts, which are likely to be larger for big purchasers, for loyal customers, and for new buyers at times when salesmen for other brands are particularly keen to increase sales penetration in a given region. Delivery charges appear to be levied in full, presumably to compensate for the large discounts given on the published selling price, but these are small since they are for delivery from regionally located manufacturer-owned branches.

Spatial Differentiation

Spatial differentiation emerges primarily through variations in the quantity and quality of the sales and maintenance services supplied by both the manufacturer's own factory branches and the franchised dealers. The factory branches of 6 of the leading firms are located in Figure 11.3. In general, brands with larger market shares (shown in Figure 11.3a) have a better representation strategically concentrated along autobahns and at their major junctions.

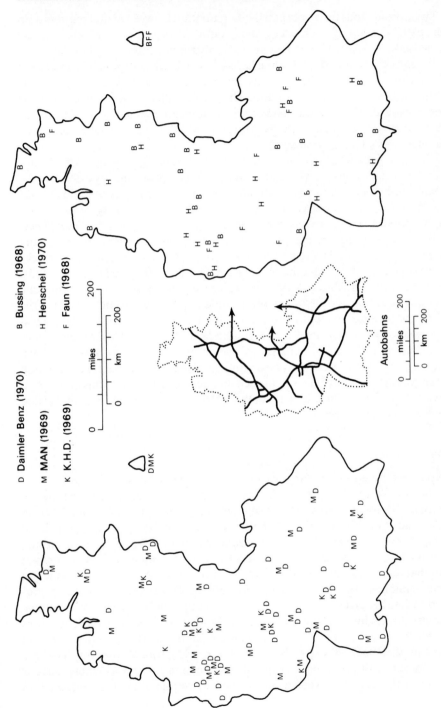

FIGURE 11.3 Location of truck-manufacturers' factory branches and autobahns. [Source: manufacturers' sales and service brochures]

The most obvious forms of spatial differentiation between manufacturers lie in the spatial density of their sales outlets and their degree of local and regional specialization. While Daimler-Benz has a distribution that largely follows the main centres of population, Bussing has 8 of its 16 branches providing a full sales and repair service not far from its factory at Salzgitter-Watenstedt in the northeast (also serving West Berlin). The spatial differentiation by dispersal is most remarkable outside the main centres of population and results in medium-sized or smaller towns, such as Münster or Oldenburg, having only one manufacturer's factory branch.

All truck producers sell all or most of their vehicles in their own factory branches, which combine wholesaling and retailing operations. By extending the organization forward to the retail stage the manufacturer is able directly to control prices, sales pressure, and discounts and, by maintaining contacts with buyers, should be able to assess changing requirements, operating experience, and attitudes to competing products. However, involvement in the selling operation varies: the Henschel network of only 10 branches sells all its trucks whereas Daimler-Benz, despite owning a network of 59 branches in 46 towns, allows separate franchised dealers to handle well over a quarter of its domestic sales. In addition, the branches service and repair trucks and supervise the franchised dealers, enabling producers to monitor product reliability and performance and to ensure a very high standard of service. This is crucial since many buyers in the 8–16 tonne g.v.w. market are too small to have their own servicing facilities. Indeed, one reason for Daimler-Benz's successful domination of this market is its large factory branch and dealer network: it aims at having a service depot every 30 kilometres (19 miles) to offer operators a quick and efficient breakdown service.

Factory Locations

Spatial differentiation can be observed in the dispersed location of the production plants (Figure 11.4). The industry has been largely centred in southern Germany, within Baden-Württemberg, Bavaria and, from 1966, in Rheinland-Pfalz (86 per cent of the trucks, and road tractors for articulated units, of over 6 tonnes g.v.w. being produced here in 1971). Except for Krupp, there is a notable absence of the industry from Nordrhein-Westfälen, in contrast with that region's second largest share of motor-vehicle components production (The Economist Intelligence Unit Ltd., 1965). Truck and road-tractor production data are given in Table 11.1. There have been only three major locational changes, MAN in 1957 and Bussing and Daimler-Benz both in 1966. All three moved into new and enlarged production plants nearby which resulted in boosting their market shares for several years. Locational dispersal has been encouraged by the need for large quantities of labour in truck assembly, but has restricted the degree of vertical integration at certain sites. It is notable that

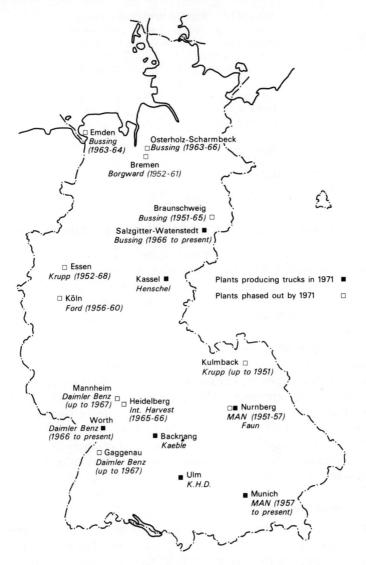

FIGURE 11.4 Location of plants producing trucks of 8–16 tonnes g.v.w.: 1951–71. [Source: Verband Der Automobilindustries, Standorte Der Automobilfabricken Im Bundesgebiet publications 1951–71]

Daimler-Benz selected Worth for its new large integrated plant in the early 1960s as that part of Germany was agriculturally depressed and offered a plentiful supply of labour.

TABLE 11.1   West German production of medium and heavy trucks and road tractors (over 6 tonnes g.v.w.) in 1971. [Source: *Verband Der Automobilindustrie*, Tatsachen und Zahlen, Table 3, 1972]

Bussing	3064
Daimler-Benz	63,382
Faun	778
Henschel	12,201
Kaeble	66
K.H.D.	13,313
MAN	13,740

SPATIAL DIFFERENCES IN COMPETITIVE PERFORMANCE

Since production and sales occur in a spatial economy and link dispersed factories and branches with buyers whose haulage requirements vary from place to place, product differentiation strategies can be compared geographically. Here the assessment of performance by leading firms in market shares and degree of market monopolization is undertaken by the 35 registration districts used since 1969 (Figure 11.5).

The spatial patterns of some districts have limitations for the drawing of inferences when used as data observations in statistical analysis. The main problem areas are Hildesheim, Braunschweig, and Osnabrück in Niedersachsen; Süd-Baden and Süd-Württemberg-Hohenzollern in Baden-Württemberg; and Bremen. Their boundary indentations could only be tidied up by mergers which would reduce the number of spatial observations and increase their size inequality. It was decided to retain the 35 districts and so maximize the number of observations untill 1971, but the boundary problems have to be borne in mind when interpreting the results.

The Use of Total Registration Data

At the registration district level data are available for the total number of vehicles registered as being in use on 1 July (Kraftfahrt-Bundesamt, 1958–71). Changes in a manufacturer's share of total registrations can result from any of four following sources:

(a) A rise or fall in a manufacturer's share of new vehicle registrations in the previous 12 months can affect its share of total registrations.

(b) The level of scrappage of a firm's vehicles below (above) the number of new registrations raises (lowers) its number of total registrations. Different manufacturers have scrappage rates varying with product quality and market-share trends. The relationship between product quality and the scrappage rate imparts

1 Schleswig-Holstein
8 Aurich
11
6 Stade
2
10
11
7 Osnabrück
3 Hannover
5 Lüneburg
35 West Berlin
15 Munster
16 Detmold
4 Hildesheim
9
12
17 Arnsberg
19 Kassel
13 Koln
14
20 Koblenz
18 Darmstadt
21 Trier
32 Unter-Franken
30 Ober-Franken
34
22 Rhein-Hessen
24
31 Mittel-Franken
29 Ober-Pfalz
23 Nord-Wurttemberg
28 Nieder-Bayern
26
33 Schwaben
27 Ober-Bayern
25 Süd-Baden

2 Hamburg
9 Braunschweig
10 Oldenburg
11 Bremen
12 Düsseldorf
14 Aachen
24 Nord-Baden
26 Süd-Wurttemberg-Hohenzollern
34 Saarland

FIGURE 11.5 Registration districts

a certain positive bias into the competitive strength of any 'quality' manufacturer when using total registration data.

(c) Any net inter-district movement of vehicle ownership affects total district level registration data: net inflow can be regarded as a measure of competitive strength and should parallel the competitive changes showing up in new registration data.

(d) The movement of trucks into, and out of, storage.

Figure 11.6 shows the brand shares of 8–16 tonne g.v.w. total truck registrations which can be compared with the new registration shares in Figure 11.2. The market-share series for total registrations shows remarkable stability, largely because of the small proportion of the total made up by new registrations. Estimated new registrations (during the 12 months to 1 July 1969) made up only 7.9 per cent of Daimler-Benz total registrations in 1969 (7.6 per cent for K.H.D. and 8.8 per cent for MAN). Apart from their stability, total registration data give a valuable indication of a firm's underlying competitive strength, and this is important because yearly fluctuations in the market shares of new registrations, which for some manufacturers are considerable, can be very misleading. A high market of share of total registrations in a particular district is evidence of a systematic and persistent spatial advantage.

The Spatial Distribution of Manufacturers' Relative Market Shares: 1959

The spatial distribution of manufacturers' competitive strengths and weaknesses can be summarized by relating the district market and national market

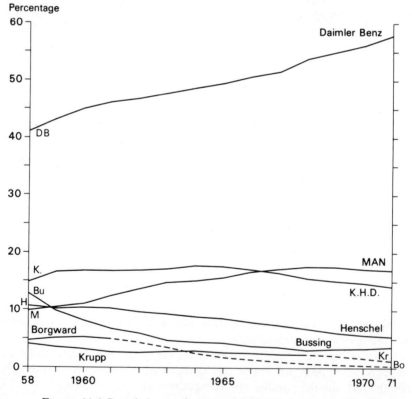

FIGURE 11.6 Brand shares of greater than 8–16 tonne g.v.w. Total truck registrations

shares of each brand. This can be expressed by the location quotient, in which a value greater than 1.0 indicates that the brand is performing better in that district than it is nationally. The spatial distribution of Daimler-Benz's market performance is illustrated in Figure 11.7.

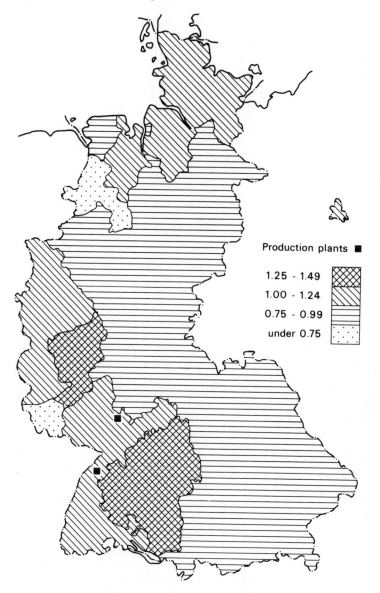

Production plants ■

1.25 - 1.49
1.00 - 1.24
0.75 - 0.99
under 0.75

FIGURE 11.7 Daimler-Benz—relative market
shares of total registrations: 1959

TABLE 11.2 Location quotients for truck brands: total registrations 1959

Registration districts	Truck brands						
	Borg-ward	Buss-ing	Daimler-Benz	Hens-chel	K.H.D.	Krupp	MAN
1. Schleswig-Holstein	1.57	1.21	1.04	0.73	1.10	0.58	0.64
2. Hamburg	1.09	1.86	0.84	1.07	1.05	1.05	0.63
3. Hannover	0.87	1.53	0.80	1.14	0.92	2.19	1.03
4. Hildesheim	1.36	1.56	0.80	1.39	0.90	1.33	0.73
5. Lüneburg	0.70	1.96	0.93	1.04	0.98	0.72	0.65
6. Stade	0.89	0.95	1.13	0.52	1.05	0.85	1.08
7. Osnabrück	1.40	1.19	0.60	1.48	1.59	0.68	0.98
8. Aurich	1.92	0.65	0.80	0.51	2.12	0.21	0.67
9. Braunschweig	1.03	3.20	0.87	0.69	0.50	1.08	0.46
10. Oldenburg	1.27	0.71	1.04	0.59	1.43	0.50	0.91
11. Bremen	2.56	0.77	0.86	0.53	1.48	0.91	0.87
12. Düsseldorf	1.03	0.94	1.02	0.91	1.09	1.42	0.73
13. Köln	0.93	0.83	1.02	0.96	1.17	0.96	0.74
14. Aachen	1.42	0.91	1.02	0.97	0.90	0.82	1.01
15. Münster	0.76	1.08	0.87	1.52	1.16	1.06	0.78
16. Detmold	1.94	1.03	0.78	1.16	1.28	1.16	0.75
17. Arnsberg	1.27	0.89	0.95	1.29	1.06	0.91	0.78
18. Darmstadt	0.83	0.92	0.98	1.30	0.99	1.31	0.87
19. Kassel	0.87	0.89	0.77	3.06	0.83	0.53	0.55
20. Koblenz	0.99	0.63	1.29	0.99	0.60	0.87	0.82
21. Trier	1.03	0.98	1.08	0.62	0.42	0.31	2.09
22. Rhein-Hessen-Pfalz	0.89	1.20	1.12	0.68	0.84	1.08	0.93
23. Nord-Württemberg	0.31	0.56	1.31	0.49	0.97	0.77	1.17
24. Nord-Baden	0.88	1.20	1.12	1.02	0.74	0.66	0.89
25. Süd-Baden	0.91	1.00	1.21	0.82	0.62	0.78	1.02
26. Süd-Württemberg	0.51	0.65	1.27	0.67	0.96	0.66	1.04
27. Ober-Bayern	0.75	0.80	0.98	0.83	1.07	0.88	1.53
28. Nieder-Bayern	2.20	0.89	0.98	0.73	0.99	0.69	1.03
29. Ober-Pfalz	1.42	0.57	0.87	0.72	1.28	0.82	1.69
30. Ober-Franken	0.67	0.80	0.95	0.86	1.03	0.94	1.66
31. Mittel-Franken	0.24	0.63	0.83	0.53	1.17	1.21	2.58
32. Unter-Franken	0.87	0.85	0.76	1.56	0.77	1.40	1.90
33. Schwaben	1.00	0.59	0.91	1.08	0.99	0.73	1.87
34. Saarland	2.66	0.51	0.42	1.22	0.66	0.42	1.75
35. W. Berlin	0.22	1.79	1.09	0.54	0.63	2.02	0.92

The districts with above average market performance are characterized by being either near to the production plants at Gaggenau and Mannheim, as in Baden-Württemberg and Rheinland-Pfalz (districts 22–26, Figure 11.5), or where competitors' production plants are absent, as in the western districts and the outliers of Stade, Oldenberg, and Schleswig-Holstein. One of Daimler-Benz's greatest assets is that the districts in which it fairs well span the densely populated industrial belt running from the Ruhr in the north to Stuttgart in the south where its branches are concentrated (Figure 11.3).

In the main, the competitors gain at the expense of Daimler-Benz in those districts where they have a production plant, or which are near to their plants. The location quotients for 1959 are given in Table 11.2. K.H.D. is the exception: most of its advantaged districts are in the far north and northwest, far from its factory in Schwaben which, in fact, has a value of 0.99, indicating only average performance. However, the K.H.D. case shows that to an extent the lack of a home district advantage can be partly overcome by developing trucks which match the specific requirements of buyers who do not have close contacts with a local producer. It illustrates well the possibilities of trading-off product differentiation against locational dispersal. Yet the spatial distribution of each manufacturer's market share points to the conclusion that locational dispersal of production plants offers considerable sales benefits under product differentiation. All leading firms, except for K.H.D. have very much larger market shares in their home districts and in adjoining ones.

Changes in the Spatial Distribution of Market Shares: 1959–71

All manufacturers experienced changes in the spatial distribution of their market shares during the period of study. The coefficient of localization (Sargant Florence, 1972) provides a periodic measure of the spatial concentration of each brand. Its extreme values are 0 for a distribution having a zero spatial variance and 1.0 for the absolute maximum degree of concentration. The coefficients of localization of each brand's market share of total registrations are given in Table 11.3. Daimler-Benz was clearly the least localized of the brands in all 3 years and the only one that became progressively less localized. However, MAN made a striking reduction in its localization coefficient between 1959 and 1965, by which time it had done much to shake off its 'home' region orientation and was in more intense competition with the other 2 nationally orientated producers, Daimler-Benz and K.H.D. The degree of localization not only differed appreciably between the several manufacturers but also increased during the 1960s. The

TABLE 11.3 Coefficients of localization at the registration district level for the leading brands of truck: total registrations 1959–71

	Truck Brand						
Year	Borgward	Bussing	Daimler-Benz	Henschel	K.H.D.	Krupp	MAN
1959	0.157	0.136	0.062	0.147	0.079	0.138	0.149
1965	0.202	0.142	0.050	0.136	0.078	0.122	0.101
1971	0.223	0.141	0.041	0.151	0.086	0.129	0.101

range of the distribution of localization coefficients rose from between 0.062 and 0.149 in 1959, up to between 0.041 and 0.151 in 1971 (Borgward excluded), corresponding with a considerable increase in the inequlity of market shares at the national level.

MARKET AREAS AS AREAS OF THE GREATEST RELATIVE ADVANTAGE

These results suggested the possibility of classifying market areas according to spatial differences in the competitive performance of the 5 leading brands. Their relative market-share patterns can be combined on one map with each district being allocated to the brand having the greatest relative advantage or shared where more than one firm had a notable relative advantage. The results of such a classification using 1971 data are given in Figure 11.8. The following criteria were used to allocate districts:

(a) the relative market share had to exceed 1.1 before a brand could be considered as having a significant relative advantage over the other brands;

(b) where two or more brands had relative market shares exceeding 1.1, the district was allocated to that brand with the highest relative share, subject to it exceeding the next highest by over 0.2 in relative market shares; otherwise the district was shared between the brands.

(c) where no brand exceeded 1.1, the brand or brands having over 1.0 were included in brackets.

The market areas follow a predictable pattern. Except for K.H.D. (and Daimler-Benz in Süd-Baden), each brand has the greatest relative advantage in its home area. The relative importance of Bussing and MAN in the west resulted partly from their relatively good representation by factory branches and dealerships. Indeed, the ability of K.H.D., Bussing, and MAN to do so well away from their areas of production is further evidence that product differentiation can reduce the distance effect. Districts shared between two brands take on the form of transitional zones.

Unfortunately, this rather easy method of classifying market areas has limited value; although Figure 11.8 clearly points out the relative spatial strengths of the different brands, it exaggerates the localization factor. For example, Henschel was the second-largest brand in Kassel, with 17.6 per cent of total 1971 registrations but was far behind Daimler-Benz with a 47 per cent share. Daimler-Benz dominated every district in 1971, as it had in the 1960s, yet its low level of sales localization means that its relative market-share values rarely diverge far from 1.0. Thus the type of market-area classification used in Figure 11.8 is useful only when all competing brands have a largely regional sales orientation. The main value of this discussion lies in its demonstration that the competitive pressure varied between districts according to which of Daimler-Benz's competitors had the strongest range of product affinities with local truck operators. The spatial differences in these competitive structures indicate variations in both the type and the intensity of competitive behaviour.

SELLER CONCENTRATION AND MARKET AREAS

Since the pioneering work of Mason (1939), industrial economists have stressed the dependence of the intensity of competitive behaviour upon the

FIGURE 11.8 Market areas having the greatest relative market share advantage—total registrations: 1971

underlying market structure (Scherer, 1970, p. 4.). Most frequently 'seller concentration' is used as an index of the state of market competition. It measures the number and size distribution of sellers and is usually expressed as a concentration ratio which equals the proportion of the market held by the largest 'n' firms.

The state of competition in each district of West Germany was estimated by the three-firm concentration ratio, henceforth referred to as CR_3. Between 1959 and 1971 the CR_3 for the West German truck market rose from 69.9 to 89.4 per cent indicating that the degree of potential monopolization had intensified. The 1971 distribution of concentration is shown in Figure 11.9. The CR_3 varied from 81.2 in Hildesheim to 94.5 in Nord-Württemberg—a range of 13.3 percentile points; this marks a reduction from the 1959 range of 28.0 points when the Saarland is included, or 19.6 when excluded. Thus the spatial variance of concentration has been reduced as the general level of concentration increased. The evidence of Figure 11.9 clearly points towards differences in the structure and intensity of competition over space and suggests that the gradings shown could be used to outline market areas. Thus a market area embracing districts with high concentration ratios is likely to be one where there is less competitive behaviour by the market participants. This approach could be applied to the 1971 situation since the same three firms comprised the CR_3 ratio in all districts except Kassel, and thus the highs and lows could be interpreted in relation to the local competitive impact of the remaining firms. But if the membership of the top three firms had varied spatially—as in 1959—the market-area classification would have required more complex criteria, with each district being classed by both its level of concentration and the membership of its CR_3. Such a classification would not have advanced the rather limited analysis of Figure 11.8 and was not pursued.

However, this account of seller concentration has achieved something. It has shown, first, that the extent of market monopolization varies significantly over space, and second, that in 1971 the areas of relatively high, medium, and low concentration all displayed a fair measure of contiguity. Consequently, competition was probably subject to systematic spatial causation since the chances of a contiguous and interpretable areal pattern of competition emerging from a random process analysis would have been very remote. Indeed, the contiguous groupings of the different levels of industrial concentration suggest that the West German truck market comprises several spatially distinct subsystems of competitive behaviour, henceforth referred to as competitive processes.

COMPETITIVE PROCESSES AND MARKET STRUCTURE

Market Areas as Spatial Competitive Subsystems

Competition in the truck market has so far been regarded as the tactical and strategic behaviour of sellers in attempting either to maintain or to increase their

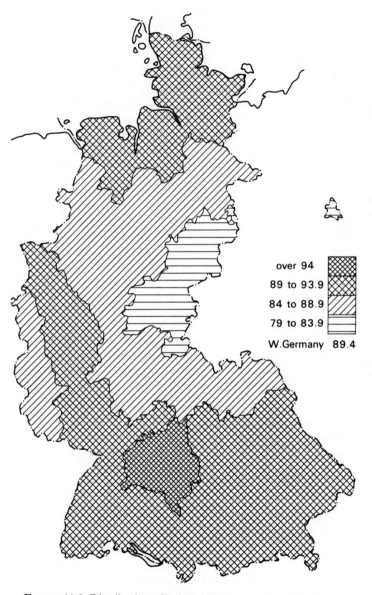

over 94

89 to 93.9

84 to 88.9

79 to 83.9

W.Germany 89.4

FIGURE 11.9 Distribution of industrial concentration 1971 [three-firm
concentration ratio]

market shares. Product differentiation is used to influence the purchasing decisions of truck operators. One way to evaluate the effectiveness of these sales efforts is to examine whether buyers stay with a brand or switch to others. A rising market share over a period would indicate successful product differentiation and, therefore, this can be used as an estimate of the competitive process.

The importance of the competitive process is that it acts as a system which, over one purchasing period, can transform the distribution of market shares (x_i) at time t into a changed (or unchanged) distribution (y_i) at time $t + 1$. The actual relative rates of transition of buyers between brands determines the extent of change in market-structure change during the purchasing period. An estimate of the purchasing transitions for a truck market describes the operation of a dynamic competitive process. Thus a market area within a product-differentiated market would be characterized by a particular route system of buyers switching between brands, together with an important element of buyer loyalty.

If the West German truck market comprised several competitive processes, these would represent spatial subsystems of the national market system rather than totally different ones. Each spatial subsystem would consist of a different group of buyers which relates to the products offered by the national producers according to the characteristics of its local or regional environment. The subsystem possibility was suggested because the same sellers competed over the whole national market, all the trucks offered were available throughout the national market, the basic market strategies were similar in all districts, government transport policy and legislation affecting the product and its usage were standard throughout the country, and the economic conditions affecting the level of industrial activity were the same everywhere, though the impact may have varied from district to district. Therefore, the pattern of competition in each district would have been primarily affected by a common set of national variables. Consequently, the expectation of a low level of subsystem independence, makes the assumption of a single national system appear plausible.

Each identifiable spatial subsystem or competitive process would represent a market area. Truck buyers within each market area would have a set of

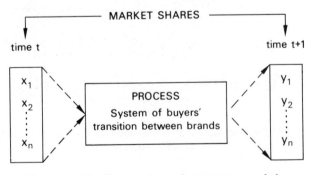

FIGURE 11.10 Changes in market structure and the competitive system

relationships with the truck brands which reflected their current, or period average, brand preferences and which would be sufficiently cohesive to cause the competitive dynamics to reach a final equilibrium distribution of brand market shares that differed from that of any other market area. In this eventuality the German market would be 'polystable' (Ashby, 1960). The expectation is that the variation in buyers' brand preferences within market area, groupings of districts with similar brand transitions, will be significantly less than that between market areas.

Market Areas as Stochastic Processes

Given the market uncertainties recognized by the motor-truck producers, it seems appropriate to adopt a probabilistic approach to estimate the rates of transition of buyers between brands. One stochastic process that appears suitable for this analysis is the first-order Markov chain. The Markov process implies that a fixed probability of purchasing a brand at time $t + 1$ is conditional only upon the brand bought in the previous purchasing period, t (and is entirely independent of the brands purchased in any earlier periods, $t-n$). However, the first-order Markov chain model has a certain amount of 'memory' (Feller, 1968) in that the experience of all brands bought before t are in a sense incorporated in the decision to buy brand i at t. This distinguishes the Markovian model from deterministic models whose predictions depend on a knowledge of all past purchases. Thus to quote Steindl (1965, p. 171), 'The Markov chain has a chain of actors connected by decisions which are the result both of chance and systematic influence.' The systematic influence is derived from the preceding purchase. A first-order chain picks up the relationship between a new truck purchase and the experience with the brand purchased last year (t). Most people employed in truck marketing think that any additional carry over to the present ($t + 1$) of experience from any years earlier than t will be minimal; any 'historic' purchases will be largely irrelevant to the present decision owing to changes such as the content and pattern of a haulier's trade, legislation, and technology. In view of this, it seems worthwhile to employ first-order Markov chain analysis.

First-order Markov Chains

The complete set of probabilities, p_{ij}, for a Markovian process are presented as a transition probability matrix, P, of the form

$$\text{Outcome states } (t + 1)$$

$$p = p_{ij} = \begin{array}{c} \text{Initial} \\ \text{states} \\ (t) \end{array} \begin{array}{c} S_1 \\ S_2 \\ \\ \\ S_r \end{array} \begin{array}{cccc} S_1 & S_2 & \cdots & S_r \\ \begin{bmatrix} p_{11} & p_{12} & \cdots & p_{1r} \\ p_{21} & p_{22} & \cdots & p_{2r} \\ , & , & \cdots & , \\ , & , & \cdots & , \\ p_{r1} & p_{r2} & \cdots & p_{rr} \end{bmatrix} \end{array}$$

As transition probabilities, the p_{ij} satisfy the conditions

$$0 \leq p_{ij} \leq 1 \tag{11.1}$$

$$\sum_{j=1}^{r} p_{ij} = 1 \text{ for } i = 1, 2, \ldots r \tag{11.2}$$

In this study, the states of the system, $S_1 \ldots S_r$, are the truck brands. Each p_{ij} represents the expected proportion of former buyers of brand i who now buy brand j.

The main diagonal of the matrix **P**, $p_{11}, \ldots, p_{rr}$, estimates the probability of repeat purchasing (buyer loyalty). The earlier discussion of the strategic application of product differentiation would lead us to expect high values for the p_{ii}, especially that for Daimler-Benz. As such, the p_{ii} will form composite indices of the effectiveness of the firms' product-differentiation strategies in fostering buyer loyalty.

The essential dynamics of the truck purchasing process are the ability to transform the share structure of the market so that if the initial distribution of market shares is given in the vector $m_i = (m_1, m_2, \ldots m_r)$ then the probable outcome distribution one period later will be given by

$$m_{j(t+1)} = \sum_{i=1}^{r} m_{i(t)} p_{ij} \tag{11.3}$$

The brand preferences of buyers which are mapped in the form of a **P** matrix become the stochastic mechanism for changing the competitive structure of the market.

Finally, another property processed by regular ergodic (buyers of one brand can possibly buy or repurchase any other available brand in a finite number of periods) Markov matrices, that is essential to a subsystem's approach, is that when taken to progressively higher powers they converge on a steady-state matrix, **A**. Every row of **A** is identical. The unique row vector, a, gives the most probable long-run equilibrium structure of market shares. It is also the unique solution to the equation

$$a\mathbf{P} = a \tag{11.4}$$

This steady-state solution is of interest not simply as a long-run forecast of the market structure, but more as a measure of the 'momentum' (Morrison *et al.*, 1971) or current competitive tendencies (Collins and Preston, 1960) of the market. This, of course, highlights the rationale of the competitive-process approach to market areas. It is not just the existing spatial distribution of market shares, or concentration ratios, that should characterize a type of market area. Rather, the areas should be classified on the basis of the competitive process at work. Thus irrespective of the initial market structures, if a number of adjoining districts have the same brand moving towards a monopoly position in approximately the same stochastic manner then they can be grouped into the same market area. The emphasis is placed on the dynamics of the process rather than the statics of the outcome states of competition.

LEAST-SQUARES ESTIMATION OF MARKOVIAN TRANSITION PROBABILITIES

The usual procedure for estimating Markov transition probabilities in models of purchasing behaviour requires knowledge of the actual number of buyers, n_{ij}, moving between each of the j brands, $(j=1, \ldots, r)$. In the case of the West German 8–16 tonne g.v.w. truck market the only data available are the distribution of purchases between the brands (market shares) at the end of each buying period. However, thanks to Miller (1952) and Goodman (1953) it is possible to obtain transition probability estimates by applying the least-squares technique to brand market-share data.

Allowing for errors in the estimated $m_{j(t+1)}$ of equation (11.3), the regression relationship becomes

$$m_{j(t+1)} = \sum_{i=1}^{r} m_{i(t)} p_{ij} + u_{j(t+1)} \qquad (11.5)$$

where, $u_{j(t+1)}$ are the errors or random distribances. The errors having the property

$$E(u_j) = 0 \qquad (11.6)$$

As observations are available for all 5 leading brands for 21 years, the truck purchasing p_{ij} can be estimated by the use of ordinary least squares. Equation (11.5) can be written in matrix form as

$$y_j = X_j p_j + u_j \qquad (11.7)$$

Least squares cannot be applied directly to (11.7) because the independent variables $m_{i(t)}$ $(i=1,\ldots,r)$ being proportions, satisfy $\sum_i m_{i(t)} = 1$. The use of ordinary least squares necessitates omitting one of the $m_{i(t)}$ brands from the X matrices. Following Telser (1963, p.279), $m_{j(t)} = 1 - \sum_i m_{i(t)}$ $(i \neq j)$ and so the right-hand term can be substituted into (11.7) which will now have r equations and $r-1$ independent variables. The jth column of $m_{i(t)} p$ can now be written as

$$m_{j(t+1)} = p_{jj} + \sum_i (p_{ij} - p_{jj}) m_{i(t)} + u_{j(t+1)} \qquad (11.8)$$

Equation (11.8) will give us direct estimates of the p_{ij}. However, Madansky (1959) has pointed out that the p_{ij} estimates are not asymptotically efficient because the errors, u_j, are correlated with a non-constant variance δ_j^2. This condition is known as heteroscedasticity and can be partially overcome by a system of weighting. Of the several weighting schemes tested by Lee *et al.* (1970) the use of the reduced variance covariance matrix, incorporated as their generalized least-squares estimator, comes out best as a measure of performance Lee *et al.*, 1970, 145–6). This estimator also satisfies conditions (11.1) and (11.2) and is employed in this study.

The Assumptions of the Model

To use time-series market-share data for the estimation of a first-order Markov chain, several assumptions have to be made:

(a) the data are generated from a first-order chain which governs every individual's truck purchasing behaviour;

(b) The participating buyer force remained constant over the period of estimation;

(c) every purchaser was restricted to the identified brands;

(d) each purchaser made a purchase every year in a manner independent of the behaviour of all other purchasers. This eliminates any 'follow the leader' type of behaviour (Anderson, 1954, p. 37).

The first assumption is crucial: without information on the movement of individuals between brands (Lee *et al.*, 1965, p. 758) the first-order assumption cannot be rigorously tested. However, several alternative, though less satisfactory, tests will be applied to the data.

The trends in brand shares move with remarkable smoothness over time and, apart from Bussing, seem to be approaching some state of equilibrium (see Figure 11.3). In fact, they closely resemble the sequence in market shares that would result from the working out of a first-order stationary Markov process (Lee *et al.*, 1970, p. 45). Assumptions (b), (c), and (d) all follow from the Markov property. The first two may become unrealistic over long periods when the membership of both the buyer population and the manufacturer force have changed. However, market entries and exits by truck purchasers have been largely concentrated among the smaller operators whose purchases make up only a small proportion of the market. Also the changes in manufacturer representation have only affected the smaller marginal brands. In the case of assumption (d), while many of the smaller haulage operators may enter the market periodically, the bulk of new trucks are purchased by medium and large operators who add to, or replace part of, their fleets every year. Furthermore, 'there is a growing concentration of truck fleets into specialist operations and the number of small operators will tend to dwindle away' (The Economist Intelligence Unit Ltd., 1970, p. 6). The more sophisticated decision-making procedures used by the larger specialist hauliers will tend to ensure independence in truck buying behaviour. However, the recognition that these assumptions do not necessarily hold for all buyers in the market means that the probability estimates are only suggestive of the process at work rather than models of reality.

TRANSITION PROBABILITY MATRICES FOR THE WEST GERMAN TRUCK MARKET

The truck purchasing system will have 4 states. The first 3 will consist of the 3 brands which have dominated the medium-sized truck market for the whole of the 1959–71 period, namely Daimler-Benz, K.H.D., and MAN. The fourth state, OTH., includes all the other brands which competed in the market (see Dorward, 1975, pp. 313–8, for a comparison with alternative 5-brand matrices). The main advantage of an 'all other' category is that by including all those firms which entered or left the market during the period it solves the problem caused by changes in the number of available brands. Of course, the heterogeneous nature of the OTH. state means that only the p_{ij}'s which describe movements between the three identified brands are meaningful indicators of behaviour. The possibility of moving to OTH. is really nothing other than an average probability of not moving to any of the three major brands. The restricted generalized least-squares estimates of the transition probabilities for the West German market over the 1958 to 1970 period are given by the matrix,

	D-B	K.H.D.	MAN	OTH.
D-B	1.0	0.0	0.0	0.0
K.H.D.	0.0	0.8255	0.1370	0.0375
MAN	0.0526	0.0594	0.8880	0.0
OTH.	0.0217	0.0960	0.0	0.8823

The annual population of operators, $N_{(t)}$, used in the weight matrix for the generalized least-squares estimates, was assumed to be proportional to the number of trucks registered in the 8–16 tonne category; the assumed number of registrations per operator was 8.

The same operator population estimates result from the alternative assumption of an operator making one new purchase every year and keeping the vehicle for the whole of its expected working life of just over 8 years. During the 1960s the average proportion of new registrations to the total was nearly 12 per cent which gives a crude estimated vehicle life of 8 years.

The high values on the main diagonal show brand loyalty to have been a very important feature of the annual registration behaviour of truck operators. The matrix describes an absorbing chain, in which operators switch between the other brands until they come to permanent rest in the Daimler-Benz brand state. Such a matrix predicts the emergence of a monopoly with Daimler-Benz as the only remaining producer. Only 5 (Hannover, Münster, Detmold, Rhein-

Hessen-Pfalz, and Ober-Pfalz), of the 35 registration district matrices were absorbing, again with Daimler-Benz having a 1.0 repeat-purchasing probability. While losing buyers to Daimler-Benz and without hope of attracting buyers from the market leader, under the market policies adopted at the time, the other brands were doomed to extinction from the market. The 27 registration districts with regular ergodic Markov matrices featured a considerable variety in purchasing behaviour: if a former purchaser of Daimler-Benz switched his custom, he would most likely have moved to MAN in 13 of the districts, to K.H.D. in 10, and have had no real marked preference in the others. Despite this, certain popular patterns of behaviour emerge across the 27 districts.

The main channel for switching into Daimler-Benz was MAN, though K.H.D. did play that role in 8 districts. In 16 K.H.D. and MAN lost buyers to each other, often characterized by high probabilities. As well as switching to MAN and Daimler-Benz, the former buyers of K.H.D. also moved to OTH. so forming its main source of new custom. This was reciprocated by OTH. buyers who primarily switched to K.H.D. in 23 districts. These predominant characteristics correspond very closely to the behavioural patterns of both the West German national new registration (Dorward, 1975) and total registration matrices. Though the probability values differ, these relationships seem to have been fairly persistent over space.

The remaining 3 matrices for Hamburg, Arnsberg, and Unter-Franken were ergodic and regular for the Daimler-Benz and MAN brands, but transient on K.H.D. and OTH. In terms of steady states, the two ergodic brands will be left to share the market between themselves. As with market structure, the patterns of buyer behaviour are heterogeneous in space. The validity of the predictions and the comparability of the matrices, however, depend on the competitive processes meeting the first-order stationary Markov chain assumptions.

The First-order Property

An F statistic was used on equation (11.8) to test the hypothesis of the movement in market shares being randomly determined. A random movement would imply a zero-order Markov Chain 'in which events occur on successive trials independently of the occurrences on preceding trials' (Telser, 1963).

The application of the unrestricted and unweighted first-order Markov model (equation 11.8) to the four brands at the national level of aggregation yielded the following multiple-correlation coefficients (R^2) and significance levels:

Dependent variables	D-B$_{(t+1)}$	K.H.D.$_{(t+1)}$	MAN$_{(t+1)}$	OTH.$_{(t+1)}$
R^2	0.99	0.95	0.99	0.99
F value	443.6	23.9	203.9	4182.1
Level of statistical significance (per cent)	0.1	0.1	0.1	0.1

The high significance levels cause the rejection of the zero-order hypothesis in favour of a first-order model.

Furthermore, these highly satisfactory outcomes were replicated at both the regional and the registration district levels for the three brands D-B$_{(t+1)}$, MAN$_{(t+1)}$, and OTH.$_{(t+1)}$ (all explanations being significant at the $F_{0.001}$ level for every spatial unit). The K.H.D.$_{(t+1)}$ equation, while generally maintaining an $F_{0.001}$ significance level, occasionally dropped to $F_{0.01}$ and, unfortunately, became insignificant in the case of Schleswig-Holstein.

A second test uses Lee *et al.* (1970, p. 141) application of the χ^2 statistic to test the goodness of fit of the restricted, weighted, first-order Markov model's brand-share predictions to those originally observed. The χ^2 statistic is given as

$$\chi^2(r-1)T = \sum_t^T \sum_i^r N(t)(m_{i(t)} - \hat{m}_{i(t)})^2 / \hat{m}_{i(t)} \qquad (11.9)$$

The predicted share $\hat{m}_i$ is assumed to be non-zero.

The West German and all the 35 registration district matrices gave market-share estimates very close to those observed. Their computed χ^2 values were all far smaller than the tabled value of 47.14 with 36 degrees of freedom at the 10 per cent significance level. Therefore, the results for the F and χ^2 statistics are consistent with the hypothesis that the brand shares at both the local and national levels are generated by first-order Markov processes. However, this is subject to the caveat that these tests are indicative rather than proof.

The Stationarity Property

The value of the steady-state predictions derived from the transition probability matrices depends upon those transition probabilities remaining constant over time. The stationarity property was tested by estimating West German national transition probability matrices for 6 periods between 1958 and 1970 by progressively eliminating either the first, or the last, observation. The resultant matrices were then multiplied by either the 1970 or 1958 vector of market shares to give predicted brand shares for either 1971 or 1959. These predictions were then weighted by the number of total truck registrations for either 1971 or 1959 and compared with the distribution of brand registrations predicted by the 1958–70 matrix using the Kolmogorov–Smirnov test. The results are given in Table 11.4. The elimination of up to 4 years from the beginning or end of the period has no significant effect on the predictive ability of the matrices. The accuracy of the predictions is very high, especially when the large size of the total registrations is taken into account (104,800 in 1959 and 193,500 in 1971). In addition, the matrices used in Table 11.4 are all remarkably similar both in structure and in individual p_{ij} values. Thus the case for stationarity appears to be quite strong.

TABLE 11.4 Kolmogorov–Smirnov tests of ability of the West German transition matrices (total registration date) to predict accurately the distribution of truck brands

1958–70 matrix predictions compared with	per cent level of statistical significance of comparisons of predictions for:	
	1971	1959
1959–70	10	
1960–70	10	
1961–70	10	
1958–69		10
1958–68		10
1958–67		10

THE TOTAL TRUCK REGISTRATION MODEL AS A SURROGATE FOR THE MEDIUM-TERM TRENDS IN NEW TRUCK SALES

When given in total registrations the temporal movements in the market shares of truck brands register the current changes in new registrations relative to the brand shares of trucks in use and so should represent the medium-term trends in competition. If this is correct, the total truck registration series should approximate the trends of the moving average for new truck registrations, which describe the 'general sweep' or secular behaviour of new truck sales. An acceptable degree of similarity in both sets of market-share time-series data would allow the matrices computed from total registrations to be used as surrogates for the underlying medium-term new truck purchasing process. The states computed from these matrices would estimate the long-run competitive outcomes for the new truck market.

In an attempt to test the total registration matrices as surrogates for the medium-term new truck purchasing processes, generalized least-squares first-order Markov probabilities were computed for West Germany and 9 regions using 5-year moving-average data for new registrations. Unfortunately, as with all moving-average series, observations were lost at each end of the period but 16 possible observations remained. The 10 matrices could all satisfactorily predict their observed market shares for their periods of estimation at the $\chi^2_{0.10}$ significance level, when weighted by the estimated number of truck buyers. However, the regional matrices were still significant at $\chi^2_{0.10}$ when weighted by total new truck registrations. Thus the 5-year moving-average data appeared to have been generated by a first-order Markov process. These 10 matrices were then compared with the 10 corresponding matrices estimated from total registration data. Generalized least-squares estimates were computed from the new registration 5-year moving-averages for several periods for which total registration data were available. The matrices computed from 1954–68 data were those for Bremen, Baden-Württemberg, and Bayern; those computed for 1955–68 were Hamburg, Niedersachsen, Nordrhein-Westfälen, Hessen, and West Germany; Rheinland-Pfalz used observations for 1956–68 and Schleswig-Holstein used 1957–68. The nearest corresponding total registration matrices were estimated for 1958–70 for West Germany, Bremen, Nordrhein-Westfälen, Hessen Rheinland-Pfalz, and Baden-Württemberg. The other regions had a closer correspondence between the above moving-average matrices and the 1959–70 total registration matrices.

The degree of similarity in the corresponding matrices was measured by means of the Kolmogorov–Smirnov 2-sample test, based on the difference between the cumulative frequency distributions of buyers moving between the brands for the two populations. All the total registration matrices closely resembled those computed from the 5-year moving-average data at the 20 per cent acceptance level. Therefore, based on the results of the Kolmogorov–Smirnov test, the hypothesis that both data series come from the same medium-term (underlying) truck competitive process can be accepted. The medium-term purchasing matrix based on West German 1955–68 5-year moving-average data is also absorbing on Daimler-Benz. Thus both this and the West German total registration 1958–70 matrix have the same steady states. This result further emphasizes the momentum of the national truck purchasing system towards monopoly.

BUYER LOYALTY AND MARKET SHARE

The transition matrices for the 35 registration districts are characterized by high probabilities on the main diagonals. This is clearly seen from a perusal of Table 11.5: thus the high level of brand loyalty noted for the national system was maintained at the local level. Yet there were considerable differences between the districts in their average levels of buyer loyalty (where r equalled the 4-brand states): the range was from 0.67 in Trier (in fact 8 districts had $\sum p_{ii}/r \leq 0.75$) to 0.95 in Ober-Pfalz.

These indices also point to differences in the spatial variation of buyer loyalty between brands. Daimler-Benz comes out with the best achievement in product-differentiation strategies in having had the highest level of buyer loyalty in 29 districts. Buyer loyalty indices levels for the 3 leading brands ranged from 0.74 to 1.0, for Daimler-Benz, 0.40 to 0.94 for K.H.D., and 0.26 to 0.98 for MAN.

Buyer loyalty is a behavioural expression of goodwill built up over several years by a firm's successful investment in product differentiation (Palda, 1964; Heflebower, 1967; Weiss, 1969; Peles, 1971). This stock should bring benefits in future years and, in particular, the greater likelihood of a steadily rising market share. To the extent that the spatial aspects of product differentiation are effective in controlling the local markets to the benefit of the firm (the achievement of high buyer loyalty), a positive relationship between the level of

TABLE 11.5 Brand loyalty for 35 registration districts (1958–70 matrices)

Registration districts	Brand loyalty indices (p_{ii})				'Modified trace' [a]
	D-B	K.H.D.	MAN	OTH.	$\sum p_{ii}/r$
1. Schleswig-Holstein	0.95	0.75	0.89	0.88	0.87
2. Hamburg	0.95	0.91	0.58	0.88	0.83
3. Hannover	1.0	0.70	0.77	0.89	0.84
4. Hildesheim	0.79	0.45	0.88	0.90	0.75
5. Lüneburg	0.95	0.85	0.92	0.90	0.91
6. Stade	0.94	0.57	0.66	0.84	0.75
7. Osnabrück	0.83	0.78	0.26	0.87	0.69
8. Aurich	0.80	0.71	0.79	0.79	0.77
9. Braunschweig	0.93	0.43	0.64	0.89	0.72
10. Oldenburg	0.94	0.92	0.88	0.78	0.88
11. Bremen	0.99	0.83	0.79	0.90	0.88
12. Düsseldorf	0.99	0.83	0.94	0.90	0.91
13. Köln	0.99	0.85	0.91	0.90	0.91
14. Aachen	0.98	0.67	0.77	0.84	0.82
15. Münster	1.0	0.74	0.82	0.87	0.86
16. Detmold	1.0	0.88	0.90	0.89	0.92
17. Arnsberg	0.98	0.94	0.90	0.90	0.93
18. Darmstadt	0.98	0.84	0.83	0.91	0.89
19. Kassel	0.97	0.85	0.93	0.91	0.92
20. Koblenz	0.89	0.66	0.74	0.83	0.78
21. Trier	0.95	0.41	0.68	0.67	0.67
22. Rhein-Hessen-Pfalz	1.0	0.69	0.85	0.86	0.85
23. Nord-Württemburg	0.99	0.75	0.82	0.80	0.84
24. Nord-Baden	0.97	0.86	0.90	0.86	0.90
25. Süd-Baden	0.96	0.63	0.78	0.81	0.80
26. Süd-Württemburg	0.95	0.72	0.65	0.84	0.79
27. Ober-Bayern	0.99	0.82	0.91	0.87	0.90
28. Nieder-Bayern	0.91	0.69	0.97	0.88	0.86
29. Ober-Pfalz	1.0	0.91	0.98	0.91	0.95
30. Ober-Franken	0.91	0.78	0.80	0.84	0.83
31. Mittel-Franken	0.79	0.76	0.58	0.84	0.74
32. Unter-Franken	0.74	0.83	0.52	0.91	0.75
33. Schwaben	0.83	0.85	0.74	0.91	0.83
34. Saarland	0.95	0.40	0.77	0.63	0.69
35. W. Berlin	0.95	0.63	0.63	0.90	0.78
West Germany	1.0	0.83	0.89	0.88	0.90

[a] Equals the average of the diagonal entries of the **P** matrix (Lipstein, 1961)

buyer loyalty in a registration district at time t and the the market share attained $(m_{j(t+1)})$ can be hypothesized. Buyer loyalty is being postulated as the activating agent between spatial product differentiation and the truck sales pay-off in terms of market share.

TABLE 11.6 Regressions on the buyer loyalty—market share relationship—35 registration districts

Brand	Structural form	Constants	Independent variable— buyer loyalty[a]	R^2
Daimler-Benz	Linear	13.82	45.137 (3.7)[b]	0.29
Daimler-Benz	Log-linear	4.07	0.736 (3.9)[b]	0.31
K.H.D.	Log-linear	2.80	0.424 (2.18)[c]	0.13

[a] The figures in brackets are the t ratios; [b] Indicates coefficient is statistically significant at the 0.1 per cent level; [c] Indicates coefficient is statistically significant at the 5 per cent level.

The 1971 market shares of brand i over 35 registration districts were regressed on the estimated level of buyer loyalty (1959–70 estimation period) of the ith brand for the corresponding districts. Separate regressions were run for each brand in both the linear and log-linear structural forms. The regression results are summarized in Table 11.6 which only includes the results for significant explanatory relationships.

In the cases of Daimler-Benz and K.H.D., the only two to show a significant relationship, the log-linear form produced better results. The relationship between market share and the preceding level of buyer loyalty was strongest for Daimler-Benz, where both structural forms managed to explain roughly 30 per cent of the spatial market share variance. The log-linear form gave an elasticity of Daimler-Benz's market share with respect to buyer loyalty of 0.74, while the corresponding elasticity for K.H.D. was much lower at 0.42. Only Daimler-Benz and K.H.D. (to a lesser extent) appear to have been able to exert a systematic control over registration district truck sales. Further work on the use of competitive process variables in explaining variations in seller concentration is reported in Dorward (1977).

LOCAL POLYSTABILITY AND SELLER CONCENTRATION

The array of steady states for the 35 registration districts (estimated from the 1958–70 total registration matrices) is given in Table 11.7. The polystability of the national system at the local level is clearly indicated by the inter-district differences in the steady-state distributions of brand shares. For example, the long-run shares of Daimler-Benz range from a low of 43.7 per cent in the MAN stronghold of Nieder-Bayern to a total monopoly in the 5 absorbing district matrices.

TABLE 11.7 Steady-state solutions and the momentum of seller concentration—35 registration districts

Registration districts	Daimler-Benz	K.H.D.	MAN	All other	CR$_3$ in steady state	Steady state CR$_3$ to 1970 actual CR$_3$
1. Schleswig-Holstein	65.7	16.9	15.5	1.9	98.1	107.8
2. Hamburg	88.4	0	11.6	0	100.0	113.9
3. Hannover	100.0	0	0	0	100.0	115.9
4. Hildesheim	50.0	17.6	20.7	11.7	88.3	110.1
5. Lüneburg	60.6	20.6	15.2	3.6	96.4	112.5
6. Stade	58.0	17.4	19.2	5.4	94.6	102.1
7. Osnabrück	51.1	23.9	15.5	9.5	90.5	105.2
8. Aurich	48.1	26.5	17.9	7.5	92.5	102.8
9. Braunschweig	64.0	10.5	14.3	11.2	88.8	109.5
10. Oldenburg	61.7	6.9	29.0	2.4	97.6	106.3
11. Bremen	86.4	6.9	6.6	0.1	99.9	110.8
12. Düsseldorf	81.3	6.5	8.7	3.5	96.5	108.2
13. Köln	85.7	6.6	7.2	0.5	99.5	110.9
14. Aachen	72.9	8.2	9.0	9.9	90.1	101.2
15. Münster	100.0	0	0	0	100.0	115.3
16. Detmold	100.0	0	0	0	100.0	115.4
17. Arnsberg	83.7	0	16.3	0	100.0	114.5
18. Darmstadt	85.5	3.1	10.9	0.5	99.5	114.3
19. Kassel	62.9	10.6	17.2	9.3	90.7	111.9
20. Koblenz	59.1	13.6	17.4	9.9	90.1	102.1
21. Trier	60.1	9.0	17.9	13.0	87.0	102.6
22. Rhein-Hessen-Pfalz	100.0	0	0	0	100.0	110.6
23. Nord-Württemburg	89.1	3.1	6.6	1.2	98.8	105.0
24. Nord-Baden	72.9	6.2	13.3	7.6	92.4	102.9
25. Süd-Baden	66.7	7.0	19.7	6.6	93.4	104.6
26. Süd-Württenburg	73.6	9.5	13.7	3.2	96.8	103.6
27. Ober-Bayern	68.6	9.4	14.6	7.4	92.6	102.1
28. Nieder-Bayern	43.7	12.2	40.0	4.1	95.9	107.9
29. Ober-Pfalz	100.0	0	0	0	100.0	112.6
30. Ober-Franken	58.1	9.3	25.1	7.5	92.5	106.8
31. Mittel-Franken	51.5	12.3	31.5	4.7	95.3	103.6
32. Unter-Franken	64.4	0	35.6	0	100.0	119.9
33. Schwaben	58.5	6.8	34.5	0.2	99.8	110.5
34. Saarland	52.0	10.9	22.1	15.0	85.0	99.4
35. W. Berlin	62.3	10.0	11.9	15.8	84.2	103.8

The ability of product differentiation to transcend distance is again evident in that both Daimler-Benz and K.H.D. have most of their higher long-run market shares away from the regions in which their plant and head offices are located. Nine of the 12 districts in which Daimler-Benz has a steady-state share of over 80 per cent have no contiguity with the production districts. Although 20 districts are within 5 percentile points of the national steady-state concentration ratio (CR_3), the range of 15.8 percentile points had slightly widened from the actual spread of seller concentration in 1971 (13.3 per cent). The West German truck market was characterized in seller concentration by a momentum towards very high concentration which differed in intensity from district to district (ranging from oligopoly, through duopoly, to monopoly). The spatial pattern of the CR_3 in the steady state can be seen more clearly in Figure 11.11. The districts of highest concentration (a CR_3 of over 94 per cent) are spread throughout West Germany, and are surrounded by districts of lower concentration on the periphery.

The final column of Table 11.7 shows how far the market was from the steady-state level of concentration in 1970, the last year of the period of probability estimation. While 20 districts were within 10 per cent of their steady-state concentration ratio, others had processes embodying greater change in the future. The greatest change was predicted in the 1971 crescent of lower concentration stretching from the centre to the north (Figure 11.11). Of course, 3 (Hannover, Münster, and Detmold) of the 6 districts of highest change were subject to absorbing chains and 2 (Arnsberg and Unter-Franken) had both K.H.D. and OTH. as transient states. If the West German truck purchasing system ever reached its final steady-state monopoly of Daimler-Benz, the polystable nature of spatial competition would collapse as each subsystem took on identical monopoly steady states. Such an outcome would be subject to the processes of competition remaining constant over time. While there were grounds for considering the total truck registration system as stationary in the period 1958 to 1970, it in no way implies stationarity after that date. In fact the acquisition of K.H.D. by Fiat in 1974 makes the predicted monopoly on Daimler-Benz a most unlikely event. Thus it is highly probable that the polystable system will remain as a long-term feature of the German market.

THE SPATIAL STATIONARITY OF THE NATIONAL PURCHASING SYSTEM

The justification for the analytical division of the national market into market areas assumes that the national purchasing process cannot satisfactorily predict the inter-brand movement of buyers at the district level because of the spatial diversity of the purchasing process. The testing of the similarity of purchasing processes over space is analogous to the testing of the stationarity (constancy) of a process over time. Hence, the spatial similarity of processes can be regarded as representing spatial stationarity. The test used to decide whether the district matrices are significantly similar or different from the national matrix is a modification of the Lee et al. (1970, p. 51) chi-square test of the hypothesis of

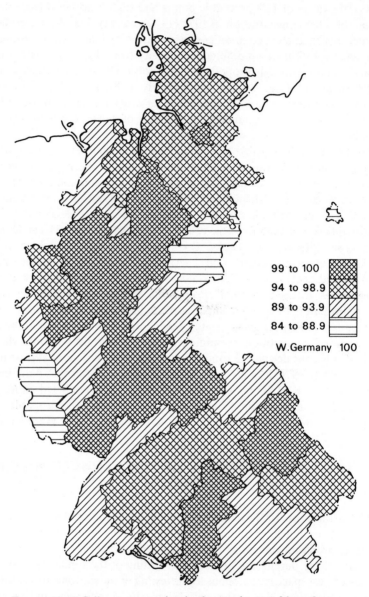

FIGURE 11.11 Seller concentration in the steady-state [three-firm
concentration ratio]

stationarity. When their summation over T periods is replaced by that over D districts, the statistic is given as

$$\chi^2 r(r-1)D = \sum_D \sum_i \sum_j n_{id(T-1)}(p_{ij(d)} - p_{ij})^2 / p_{ij} \qquad (11.10)$$

where $p_{ij(d)}$ is the generalized least-squares probability estimate for district d, $d = 1, \ldots, D$; $n_{id(T-1)}$ is the estimated number of truck operators of brand in district d at time $T-1$; the estimation period being of length T, $t = 1, \ldots, T$; the p_{ij} are the elements of the national $\mathbf{P}$ matrix having r brand states (zero values are switched with the corresponding $p_{ij(d)}$ so as to give determinate solutions); and n_{id} is the estimated number of truck operators of brand i in district d in 1969. With $D = 35$, each district matrix is compared with that for West Germany and the 35 χ^2 values are summed to give the stationarity statistic. In computing this statistic each row (brand) of the district and national matrices can be compared separately. This follows a procedure used by Goodman (1962) to study the spatial stationarity of each of the separate brands. The merit of this disaggregated study of the brands is that whenever the χ^2 value for the matrices exceeds the tabled value, it permits the main brand source of heterogeneity to be identified. In this case the statistic is distributed with $(r-1)D$ degrees of freedom.

The inability of the 1958–70 West German matrix to estimate satisfactorily the inter-brand transitional movements of truck operators for all the districts is shown in Table 11.8. The chi-square value for the 35 matrices at 3670.16 is over 7 times greater than the tabled value at the 0.1 per cent significance level. Thus on the basis of sampling theory, the hypothesis of the national competitive system having been stationary over space is rejected.

When the corresponding rows of the national and each district's matrices were

TABLE 11.8 The chi-square values for the test of goodness of fit of the West German $\mathbf{P}$ matrix and individual brand-states to the $\mathbf{P}$ matrices and individual brand-states for the registration districts: 1958–70

Sets of matrices and brand states	No. of regions/ registration districts	Sum of χ^2 values[a]	Degrees of freedom	Tabled values:[b] $\chi^2_{0.001}$
Daimler-Benz	35	618.32	105	153.95
K.H.D.	35	741.61	105	153.95
MAN	35	2006.96	105	153.95
OTH.	35	303.27	105	153.95
Matrix total (4 brands)	35	3670.16	420	513.78
OTH.[c]	33	132.07	99	146.64

[a] Each brand is weighted by the estimated number of truck operators in that brand state in 1969.
[b] Calculated by normal approximation $= \frac{1}{2}(Z + \sqrt{2n-1})^2$.
[c] Koblenz ($\chi^2 = 107.79$) and the Saarland ($\chi^2 = 63.4$) are excluded.

compared for goodness of fit, the MAN brand, by contributing nearly 55 per cent of the matrix total χ^2 sum, was found to be the main source of spatial heterogeneity. However, all 4 brands failed their respective spatial stationarity tests, although in the case of OTH. this was only because of the high χ^2 values for Koblenz and the Saarland. When they were excluded the OTH. brand was spatially stationary at the 1 per cent level. The relatively low spatial heterogeneity of the OTH. brand is only to be expected, given its characteristic as a miscellaneous brand state. The aggregating of the minor brands would inevitably smooth out their relatively high individual spatial variation. The lack of stationarity in the case of Daimler-Benz is a little surprising, especially in the light of the low spatial variance of its buyer loyalty and the absorbing and near-absorbing properties (where $p_{11} \geq 0.99$) of 9 of the district matrices. However, despite having approximately 55 per cent of the national market, it only contributed 16.8 per cent of the matrix total χ^2 sum, which was a lower proportion than that arising from the other two leading brands. An inventory of the 7 districts for which the national matrix was a statistically acceptable surrogate is summarized by levels of significance in Figure 11.12. Even so, when the 5 districts having individual brand vectors significantly similar to the national estimates—though failing the overall matrix test—are included, the resultant 12 districts accounted for 33.8 per cent of total truck registrations in 1971. As might be expected 6 of the districts in Figure 11.12 had matrices which were absorbing or virtually absorbing on Daimler-Benz.

THE CHI-SQUARE CLASSIFICATION OF MARKET AREAS

The final task is to examine the spatial distribution of the 35 district matrices to see whether they fall into any form of areal grouping, each group containing matrices having a contiguous matching of truck purchasing behaviour. The resultant groups of matrices would be defined as market areas. If the matrices show little spatial association with those of neighbouring districts, the market areas could be as numerous as the districts and therefore subject to highly localized types of buyer behaviour. On the other hand, any marked propensity for regionalized groupings will justify the original delimitation of the market as being one that is orientated to a regional transport function. In the latter case, each market area behavioural type would have been subjected to its own set of regional (multi-district) characteristics of industry, trade and conditions of transport. Unfortunately, the form of the data permits only 35 spatial observations on rather large areal tracts. The delimitation of market areas must be based on finding significant discontinuities in both the values of the probabilities and the structure of the movements of buyers between brands in the matrices of the 35 registration districts. Thus the delimitation exercise is constrained to follow the boundaries of the registration districts. As a result, the mapped transition from one competitive process to another will inevitably be

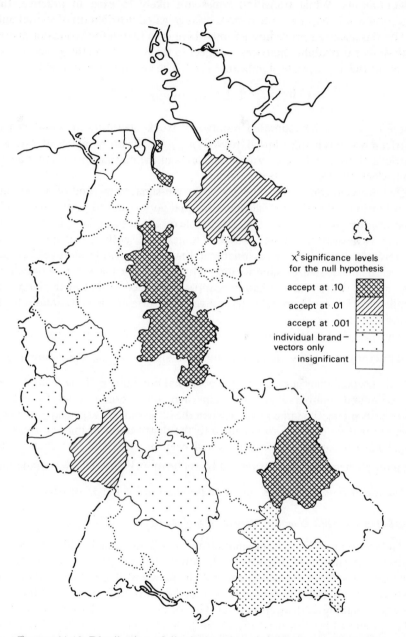

FIGURE 11.12 Distribution of district matrices significantly similar to the national system

discontinuous. While transition zones are likely to exist in practice, their detection would require a much more disaggregated distribution of spatial units.

The classification procedure adopted here is to search for groups of districts with similar probability matrices—subject to them satisfying the χ^2 goodness of fit test at the appropriate significance level. The chi-square test used is given as

$$\chi^2 r(r-1) = \sum_i \sum_j n_{id(T-1)}(p_{ij(d)} - p_{ij})^2 / p_{ij} \qquad (11.11)$$

where $n_{id(T-1)}$ is the estimated number of truck operators in brand i in the district d which is being allotted in 1969; $p_{ij(d)}$ are the probabilities of that same district's matrix, and the p_{ij} are the elements of the matrix for the other district with which the former is being paired.

One problem confronting the use of the chi-squared method of market area classification is that the districts have unequal population sizes, N_d. In the initial classification, matrix similarity is acceptable on the basis of the n_i for the smaller of the two districts being paired. Though not entirely satisfactory, this compromise appears to be reasonable in that if both district matrices had been derived from equal-sized samples drawn from the same market-area population (the smaller district having had its sample size raised to that of the larger) the smaller district would probably have given more acceptable p_{ij} estimates for the larger one.

One way of moderating the effect of unequal populations, or sample sizes, is to weight every pairing by an equal population size, $N = \sum_i n_i$, while retaining the actual observed differences in the proportional breakdown of the N into the n_{id}; the estimated number of operators in each initial brand state. Though not necessarily giving the same χ^2 value when the observed and expected districts are reversed it does provide an insight into the distribution of market areas that might have occurred if the districts had been of equal size. A variant of this weighting scheme was used in a second classification. Every $\sum_i n_{id}$ was made equal to the mean estimated truck operator population for the 35 districts.

Market Areas with Unequal District Populations

The grouping of districts into market areas, with the actual N differing between districts, is shown in Figure 11.13. After applying the $\chi^2_{0.001}$ probability criterion, 25 of the districts were successfully paired with one or more of the other districts. Nord- and Süd-Baden were added even though they failed the $\chi^2_{0.001}$ criterion, making 27 districts in total. The former had χ^2 values of 34.5 and 34.7 when predicted by Arnsberg and Darmstadt, respectively—only just exceeding the tabled value of 32.9. Süd-Baden had a χ^2 value of 33.3 when paired with Ober-Franken. These pairings were classified into 8 multi-district market areas. The largest grouping, signified by 1, contains 12 districts divided into 3 separate

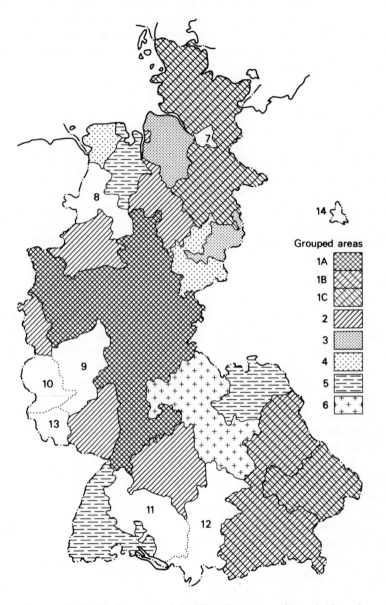

FIGURE 11.13 Market areas of the West German medium-sized truck
industry: chi-squared classification

areal blocs. The central bloc, 1A, forms the largest market area; its 7 contiguous districts accounting for 34.2 per cent of total national truck registration in 1969. Nieder-Bayern has been included in 1C owing to its significant similarity with Schleswig-Holstein. Its total lack of significance when paired with Ober-Bayern or Ober-Pfalz excluded it from 1B. To some extent Schleswig-Holstein and Nieder-Bayern can be regarded as having been members of a special subset of the 12 districts in 1. Market area 2 incorporates 6 districts totalling 18.4 per cent of national truck registrations in 1969. It takes the form of a discontinuous belt surrounding 1A, with only Bremen and Hannover being contiguous. Three of the remaining 4 groupings cover peripherally located districts which lack contiguity. The exception was the Unter-Franken and Mittel-Franken pairing. The 8 districts which could not be grouped must have been subject to the dominating influence of local competitive conditions. Certainly both the Saarland and West Berlin were very much influenced by special economic and political forces. The 16 resulting market areas (8 grouped, 8 unpaired) are based on 14 distinct truck purchasing processes. Such a large number does point to the considerable influence exerted by local forces upon the truck purchasing decision.

Market Areas with Equal District Populations

When the mean district truck operator population $\sum N_d/D$ was used in weighting the probability pairings, the number of significantly paired districts dropped from 25 to 19 which showed exactly the same distribution as in Figure 11.13. The weakness of this weighting scheme is that it penalizes those paired districts whose estimated populations were both below the mean for all districts. It is possible that more of these pairings would have been significant if the p_{ij}s had been estimated from samples as large as the all-district mean (2.86 per cent of the national market). Thus by incorporating this possibility as an assumption, the classification criterion has been relaxed to include those pairings which were significantly similar only when given their actual estimated operator populations, subject to both populations being below the all-district mean.

The result of this modification is to increase the number of significantly paired districts back to 25 because market areas 3, 4, and 6 are returned to the classification. The only remaining alteration from Figure 11.9 is the exclusion of both Süd-Baden and Nieder-Bayern. However, the latter may be reincluded in 1C on the grounds that its pairings with Schleswig-Holstein gave a χ^2 value of 34.9 which only just exceeded the tabled $\chi^2_{0.001}$ value of 32.9. This alternative approach to weighting has served only to reinforce the market-area classification of Figure 11.13. Consequently, the chi-square criterion appears to be relatively insensitive to the alternative weighting schemes.

The chi-square method has performed reasonably well as a market-area classification procedure, the one weakness being its inability to determine an optimal grouping (Spence and Taylor, 1969). It leaves both the allocation of districts—to the appropriate market area—and the selection of the level of statistical significance to largely subjective criteria. Given the difficulties in estimating the brand operator populations which are used as weights in the chi-square classifications, it appeared advisable to attempt an alternative form of classification which would simply group the matrix probabilities rather than the movement of operators between brands.

THE HIERARCHICAL GROUPING OF MARKET AREAS

The Ward (1963) hierarchical grouping technique, unlike the chi-square method does not weight the matrices and their initial brand states. The technique is based on the Pythagoras sum of squares equation generalized to measure distances between points in an 'n'-dimensional space. The programme used for the computations was developed by Baker (1974). The matrices are treated as observations on 16 variables (the p_{ij}s). To examine the degree of correspondence between the hierarchical grouping classification of the matrices and that derived from the chi-square tests, the grouping of the 26 most closely associated district matrices was extracted. The resulting classification into 8 multi-district market areas is shown in Figure 11.14. The market area groupings of the 26 districts closely match those given in Figure 11.13 but Aurich and Hildesheim are no longer paired, Süd-Württemberg Hohenzollern is now included to form a new market area with neighbouring Süd-Württemberg. (for this latter grouping to have been permissible under the $\chi^2_{0.001}$ probability level each operator would have been required to run at least 26 trucks rather than the 8 assumed), and Lüneburg is detached from Schleswig-Holstein.

The Ward classification was checked by Demirmen's (1969) discriminant iteration analysis computer programme and found to be optimal. The F test on the average matrices for the multi-district market areas yielded a value of 7.23 which was significant at $F_{0.001}$. Consequently, the internal variations in the transitional probabilities of the market areas are significantly lower than the inter-market-area variations. The evidence appears to verify the hypothesis outlined above of the market areas taking the form of several spatial subsystems of the one national market system. Indeed, the low-to-moderate differences between the mean p_{ij} values of the market areas points towards the existence of an important measure of subsystem interconnectedness in both communications and economic variables.

The truck purchasing subsystems which are classified into the grouped market areas of Figure 11.14 can now be examined in more detail. The average matrices for the 8 grouped market areas are presented in Table 11.9. The largest purchasing subsystem in terms of market coverage operated in the market areas 1A and 1B (classified separately in Figure 11.10 owing to their distance separation). These two market areas included nearly 43 per cent of the trucks registered in 1969. The competitive process is characterized by very large buyer

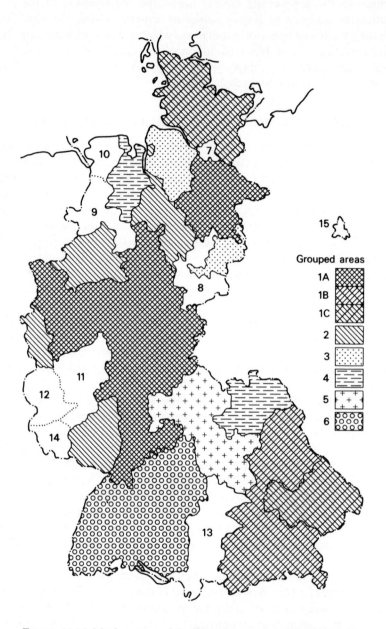

FIGURE 11.14 Market areas of the West German medium-sized truck
industry: grouping of 26 districts

TABLE 11.9 The average transition probability matrices for the multi-district market areas shown on Figure 11.4 generalised least-squares estimates: 1958–70

Market areas

Market areas		D-B	K.H.D.	MAN	OTH.		D-B	K.H.D.	MAN	OTH.
1A + 1B	D-B	0.98	0.01	0.005	0.005	4	0.92	0.01	0.07	0.0
	K.H.D.	0.03	0.86	0.09	0.02		0.01	0.85	0.04	0.10
	MAN	0.08	0.01	0.91	0.0		0.15	0.0	0.84	0.0
	OTH.	0.03	0.08	0.0	0.89		0.09	0.10	0.0	0.81
1C	D-B	0.93	0.06	0.0	0.01	5	0.76	0.0	0.24	0.0
	K.H.D.	0.17	0.72	0.11	0.0		0.0	0.80	0.15	0.05
	MAN	0.03	0.04	0.93	0.0		0.41	0.04	0.55	0.0
	OTH.	0.04	0.08	0.0	0.88		0.0	0.12	0.0	0.88
2	D-B	0.99	0.0	0.0	0.01	6	0.97	0.03	0.0	0.0
	K.H.D.	0.05	0.72	0.21	0.02		0.02	0.70	0.17	0.11
	MAN	0.03	0.16	0.80	0.01		0.14	0.11	0.75	0.0
	OTH.	0.02	0.11	0.0	0.87		0.02	0.16	0.0	0.82
3	D-B	0.93	0.0	0.05	0.02	West German national system	1.0	0.0	0.0	0.0
	K.H.D.	0.30	0.50	0.20	0.0		0.0	0.82	0.14	0.04
	MAN	0.0	0.35	0.65	0.0		0.05	0.06	0.89	0.0
	OTH.	0.01	0.12	0.01	0.86		0.02	0.10	0.0	0.88

loyalties on all brands, with Daimler-Benz in particular having been only two percentile points removed from becoming as absorbing state. The behaviour of the truck operators was similar to that of the national system; the chief difference being the estimation of a lower level of competition between MAN and K.H.D. The market area 1C, though classified separately, was really a special case of 1A + 1B, the main difference being the greater interchanges between the customers of K.H.D. and MAN and K.H.D. and Daimler-Benz in the case of 1C.

The purchasing process characterizing market area 2 affected nearly 12 per cent of 1969 national truck registrations. With 3 (Hannover, Münster and Rhein-Hessen) of the 5 districts having had absorbing chains it is not surprising to see that the average Markov chain was nearly absorbing ($p_{ii} = 0.994$). Even so, it was further removed from the national system than 1A + 1B or 1C because of the lower buyer loyalties predicted for K.H.D. and MAN, as a result of the very intense competition between them.

Market area 6 contained just over 13 per cent of 1969 national truck registrations and formed a contiguous zone around Daimler-Benz's production plant at Gaggenau; as might be expected, it again had a very high p_{ii} for Daimler-Benz. Market area 3, comprising Stade and Braunschweig, was principally characterized by the extremely intense competition between MAN and K.H.D. with the latter brand losing to Daimler-Benz. Market area 4 seemed to operate as a slightly more competitive version of 1A + 1B.

Market area 5 takes on a special significance as a zone of transition between 1A + 1B and 6. In this manner it formed a wedge between the zones of influence of Daimler-Benz in the west and MAN in the southeast. In both 5 and in Schwaben, these two brands were locked in intense competition which resulted in a major fall in their levels of buyer loyalty. This is the only multi-district market area where Daimler-Benz appeared to be under pressure from a competitor. The 9 remaining unpaired districts, market areas 7–15, have been excluded from this analysis owing to their relative dissimilarity both with the foregoing classified areas and with each other.

The Spatial Implications of a Marketing Strategy

The main lesson of this study is that a market strategy incorporating product differentiation can have considerable spatial implications. The spatial variation in truck purchasing preferences as indicated by the spatial variation in purchasing probabilities demands that manufacturers recognize the spatial dimension in their planning of product development, sales outlets, and after-sales service. The success of Daimler-Benz in developing the widest range of relatively superior trucks can be attributed to the synthesis it achieved in the spatial and the non-spatial dimensions of its market strategy. No doubt its establishment of an intensive network of strategically located factory branches and dealerships provided a direct channel for receiving valuable ante-production and post-transaction information on the spatially diverse truck needs of buyers. Although the other firms had sales and repair outlets, they seemed to have been unable to realize their potential effectively. Daimler-Benz alone managed systematically to reduce its spatial inequality of performance throughout the 1958 to 1971 period. This indicates the use of its factory branches as a means of shaping competition dynamically in its favour.

CONCLUSIONS

This investigation into the possibility of spatially segmenting national markets into market areas on the basis of variations in the pattern and intensity of competition has achieved a breakthrough in the analysis of market areas within product-differentiated industries. It is now possible for overlapping sales territories to be subdivided into as many market areas as there are distinctly different competitive processes. Each market area can consist of several districts or regions so long as their purchasing probabilities are significantly similar.

The application of this approach to the West German medium-sized truck industry between 1958 and 1971 has confirmed the principal hypothesis of several significantly different market areas existing within this product-differeniated market. The number of market areas delimited depended upon the criteria used for classification: the chi-square classification gave 16 market areas and the Ward hierarchical grouping gave 17. Although using different techniques, both these classifications gave matched pairings for nearly all those districts having similar purchasing processes.

The fact that most of the districts sharing similar truck purchasing processes were contiguous enabled the delimitation of regionalized market areas. Large areas of the West German truck market had a market regional orientation in buyer preference functions. Hence, buyers within the neighbouring districts of a market area in all likelihood shared a common set of purchasing considerations which led to a high level of behavioural contagion. Thus the market areas take on the form of subsystems of a national behavioural system, each differing by the degree to which its purchasing behaviour adapts to local and regional transport conditions.

The number and spatial distribution of the market areas delimited in this investigation do not lend themselves to any simple explanation. The spatial variation in the Markovian purchasing probabilities is the net result of the spatial interaction of a set of complex variables, including the location of production, the characteristics of the regional pattern of industry, trade, and transport, the strength of buyer–seller communications, and the effectiveness of the firms' product differentiation activities. Many of these variables are ill-defined and require further research before they can be adequately specified for use in quantitative analysis.

Although the competitive-process approach to the analysis of market areas in product-differentiated industries has proved satisfactory in the case of the West German medium-sized truck industry, it requires further examination for other markets of the same industry and for other product-differentiated industries. The author is currently extending the analysis to cover both the motor car and truck markets of 16 West European countries. It is also hoped that applications can be made in several consumer non-durable product groups where the products differ in: the form of product differentiation; purchasing period; buyer type; and circumstances of purchase. In this way it is hoped to test the generality of the proposition that the overlapping sales territories in product-differentiated markets are divisible into spatially segmented market areas.

Further research is required into the performance of alternative methods of estimating the competitive process, especially into those methods based on behavioural states (patterns of buyer behaviour in the form of brand purchasing probabilities or seller behaviour in the form of price and non-price competitive activities). The stationary first-order Markov process estimated from time-series market-share data, while applicable in the West German truck industry, is unlikely to be a suitable model when estimating brand purchasing probabilities over long time periods and where buyer preferences frequently change as a result of changes in fashion or technology. Experimentation should be undertaken not only with models of variable purchasing probabilities which are functions of certain variables such as price or advertising (Telser, 1963) but also with other estimators of buyer loyalty (Ehrenberg, 1972; Bass, 1974; Herniter, 1974).

Unlike the traditional concepts of the market area, as given by Fetter (1924), Lösch (1954), or Greenhut (1970), the competitive-process concept cannot be used to determine the optimum size and shape of the market area. However, it is not restricted to the delimitation of quasi-monopolist sales territories and can be used to segment the overlapping sales territories found in product-differentiated environments. By employing approaches such as those adopted here, researchers should be able to make good some of the present empirical under-development of market-area analysis. The build-up of a significant body of empirical research in this field may eventually lead to the development of a theory of oligopolistic spatial competition under the condition of product differentiation.

References

Ahnström, L., 1973, *Styrande och Ledande Verksamhet i Västeuropa: en Ekonomisk-Geografisk Studie* (Stockholm:Ekonomiska Forskningsinstitutet vid Handelshögskolan i Stockholm).

Albach, H., 1965, 'Zur Theorie des wachsenden Unternehmens', in W. Krelle (Ed.), *Theorien des Einzelwirtschaftlichen und des Gesamtwirtschaftlichen Wachstums* (Berlin: Duncker & Humblot), 9–97.

Alchian, A. A., 1950, 'Uncertainty, evolution, and economic theory', *The Journal of Political Economy*, **58**, 211–21.

Alonso, W., 1967, 'A reformulation of classical location theory and its relation to rent theory', *Regional Science Association Papers*, **19**, 23–44.

Anderson, T. W., 1954, 'Probability models for analyzing time changes in attitudes' in P. F. Lazarsfeld (Ed.), *Mathematical Thinking in the Social Sciences* (Glencoe, Ill.: The Free Press), 17–66.

Ansoff, H. I., 1957, 'Strategies for diversification', *Harvard Business Review*, **35**(5), 113–24.

Ansoff, H. I., 1965, *Corporate Strategy: An Analytic Approach to Business Policy for Growth and Expansion* (New York: McGraw-Hill).

Argyris, C., 1973a, 'Some limits of rational man organizational theory', *Public Administration Review*, **33**, 253–67.

Argyris, C., 1973b, 'Organization man: rational and self-actualizing', *Public Administration Review*, **33**, 354–7.

Armstrong, A. and Silberston, A., 1965, 'Size of plant, size of enterprise and concentration in British manufacturing industry, 1935–58', *Journal of the Royal Statistical Society*, **128A**, 395–420.

Ashby, W. R., 1960, *Design for a Brain: The Origin of Adaptive Behaviour* (New York:Wiley).

Atkins, D.H.W., 1973, 'Employment change in branch and parent manufacturing plants in the UK: 1966–71'. *Trade and Industry*, **12**, 437–9.

Auerbach, F., 1913, 'Das Gesetz der Bevölkerungskonzentration', *Petermann's Mitteilungen*, **59**, 74–6.

Back, R. *et al.*, 1974, *Industrial Location Patterns: A Multidimensional Analysis of Relationships Between Firms and Regions* (Stockholm: Ekonomiska Forskningsinstitutet vid Handelshögskolan i Stockholm).

Baker, L., 1974, *A Selection of Geographical Computer Programmes* (London School of Economics, Department of Geography, Geographical Papers No. 6).

Bandman, M. K., 1976, *Modelling of Territorial Production Complexes* (3 vols) (Novosibirsk:Institute of Economics and Organization of Industrial Production, U.S.S.R. Academy of Sciences—Siberian Branch).

Barber, C. L., 1971, *Report of the Royal Commission on Farm Machinery* (Ottawa: Information Canada).

Barlow, A. T., 1977, 'Industrial location and medium sized towns: plant entry and local labour market structure' (paper presented to the SSRC Urban and Regional Economics Study Group, University of Glasgow, December 1977).

Barr, B. M., 1974, 'The changing impact of industrial management and decision-making on the locational behaviour of the Soviet firm', in F. E. I. Hamilton (Ed.), *Spatial Perspectives on Industrial Organization and Decision-making* (London: Wiley), 411–46.

Barr, B. M. and Fairbairn, K. J., 1974, 'Some observations on the environment of the firm: locational behavior of kraft pulp mills in the interior of British Columbia', *The Professional Geographer*, **26**, 19–26.

Bass, F. M., 1974, 'The theory of stochastic preference and brand switching', *Journal of Marketing Research*, **11**, 1–20.

Bassett, K. and Haggett, P., 1971, 'Towards short-term forecasting for cyclic behaviour in a regional system of cities', in M. Chisholm, A. E. Frey, and P. Haggett (Eds.) *Regional Forecasting* (London: Butterworths), 389–413.

Bater, J. H. and Walker, D. B., 1970, 'Further comments on industrial location and linkage', *Area*, No. 4, 59–63.

Baumback, C. M. *et al.*, 1973, *How to Organize and Operate a Small Business* (Englewood Cliffs:Prentice-Hall).

Baumol, W. J., 1959, *Business Behavior, Value and Growth* (New York: Macmillan).

Baumol, W. J., 1962, 'On the theory of expansion of the firm', *The American Economic Review*, **52**, 1078–87.

Beard, T. R. and Scott, L. C., 1975, 'Revenue projections for Louisiana state government, fiscal years 1974–75—1979–80', *Louisiana Business Review*, **29** (February), 2–5, 11–14, 16.

Beaumont, P. B., 1977, 'Assessing the performance of assisted labour mobility policy in Britain', *Scottish Journal of Political Economy*, **24**, 55–65.

Beckmann, M. J., 1971, 'Market share, distance and potential', *Regional and Urban Economics*, **1**, 3–18.

Beckmann, M. J., 1972, 'Equilibrium versus optimum: spacing of firms, and patterns of market areas', in R. Funck (Ed.), *Recent Developments in Regional Science* (London: Pion), 50–62.

Berle, A. A. and Means, G. C., 1932, *The Modern Corporation and Private Property* (New York:Macmillan).

Bernasek, M. and Kubinski, Z. M., 1963, 'Agricultural machinery and implements', in A. Hunter (Ed.), *The Economics of Australian Industry: Studies in Environment and Structure* (Melbourne University Press), 460–93.

Berry, B. J. L., 1961, 'City size distributions and economic development', *Economic Development and Cultural Change*, **9**, 573–88.

Beyers, W. B. and Krumme, G., 1974, 'Multiple products, residuals and location theory', in F. E. I. Hamilton (Ed.), *Spatial Perspectives on Industrial Organization and Decision-making* (London:Wiley), 77–104.

Bobo, J. R. and Charlton, J. M., 1974, *Statistical Abstract of Louisiana* [5th edn.] (University of New Orleans, College of Business Administration).

Boddewyn, J. J., 1976–77, 'External affairs roles in U.S. multinationals operating in Western Europe', *International Studies of Management and Organization*, **6**, 185–203.

Boon, G. T., 1974, 'A household survey of unemployment in Ashington and Bedlington', *Regional Studies*, **8**, 175–84.

Bora, G., 1977, 'The stages of development in the industrial system of Budapest' (unpublished paper presented to the Conference of the IGU Commission on Industrial Systems, Krakow, Poland, August 1977).

Böventer, E. von, 1963a, 'Bemerkungen zur optimalen Standortspolitik der Einzelunternehmung', *Jahrbuch für Sozialwissenschaft*, **14**, 440–61.

Böventer, E. von, 1963b, 'Towards a united theory of spatial economic structure', *Regional Science Association Papers*, **10**, 163–87.

Bramhall, D. F., 1969, 'An introduction to spatial general equilibrium', in G. J. Karaska and D. F. Bramhall, *Locational Analysis for Manufacturing: A Selection of Readings* (Cambridge, Mass.: M.I.T. Press), 467–76.

Brash, D. T., 1966, *American Investment in Australian Industry* (Canberra: Australian National University Press).

Brechling, F., 1967, 'Trends and cycles in British regional unemployment', *Oxford Economic Papers*, **19** New Series, 1–21.

Brockhoff, K., 1966, *Unternehmenswachstum und Sortimentsänderungen* (Cologne: Westdeutscher Verlag).

Bronfenbrenner, M., 1956, 'Potential monopsony in labor markets', *Industrial and Labor Relations Review*, **9**, 577–88.

Bunting, R. L., 1962, *Employer Concentration in Local Labor Markets* (Chapel Hill: University of North Carolina Press).

Burford, R. L. and Hargrave, C. H., 1973, *An Input–Output Study of the Louisiana Economy* (Baton Rouge: Louisiana State University, College of Business Administration).

Business Statistics Office, 1975, *Business Monitor, 1972*, Analyses of United Kingdom manufacturing (local) units by employment size (London:HMSO).

Buzlyakov, N., 1973, *Welfare: The Basic Task* (Moscow: Progress Publishers).

Cameron, G. C. and Clark, B. D., 1966, *Industrial Movement and the Regional Problem* (University of Glasgow, Social and Economic Studies, Occasional Paper No. 5).

Central Statistical Office, 1970, *Input–Output Tables for the United Kingdom 1963*, Studies in Official Statistics No. 16 (London:HMSO).

Chamberlin, E. H., 1946, *The Theory of Monopolistic Competition: A Re-orientation of the Theory of Value* (Cambridge, Mass.: Harvard University Press).

Chandler, A. D., 1962, *Strategy and Structure: Chapters in the History of the Industrial Enterprise* (Cambridge, Mass.: M.I.T. Press).

Chapman, K., 1974, 'Corporate systems in the United Kingdom petrochemical industry', *Annals of the Associations of American Geographers*, **64**, 126–37.

Chisholm, M., 1967, 'General systems theory and geography', *Transactions of the Institute of British Geographers*, **42**, 45–52.

Chisholm, M., 1971, 'In search of a basis for location theory: micro-economics or welfare economics?', *Progress in Geography*, **3**, 111–33.

Cohen, M. D. *et al.*, 1972, 'A garbage can model of organizational choice', *Administrative Science Quarterly*, **17**, 1–25.

Collins, L., 1973, 'Industrial size distributions and stochastic processes', *Progress in Geography*, **5**, 119–65.

Collins, L. and Walker, D. F., 1975a, 'A perspective', in L. Collins and D. F. Walker (Eds.), *Locational Dynamics of Manufacturing Activity* (London:Wiley), 1–15.

Collins, L. and Walker, D. F. (Eds.) 1975b, *Locational Dynamics of Manufacturing Activity* (London:Wiley).

Collins, N. R. and Preston, L., 1960, 'Growth and turnover of food processing firms', *Proceedings of the Annual Meeting of the Western Farm Economics Association* (Stanford University Press), 297–314.

Committee of Inquiry on Small Firms, 1971, *Report* (London: HMSO).

Cox, K. R., 1973, *Conflict, Power and Politics in the City: A Geographic View* (New York: McGraw-Hill).

Cracco, E. and Van Campenhoudt, J. M., 1976–77, 'L' internationalisation des entreprises européenes: cas de la Belgique', *Annals de sciences économiques appliquées* (Louvain), **33**, 61–83.

Curwen, P. J., 1974, *Managerial Economics* (London: Macmillan).

Cyert, R. M. and March, J. G., 1963, *A Behavioral Theory of the Firm* (Englewood Cliffs: Prentice-Hall).

DAFSA, 1973, 'Voitures particulières en Europe' (Paris).

Dahmén, E., 1970, *Entrepreneurial Activity and the Development of Swedish Industry, 1919–1939* (Homewood, Ill.:Irwin).

Demirmen, F., 1969, *Multivariate Procedures and Fortran IV Program for Evaluation and Improvement of Classifications* (Stanford University, Geology Department).

Dent, J. K., 1959, 'Organizational correlates of the goals of business managements', *Personnel Psychology*, **12**, 365–93.

Desai, M., 1974, *Marxian Economic Theory* (London: Gray-Mills Publishing).

Devletoglou, N. E., 1965, 'A dissenting view of duopoly and spatial competition', *Economica*, **32** New Series, 140–60.

Dicken, P., 1971, 'Some aspects of the decision making behavior of business organizations', *Economic Geography*, **47**, 426–37.

Dill, W. R., 1958, 'Environment as an influence on managerial autonomy', *Administrative Science Quarterly*, **2**, 409–43.

Division of Administration, 1970–71 through 1975–76, 'Where the tax dollar came from', *Financial Statement, Fiscal Year* (Baton Rouge:State of Louisiana).

Dobb, M., 1940, 'The trend of modern economics', *Political Economy and Capitalism* (London:Routledge).

Dorward, N. M. M., 1975, 'An analysis of the market areas of the West German motor truck industry', unpublished Ph.D. dissertation (London School of Economics).

Dorward, N. M. M., 1977, 'Market structure and buyer loyalty: a case study of the West German truck market', *The Journal of Industrial Economics*, **26**, 115–35.

Downie, J. 1958, *The Competitive Process* (London: Duckworth).

Drewnowski, J., 1974, *On Measuring and Planning the Quality of Life* (The Hague: Mouton).

Edwards, R. S. and Townsend, H., 1961, *Business Enterprise: Its Growth and Organisation* (London:Macmillan).

Ehrenberg, A. S. C., 1972, *Repeat-Buying: Theory and Applications* (Amsterdam:North-Holland).

Emery, F. E. (Ed.), 1969, *Systems Thinking* (Harmondsworth:Penguin).

Executive Office of the President of the United States, 1977, *The Budget of the United States Government, 1978—Appendix* (Washington: Government Printing Office).

Fearn, R. M., 1975, 'Cyclical, seasonal, and structural factors in area unemployment rates', *Industrial and Labor Relations Review*, **28**, 424–31.

Feller, W., 1968, *An Introduction to Probability Theory and Its Applications*, Vol. 1 (New York:Wiley).

Fetter, F. A., 1924, 'The economic law of market areas', *The Quarterly Journal of Economics*, **38**, 520–9.

Fleming, D. K. and Krumme, G., 1968, 'The "Royal Hoesch union": case analysis of adjustment patterns in the European steel industry', *Tijdschrift voor Economische en Sociale Geografie*, **59**, 177–99.

Fredriksson, C. and Lindmark, L., 1976, *Nationella och Lokala Produktionssystem: En Strukturstudie av Svenskt Näringsliv* (University of Umeå, Department of Business Administration and Economics).

Friedman, M., 1953, 'The methodology of positive economics', in *Essays in Positive Economics* (University of Chicago Press), 3–43.

Friedmann, J., 1966, *Regional Development Policy: A Case Study of Venezuela* (Cambridge, Mass.: M.I.T. Press).

Galbraith, J. K., 1973, *Economics and the Public Purpose* (Boston: Houghton Mifflin).

Galbraith, J.K., 1974, *The New Industrial State* (Harmondsworth: Penguin).

Gannon, C. A., 1973, 'Optimization of market share in spatial competition', *Southern Economic Journal*, **40**, 66–79.

Goddard, J. B., 1968, 'Multivariate analysis of office location patterns in the city centre: a London example', *Regional Studies,* **2,** 69–85.

Goddard, J. B., 1971, 'Office communications and office location: a review of current research', *Regional Studies,* **5,** 263–80.

Goddard, J. B., 1978, 'The location of non-manufacturing activities within manufacturing industries', in F. E. I. Hamilton (Ed.), *Contemporary Industrialization: Spatial Analysis and Regional Development* (London:Longman), 62–85.

Gokhman, V. M., Gorkin, A. P., and Smirnyagin, L. V., 1976, 'Structural approach to economico-geographical systems study (in application to "manufacturing of the country" system)', in V. M. Gokhman *et al.* (Eds.), *International Geography '76: Economic Geography* (Moscow: 23rd International Geographical Congress), 29–33.

Goodman, J. F. B., 1970, 'The definition and analysis of local labour markets: some empirical problems', *British Journal of Industrial Relations,* **8,** 179–96.

Goodman, L. A., 1953, 'A further note on "Finite Markov Processes in Psychology"', *Psychometrika,* **18,** 245–8.

Goodman, L. A., 1962, 'Statistical methods for analyzing processes of change', *The American Journal of Sociology,* **68,** 57–78.

Gordon, R. A., 1945, *Business Leadership in the Large Corporation* (Washington:The Brooking Institute).

Gorkin, A. P., Gokhman, V. M., and Smirnyagin, L. V., 1976, 'Territorial'naya struktura promyshlennosti [The territorial structure of industry]', *Izvestiya Akademii Nauk SSSR Seriya Geograficheskaya,* No. 6, 107–14 (in Russian).

Gorkin, A. P., and Smirnyagin, L. V., 1973, 'O faktorakh i usloviyakh razmeschenniya kapitalisticheskoy promyshlennosti' [concerning the factors and conditions of the location of capitalist industry], *Izvestiya Akademii Nauk SSSR Seriya Geografiya,* **1,** 68–74.

Graaff, J. der, 1957, *Theoretical Welfare Economics* (Cambridge University Press).

Graham, B. *et al.,* 1962, *Security Analysis: Principles and Technique* (New York: McGraw-Hill).

Granberg, A. G., 1976, *Spatial National Economic Models* (Novosibirsk: Institute of Economics and Organization of Industrial Production, U.S.S.R. Academy of Sciences—Siberian Branch).

Greenhut, M. L., 1956, *Plant Location in Theory and in Practice: The Economics of Space* (Chapel Hill: University of North Carolina Press).

Greenhut, M. L., 1963, *Microeconomics and the Space Economy: The Effectiveness of an Oligopolistic Market Economy* (Chicago: Scott Foresman).

Greenhut, M. L., 1970, *The Theory of the Firm in Economic Space* (New York: Appleton-Century-Crofts).

Greig, M. A., 1971, 'The regional income and employment multiplier effects of a pulp mill and paper mill', *Scottish Journal of Political Economy,* **18,** 31–48.

Griliches, Z., 1960, 'The demand for a durable input: farm tractors in the United States, 1921–57', in A. C. Harberger (Ed.), *The Demand for Durable Goods* (University of Chicago Press), 181–207.

Gripaios, P., 1977, 'Industrial decline in London: an examination of its causes', *Urban Studies,* **14,** 181–9.

Groo, E. S., 1971, 'Choosing foreign locations: one company's experience', *Columbia Journal of World Business,* **6**(5), 71–8.

Gudgin, G., 1976, 'Establishment based data in studies of employment growth and location', in J. K. Swales (Ed.) *Establishment Based Research: Conference Proceedings* (University of Glasgow, Urban and Regional Studies Discussion Papers No. 22).

Gujarati, D., 1972, 'The behaviour of unemployment and unfilled vacancies: Great Britain, 1958–1971', *The Economic Journal,* **82,** 195–204.

Gullander, S., 1976, 'Joint ventures in Europe: determinants of entry', *International Studies of Management and Organization*, **6**, 85–111.

Gutenberg, E., 1961, *Grundlagen der Betriebswirtschaftslehre, 1. Band: Die Produktion* (Berlin: Springer-Verlag).

Haddad, P. R. and Schwartzman, J., 1974, 'A space cost curve of industrial location', *Economic Geography*, **50**, 141–3.

Haggett, P., 1965, *Locational Analysis in Human Geography* (London: Arnold).

Håkansson, H. and Wootz, B., 1975, *Företags inköpsbeteende* (Lund: Studentlitteratur).

Hall, P. *et al.*, 1973, *The Containment of Urban England* (London:Allen and Unwin).

Hamilton, F. E. I., 1967, 'Models of industrial location', in R. J. Chorley and P. Haggett (Eds.), *Models in Geography* (London: Methuen), 361–424.

Hamilton, F. E. I., 1974a, 'A view of spatial behaviour, industrial organizations and decision-making', in F. E. I. Hamilton (Ed.), *Spatial Perspectives on Industrial Organization and Decision-making* (London:Wiley) 3–43.

Hamilton, F. E. I., 1974b, 'Self-management: the Yugoslav case', in F. E. I. Hamilton (Ed.), *Spatial Perspectives on Industrial Organization and Decision-making* (London:Wiley), 449–59.

Hamilton, F. E. I. (Ed.), 1974c, *Spatial Perspectives on Industrial Organization and Decision-making* (London:Wiley).

Hamilton, F. E. I., 1978a, 'The changing milieu of spatial industrial research', in F. E. I. Hamilton (Ed.), *Contemporary Industrialization: Spatial Analysis and Regional Development* (London: Longman), 1–19.

Hamilton, F. E. I., 1978b, 'Aspects of industrial mobility in the British economy', *Regional Studies*, **12**, 153–65.

Hamilton, F. E. I., 1978c, 'Multinational enterprise and the E.E.C.', in F. E. I. Hamilton (Ed.), *Industrial Change: International Experience and Public Policy* (London: Longman), 24–41.

Harrop, K. J., 1973, *Nuisances and their Externality Fields* (University of Newcastle, Department of Geography, Seminar Paper No. 23).

Harvey, D., 1969, *Explanation in Geography* (London:Arnold).

Harvey, D., 1973, *Social Justice and the City* (London:Arnold).

Heady, E. O. and Tweeten, L. G., 1963, *Resource Demand and Structure of the Agricultural Industry* (Ames:Iowa State University Press).

Heal, D. W., 1974, 'Ownership, control and location decisions: the case of the British steel industry since 1945', in F. E. I. Hamilton (Ed.), *Spatial Perspectives on Industrial Organization and Decision-making* (London:Wiley), 265–84.

Hedberg, B. L. T. *et al.*, 1976, 'Camping on seesaws: prescriptions for a self-designing organization', *Administrative Science Quarterly*, **21**, 41–65.

Heflebower, R. B., 1967, 'The theory and effects of nonprice competition', in R. E. Kuenne (Ed.), *Monopolistic Competition Theory: Studies in Impact: Essays in Honor of Edward H. Chamberlin* (New York:Wiley), 177–201.

Herniter, J. D., 1974, 'A comparison of the entropy. model and the Hendry model', *Journal of Marketing Research*, **11**, 21–9.

Hildebrand, G. H. and Mace, A., 1950, 'The employment multiplier in an expanding industrial market: Los Angeles County, 1940–47, *The Review of Economics and Statistics*, **32**, 241–9.

Hill, R. W., 1973, *Marketing Technological Products to Industry* (Oxford:Pergamon Press).

Hirschman, A. O., 1958, *The Strategy of Economic Development* (New Haven: Yale University Press).

Hodges, M., 1974, *Multinational Corporations and National Government: A Case Study of the United Kingdom's Experience 1964–1970* (Farnborough: Saxon House).

Homs, J., 1918, *Agricultural Implements and Machinery in Australia and New Zealand*, Special Agents Series-No. 166, Bureau of Foreign and Domestic Commerce, Department of Commerce (Washington:Government Printing Office).

Hoover, E. M., 1937, *Location Theory and the Shoe and Leather Industries* (Cambridge, Mass.:Harvard University Press).

Hoover, E. M., 1948, *The Location of Economic Activity* (New York: McGraw-Hill).

Hoover, E. M., 1967, 'Some programmed models of industry location', *Land Economics*, **43**, 303–11.

Hörnell, E. *et al.*, 1973, *Export och Utlandsetableringar* (Stockholm: Almqvist & Wiksell).

Hotelling, H., 1929, 'Stability in competition', *The Economic Journal*, **39**, 41–57.

Hunt, E. K., 1972, 'Economic scholasticism and capitalist ideology', in E. K. Hunt and J. G. Schwarz (Eds.), *A Critique of Economic Theory* (Harmondsworth: Penguin), 186–93.

Hyson, C. D. and Hyson, W. P., 1950, 'The economic law of market areas', *The Quarterly Journal of Economics*, **64**, 319–27.

International Labour Office, 1961, *Services for Small-scale Industry* (Studies and Reports, New Series, No. 61) (Geneva: ILO).

Isard, W., 1956, *Location and Space Economy* (Cambridge, Mass.: M.I.T. Press).

Isard, W., 1960, *Methods of Regional Analysis: An Introduction to Regional Science* (Cambridge, Mass.: M.I.T. Press).

Isard, W. *et al.*, 1969, *General Theory: Social, Political, Economic, and Regional* (Cambridge, Mass.: M.I.T. Press).

Isard, W. *et al.*, 1972, *Ecologic-Economic Analysis for Regional Development: Some Initial Explorations with Particular Resource Use and Environmental Planning* (New York: The Free Press).

Jackman, R. A., 1975, 'The problem of externalities in a spatial economy', in E. L. Cripps (Ed.), *Regional Science—New Concepts and Old Problems* (London: Pion), 18–30.

Jacobs, J., 1969, *The Economy of Cities* (New York:Random House).

James, B. S. G., 1964, 'The incompatibility of industrial and trading cultures: a critical appraisal of the growth-point concept', *The Journal of Industrial Economics*, **13**, 90–4.

Jenner, R. A., 1966, 'An information version of pure competition', *The Economic Journal*, **76**, 786–805.

Jewkes, J. *et al.*, 1961, *The Sources of Invention* (London:Macmillan).

Johanson, J. and Wiederscheim-Paul, F., 1975, 'The internationalization of the firm—four Swedish cases', *Journal of Management Studies*, **12**, 305–22.

Kahn, H. R., 1964, *Repercussions of Redundancy* (London:Allen and Unwin).

Karaska, G. J. and Linge, G. J. R., 1979, 'Applicability of the model of the territorial production complex outside the USSR', *Proceedings of the Seventeenth European Regional Science Association* (in press).

Kaufmann, O., 1972, 'Strategies of expansion and organization developments in European and American firms', *Journal of Management Studies*, **9**, 82–96.

Keeble, D. E. and Hauser, D. P., 1971, 'Spatial analysis of manufacturing growth in outer south-east England 1960–1967: 1. hypotheses and variables', *Regional Studies*, **5**, 229–61.

Kennelly, R. A., 1954–5, 'The localization of the Mexican steel industry', *Revista Geografica*, **15**, 105–29; **16**, 199–213; **17**, 60–77.

Kenny, S., 1977, 'The measurement of sub-regional industrial specialization', *Area*, **9**, 220–3.

Keuning, H. J., 1960, 'Approaching economic geography from the point of view of the enterprise', *Tijdschrift voor Economische en Sociale Geografie*, **51**, 10–11.

Kibal'chich, O. A., 1977, 'Territorial'no-proizvodstvennye Kompleksy (Territorial-Production Complexes)', in: *Novye Territorial'nye Kompleksy SSSR*, (Moscow: Mysl), 7–44.

King, L. *et al.*, 1972, 'Cyclical fluctuations in unemployment levels in U.S. metropolitan areas', *Tijdschrift voor Economische en Sociale Geografie*, **63**, 345–52.

Kipnis, B. A., 1977, 'The impact of factory size on urban growth and development', *Economic Geography*, **53**, 295–302.

Koopmans, T. C. and Beckmann, M. J., 1957, 'Assignment problems and the location of economic activities', *Econometrica*, **25**, 53–76.

Kraftfahrt-Bundesamt, 1958–71, *Bestand an Kraftfahrzeugen und Kraftfahrzeuganhängern* (Flensburg: Murwik).

Krumme, G., 1969, 'Toward a geography of enterprise', *Economic Geography*, **45**, 30–40.

Krumme, G., 1970, 'The interregional corporation and the region: a case study of Siemens' growth characteristics and response patterns in Munich, West Germany', *Tijdschrift voor Economische en Sociale Geografie*, **61**, 318–33.

Kuhn, H. W. and Kuenne, R. E., 1962, 'An efficient algorithm for the numerical solution of the generalized Weber problem in spatial economics', *Journal of Regional Science*, **4**(2), 21–33.

Kuhn, T. S., 1962, *The Structure of Scientific Revolutions* (University of Chicago Press: International Encyclopedia of Unified Science, **2**(2)).

Lancaster, K. J., 1966, 'A new approach to consumer theory', *The Journal of Political Economy*, **74**, 132–57.

Lance, G. N. and Williams, W. T., 1966, 'Computer programs for hierarchical polythetic classification (similarity analyses)', *Computer Journal*, **9**, 60–4.

Lange, D., 1977, 'Journal projections for 1977. There's an upbeat to Journal's forecast of oil activity in 1977', *Oil and Gas Journal*, **75**(5), 105–21.

Law, D. 1964, 'Industrial movement and locational advantage', *The Manchester School of Economic and Social Studies*, **32**, 131–54.

Lawrence, P. R. and Lorsch, J. W., 1967, *Organization and Environment: Managing Differentiation and Integration* (Boston: Harvard University, Graduate School of Business Administration, Division of Research).

Lea, A. C., 1973, *Location-Allocation Systems: An Annotated Bibliography* (University of Toronto, Department of Geography, Discussion Paper No. 13).

Lee, T. C., *et al.*, 1965, 'On estimating the transition probabilities of a Markov process', *Journal of Farm Economics*, **47**, 742–62.

Lee, T. C. *et al.*, 1970, *Estimating the Parameters of the Markov Probability Model from Aggregate Time Series Data* (Amsterdam:North-Holland).

Leigh, R. and North, D., 1978, 'Acquisitions in British industries: implications for regional development', in F. E. I. Hamilton (Ed.), *Contemporary Industralization: Spatial Analysis and Regional Development* (London: Longman), 158–81.

Lerner, A. P. and Singer, H. W., 1937, 'Some notes on duopoly and spatial competition', *The Journal of Political Economy*, **45**, 145–86.

Lever, W. F., 1972, 'Industrial movement, spatial association and functional linkages', *Regional Studies*, **6**, 371–84.

Lever, W. F., 1974, 'Changes in local income multpliers over time', *Journal of Economic Studies*, **1** New Series, 98–112.

Lever, W. F., 1975, 'Mobile industry and levels of integration in subregional economic structures', *Regional Studies*, **9**, 265–78.

Lewis, W. A., 1945, 'Competition in retail trade', *Economica*, **12** New Series, 202–34.

Lichfield, N., 1971, 'Cost-benefit analysis in planning: a critique of the Roskill Commission', *Regional Studies*, **5**, 157–83.

Linge, G. J. R., 1978a, 'Relocation of employment', in P. Scott (Ed.), *Australian Cities and Public Policy* (Melbourne:Georgian House), 59–71.

Linge, G. J. R., 1978b, 'The Australian environment and industrial location analysis', in F. E. I. Hamilton (Ed.), *Industrial Change: International Experience and Public Policy* (London:Longman), 144–54.

Lipstein, B., 1961 'Tests for test marketing', *Harvard Business Review,* **39**(2), 74–7.

Lloyd, P. E. and Dicken, P., 1972, *Location in Space: A Theoretical Approach to Economic Geography* (New York:Harper & Row).

Lloyd, P. E. and Mason, C. M., 1976, 'Establishment based data for the study of intraurban and subregional industrial change: the Manchester study', in J. K. Swales (Ed.) *Establishment Based Research: Conference Proceedings* (University of Glasgow, Urban and Regional Studies Discussion Papers No. 22).

Loasby, B. J., 1971, 'Hypothesis and paradigm in the theory of the firm', *The Economic Journal,* **81**, 863–85.

Lojkine, J., 1976, 'Contribution to a Marxist theory of capitalist urbanization', in C. G. Pickvance (Ed.), *Urban Sociology: Critical Essays* (London: Tavistock), 119–46.

Lösch, A., 1954, *The Economics of Location,* translated by W. H. Woglom assisted by W. F. Stolper (New Haven:Yale University Press).

Lovell, M., 1970, 'Product differentiation and market structure', *Western Economic Journal,* **8**, 120–43.

Luttrell, W. F., 1962, *Factory Location and Industrial Movement: A Study of Recent Experience in Great Britain,* Vol. 1 (London:National Institute of Economic and Social Research).

McCrone, G., 1969, *Regional Policy in Britain* (London:Allen and Unwin).

McDermott, P. J., 1973, 'Spatial margins and industrial location in New Zealand', *New Zealand Geographer,* **29**, 64–74.

McGuire, J. W. *et al.,* 1962, 'Executive incomes, sales and profits', *The American Economic Review,* **52**, 753–61.

Mackay, D. I. *et al.,* 1971, *Labour Markets under Different Employment Conditions* (London:Allen and Unwin).

McLean, I. W., 1973a, 'Growth and technological change in agriculture: Victoria 1870–1910', *The Economic Record,* **49**, 560–74.

McLean, I. W., 1973b, 'The adoption of harvest machinery in Victoria in the late nineteenth century', *Australian Economic History Review,* **13**, 41–56.

McNee, R. B., 1958, 'Functional geography of the firm, with an illustrative case study from the petroleum industry', *Economic Geography,* **34**, 321–37.

McNee, R. B., 1960, 'Toward a more humanistic economic geography: the geography of enterprise', *Tijdschrift voor Economische en Sociale Geografie,* **51**, 201–6.

McNee, R. B., 1961, 'Centrifugal-centripetal forces in international petroleum company regions', *Annals of the Association of American Geographers,* **51**, 124–38.

McNee, R. B., 1964, 'The economic geography of an international petroleum firm', in R. S. Thoman and D. J. Patton (Eds.), *Focus on Geographic Activity: A Collection of Original Studies* (New York:McGraw-Hill), 98–107.

McNee, R. B., 1972, 'An inquiry into the goal or goals of the enterprise: a case study', *The Professional Geographer,* **24**, 203–9.

McNee, R. B., 1974, 'A systems approach to understanding the geographic behaviour of organizations, especially large corporations', in F. E. I. Hamilton (Ed.), *Spatial Perspectives on Industrial Organization and Decision-making* (London:Wiley), 47–75.

Madansky, A., 1959, 'Least squares estimation in finite Markov processes', *Psychometrika,* **24**, 137–44.

March, J. G., 1971, 'The technology of foolishness' [mimeo] (Stanford University, Graduate School of Education).

Marris, R., 1964, *The Economic Theory of 'Managerial' Capitalism* (London: Macmillan).

Marx, K. and Engels, F., 1961, *Sochetaniya (Collected Works)*, [2nd edn.], 18 (Moscow: Gospolitizdat).

Mason, E. S., 1939, 'Price and production policies of large-salce enterprise', *The American Economic Review*, **29** (Supplement), 61–74.

Massey, D., 1974, *Towards a Critique of Industrial Location Theory* (London: Centre for Environmental Studies).

Massey, D. B., forthcoming, *Industrial Location and the Economy* (London:Macmillan).

Massey, D. B. and Meegan, R. A., 1978, *Industrial Location Project: Final Report* (London: Centre for Environmental Studies).

Meyer, H. E., 1977, 'This communist internationale has a capitalist accent', *Fortune*, February, 134–48.

Miller, G. A., 1952, 'Finite Markov processes in psychology', *Psychometrika*, **17**, 149–67.

Mills, E. S., 1970, 'The efficiency of spatial competition', *Regional Science Association Papers*, **25**, 71–82.

Mills, E. S. and Lav, M. R., 1964, 'A model of market areas with free entry', *The Journal of Political Economy*, **72**, 278–88.

Mishan, E. J., 1967, *The Costs of Economic Growth* (London: Staples Press).

Morrison, D. G. *et al.*, 1971, 'The effect of nonhomogeneous populations on Markov steady-state probabilities', *Journal of the American Statistical Association*, **66**, 268–74.

Moseley, M. J., 1973, 'The impact of growth centres in rural regions—II: an analysis of spatial 'flows' in East Anglia', *Regional Studies*, **7**, 77–94.

Moses, L. N., 1958, 'Location and the theory of production', *The Quarterly Journal of Economics*, **72**, 259–72.

Murata, K., 1978, 'The limits of regional agglomeration and social cost', in F. E. I. Hamilton (Ed.), *Contemporary Industrialization: Spatial Analysis and Regional Development* (London: Longman), 37–44.

Myrdal, G., 1957, *Economic Theory and Under-developed Regions* (London: Duckworth).

Myrdal, G., 1973, *Against The Stream: Critical Essays on Economics* (New York: Pantheon).

NATO, 1976, *East–West Technological Co-operation* (Brussels:NATO Directorate of Economic Affairs).

Needham, D., 1970, *Economic Analysis and Industrial Structure* (London: Holt, Rinehart, and Winston).

Nekrasov, N., 1974, *The Territorial Organisation of Soviet Economy* (Moscow:Progress Publishers).

Nordhaus, W. and Tobin, J., 1972, 'Is growth obsolete?', *Economic Growth* (New York: National Bureau of Economic Research; Columbia University Press).

North, D. C., 1955, 'Location theory and regional economic growth', *The Journal of Political Economy*, **63**, 243–58.

North, D. C., 1959, 'Agriculture in regional economic growth', *Journal of Farm Economics*, **41**, 943–51.

North, D. J., 1973, *The Process of Locational Change in Different Manufacturing Organisations* (University College London, Department of Geography, Occasional Paper No. 23).

North, D. J., 1974, 'The process of locational change in different manufacturing organizations', in F. E. I. Hamilton (Ed.), *Spatial Perspectives on Industrial Organization and Decision-making* (London:Wiley), 213–44.

Pahl, R. E., 1977, ' "Collective consumption" and the state in capitalist and state socialist societies', in R. Scase (Ed.), *Industrial Society: Class, Cleavage and Control* (London: Allen and Unwin), 153–71.

Palander, T., 1935, *Beitrage zur Standortstheorie* (Uppsala: Almqvist & Wiksell).

Palda, K. S., 1964, *The Measurement of Cumulative Advertising Effects* (Englewood Cliffs:Prentice-Hall).

Parry, T. G., 1974, 'Technology and the size of the multinational-corporation subsidiary: evidence from the Australian manufacturing sector', *The Journal of Industrial Economics*, **23**, 125–34.

Parsons, G. F., 1972, 'The giant manufacturing corporations and balanced regional growth in Britain', *Area*, **4**, 99–103.

Patton, A., 1961, *Men, Money and Motivation; Executive Compensation as an Instrument of Leadership* (New York:McGraw-Hill).

Peles, Y., 1971, 'Rates of amortization of advertising expenditures', *The Journal of Political Economy*, **79**, 1032–58.

Penrose, E. T., 1959, *The Theory of the Growth of the Firm* (Oxford: Blackwell).

Perlmutter, H. V., 1971–72, 'Towards research on the development of nations, unions, and firms as worldwide institutions', *International Studies of Management and Organization*, **1**, 419–49.

Perroux, F. 1950, 'The domination effect and modern economic theory', *Social Research*, **17**, 188–206.

Perroux, F., 1955, 'Note sur la notion de "pôle de croissance"', *Matériaux pour une analyse de la croissance économique*, (Cahiers de l' Institut de Science Economique Appliquée, Série D, No. 8).

Pollard, S., 1965, *The Genesis of Modern Management: A Study of the Industrial Revolution in Great Britain* (London:Arnold).

Pred, A., 1967, *Behavior and Location: Foundations for a Geographic and Dynamic Location Theory Part I* (Lund Studies in Geography, Series B, No. 27).

Pred, A., 1969, *Behavior and Location: Foundations for a Geographic and Dynamic Location Theory Part II* (Lund Studies in Geography, Series B, No. 28).

Pred, A. R., 1973, 'The growth and development of systems of cities in advanced economies', in A. R. Pred and G. E. Törnqvist, *Systems of Cities and Information Flows: Two Essays* (Lund Studies in Geography, Series B, No. 38).

Pred, A. R., 1976, 'The interurban transmission of growth in advanced economies: empirical findings versus regional-planning assumptions', *Regional Studies*, **10**, 151–71.

Pred, A. R., 1977, *City-Systems in Advanced Economies: Past Growth, Present Processes and Future Development Options* (London:Hutchinson).

Ramström, D., 1967, *The Efficiency of Control Strategies* (Stockholm:Almqvist & Wiksell).

Rasmussen, A., 1955, *Pristeori Eller Parameterteori: Studier Omkring Virksomhedens Afsaetning* (Copenhagen: Skrifter fra instituttet for salgsorganisation og reklame, No. 16).

Rawstron, E. M., 1958 'Three principles of industrial location', *The Institute of British Geographers Transactions and Papers*, No. 25, 135–42.

Ray, D. M., 1971, 'The location of United States manufacturing subsidiaries in Canada', *Economic Geography*, **47**, 389–400.

Rayner, A. J. and Cowling, K., 1967, 'Demand for a durable input: an analysis of the United Kingdom market for farm tractors', *The Review of Economics and Statistics*, **49**, 590–8.

Rayner, A. J. and Cowling, K., 1968, 'Demand for farm tractors in the United States and the United Kingdom', *American Journal of Agricultural Economics*, **50**, 896–912.

Rees, J., 1972, 'The industrial corporation and location decision analysis', *Area*, **4**, 199–205.

Rees, J., 1974, 'Decision-making, the growth of the firm and the business environment', in

F. E. I. Hamilton (Ed.), *Spatial Perspectives on Industrial Organization and Decision-making* (London: Wiley), 189–211.

Rees, J., 1978, 'Manufacturing change, internal control and government spending in a growth region of the U.S.A.', in F. E. I. Hamilton (Ed.), *Industrial Change: International Experience and Public Policy.* (London: Longman), 155–74.

Reiter, S. and Sherman, G. R., 1962, 'Allocating indivisible resources affording external economies or diseconomies', *International Economic Review*, **3**, 108–35.

Revenko, A. F., 1971 *Promyshlenniye statistiki S.Sh.A.* [*Industrial Statistics of the U.S.A.*] (Moscow: Statistika).

Richardson, H. W., 1969, *Regional Economics: Location Theory, Urban Structure and Regional Change* (London: Weidenfeld and Nicolson).

Richter, C. E., 1969, 'The impact of industrial linkages on geographic association', *Journal of Regional Science*, **9**, 19–28.

Rimmer, P. J., 1969, *Manufacturing in Melbourne* (Canberra: Australian National University, Department of Human Geography Publication HG/2).

Roberts, D. R., 1956, 'A general theory of executive compensation based on statistically tested propositions, *The Quarterly Journal of Economics*, **70**, 270–94.

Robinson, D., 1968, *Wage Drift, Fringe Benefits and Manpower Distribution* (Paris: OECD).

Rydén, B., 1971, *Fusioner i Svensk Industri: En Kartläggning och Orsaksanalys av Svenska Industriföretags fusionsverksamhet 1946–69* (Stockholm: Industriens Utrendningsinstitut).

Sadler, P. *et al.*, 1973, 'Regional income multipliers: the Anglesey Study' (Bangor, University College of North Wales, Occasional Paper in Economics No. 1).

Sales, A., 1972–73, 'The firm and the control of its environment', *International Studies of Management and Organization*, **2**, 230–57.

Salt, J., 1967, 'The impact of the Ford and Vauxhall plants on the employment situation of Merseyside, 1962–65', *Tijdschrift voor Economische en Sociale Geografie*, **58**, 245–58.

Samuelson, P. A., 1973, *Economics* [9th edn.] (New York: McGraw-Hill).

Sant, M. E. C., 1970, 'Age and area in industrial location; a study of manufacturing establishments in East Anglia', *Regional Studies*, **4**, 349–58.

Sant, M. E. C., 1973, *The Geography of Business Cycles: A Case Study of Economic Fluctuations in East Anglia, 1951–68* (London School of Economics, Department of Geography, Geographical Papers No. 5).

Sargant Florence, P., 1972, *The Logic of British and American Industry: A Realistic Analysis of Economic Structure and Government* (London: Routledge & Kegan Paul).

Saussy, G. A. *et al.*, 1976, *Final Report, The Fiscal Impact of Energy Resource Depletion on Louisiana* [a report to the Louisiana State Conservation Department] (University of New Orleans, College of Business Administration).

Sayles, L. R., and Chandler, M. K., 1971, *Managing Large Systems: Organizations for the Future* (New York: Harper & Row).

Scherer, F. M., 1970, *Industrial Market Structure and Economic Performance* (Skokie, Ill.: Rand McNally).

Schumpeter, J. A., 1934, *The Theory of Economic Development: An Inquiry into Profits, Capital, Credit, Interest, and the Business Cycle,* translated by R. Opie (Cambridge, Mass.: Harvard University Press).

Scott, R. M., and Austin, M. P., 1971, 'Numerical classification of land systems using geomorphological attributes', *Australian Geographical Studies*, **9**, 33–40.

Sheridan, K., 1974, *The Firm in Australia: A Theoretical and Empirical Study of Size, Growth and Profitability* (Melbourne: Nelson).

Simon, H. A., 1957, *Models of Man Social and Rational: Mathematical Essays on Rational Human Behavior in a Social Setting* (New York: Wiley).

Simon, H. A., 1959, 'Theories of decision-making in economics and behavioral science', *The American Economic Review*, **49**, 253–83.

Simon, H. A., 1973, 'Organization man: rational or self-actualizing?', *Public Administration Review*, **33**, 346–53.

Smart, M. W., 1974, 'Labour market areas: uses and definitions', *Progress in Planning*, **2**, 239–353.

Smith, D. M., 1966, 'A theoretical framework for geographical studies of industrial location', *Economic Geography*, **42**, 95–113.

Smith, D. M., 1970a, 'On throwing out Weber with the bathwater: a note on industrial location and linkage', *Area*, No. 1, 15–18.

Smith, D. M., 1970b, 'The location of the British hosiery industry since the middle of the nineteenth century', in R. H. Osborne *et al.* (Eds.), *Geographical Essays in Honour of K. C. Edwards* (University of Nottingham, Department of Geography), 71–9.

Smith, D. M., 1971, *Industrial Location: An Economic Geographical Analysis* (New York: Wiley).

Smith, D. M., 1974, 'Who gets what where, and how: a welfare focus for Human Geography', *Geography*, **59**, 289–97.

Smith, D. M., 1977, *Human Geography: A Welfare Approach* (London: Arnold).

Smith, D. M. and Lee, T. H., 1970, *A Programmed Model for Industrial Location Analysis* (Carbondale, South Illinois University, Department of Geography, Discussion Paper No. 1).

Smithies, A., 1941, 'Optimum location in spatial competition', *The Journal of Political Economy*, **49**, 423–39.

Spence, N. A. and Taylor, P. J., 1969, 'Quantitative methods in regional taxonomy' [paper presented at the International Geographical Union Commission on Quantitative Methods Conference, London School of Economics, August 1969].

Spooner, D. J., 1972, 'Industrial movement and the rural periphery: the case of Devon and Cornwall', *Regional Studies*, **6**, 197–215.

Staley, E. and Morse, R., 1965, *Modern Small Industry for Developing Countries* (New York: McGraw-Hill).

Starbuck, W. H., 1971, 'Organizational growth and development' in W. H. Starbuck (Ed.), *Organizational Growth and Development* (Harmondsworth: Penguin), 11–141.

Steed, G. P. F., 1968, 'The changing milieu of a firm: a case study of a shipbuilding concern', *Annals of the Association of American Geographers* **58**, 506–25.

Steed, G. P. F., 1971a, 'Internal organization, firm integration, and locational change: the Northern Ireland linen complex, 1954–64', *Economic Geography*, **47**, 371–83.

Steed, G. P. F., 1971b, 'Plant adaptation, firm environments and location analysis', *The Professional Geographer*, **23**, 324–8.

Steed, G. P. F., 1971c, 'Forms of corporate-environmental adaptation', *Tijdschrift voor Economische en Sociale Geografie*, **62**, 90–4.

Steed, G. P. F., 1971d, 'Locational implications of corporate organization of industry', *The Canadian Geographer*, **15**, 54–7.

Steed, G. P. F., 1974, 'The Northern Ireland linen complex, 1950–1970', *Annals of the Association of American Geographers*, **64**, 397–408.

Steindl, J., 1965, *Random Processes and the Growth of Firms: A Study of the Pareto Law* (London: Griffin).

Stevens, B. H., 1961, 'An application of game theory to a problem in location strategy', *The Regional Science Association Papers and Proceedings*, **7**, 143–58.

Stevenson, G. M., 1972, 'Noise and the urban environment', in T. R. Detwyler and

M. G. Marcus and Contributors, *Urbanization and Environment* (Belmont, Calif.: Duxbury Press), 195–228.

Stimson, R. J., 1970, 'Hierarchical classificatory methods: an application to Melbourne population data', *Australian Geographical Studies*, **8**, 149–72.

Stopford, J. M. and Haberich, K. O., 1976, 'Ownership and control of foreign operations', *Journal of General Management*, **3**, No. 4, 3–20.

Stubbs, P., 1972, *The Australian Motor Industry: A Study in Protection and Growth* (Melbourne: Cheshire).

Taylor, J., 1972, 'The behaviour of unemployment and unfilled vacancies: Great Britain, 1958–71. An alternative view', *The Economic Journal*, **82**, 1352–65.

Taylor, J., 1975, *Problems of Minimum Cost Location: The Kuhn and Kuenne Algorithm* (University of London, Queen Mary College, Department of Geography, Occasional Papers No. 4).

Taylor, M. J., 1970, 'The location decisions of small firms', *Area*, No. 2, 51–4.

Telser, L. G., 1963, 'Least-squares estimates of transition probabilities', in C. Christ *et al.*, *Measurement in Economics: Studies in Mathematical Economics and Econometrics in Memory of Yehuda Grunfeld* (Stanford University Press), 270–92.

Telser, L. G., 1964, 'Advertising and competition', *The Journal of Political Economy*, **72**, 537–62.

Terreberry, S., 1967–68, 'The evolution of organizational environments', *Administrative Science Quarterly*, **12**, 590–613.

Textile and Clothing Board, 1977, *Clothing Inquiry: A Report to the* [Canadian] *Minister of Industry, Trade and Commerce* (Ottawa).

The Economist Intelligence Unit Ltd, 1965, 'The structure of the West German vehicle components industry', *Motor Business*, No. 42, 1–10.

The Economist Intelligence Unit Ltd, 1970, 'Trends in the truck industries of the European Common Market', *Motor Business*, No. 63, 1–17.

Thomas, J. J., 1973, *An Introduction to Statistical Analysis for Economists* (London: Weidenfeld & Nicolson).

Thompson, G. E., 1959, 'An investigation of the local employment multiplier', *The Review of Economics and Statistics*, **41**, 61–7.

Thompson, J. D., 1967, *Organizations in Action: Social Sciences Bases of Administrative Theory* (New York: McGraw-Hill).

Thompson, J. D. and McEwen, W. J., 1958, 'Organizational goals and environment', *American Sociological Review*, **23**, 23–31.

Thompson, W. R., 1965, *A Preface to Urban Economies* (Baltimore: The Johns Hopkins Press).

Thorngren, B., 1970, 'How do contact systems affect regional development?', *Environment and Planning*, **2**, 409–27.

Thorngren, B., 1977, 'Telekommunikationer och samhällsstruktur' [mimeo] (Stockholm School of Economics, EFI).

Tiebout, C. M., 1957, 'Location theory, empirical evidence and economic evolution', *The Regional Science Association Papers and Proceedings*, **3**, 74–86.

Törnqvist, G. E., 1973, 'Contact requirements and travel facilities', in A. R. Pred and G. E. Törnqvist, *Systems of Cities and Information Flows: Two Essays* (Lund Studies in Geography, Series B, No. 38).

Touraine, A. *et al.*, 1967, 'Mobilité des entreprises et structures urbaines', *Sociologie du Travail*, **9**, 369–405.

Townroe, P. M., 1971. *Industrial Location Decisions: A Study in Management Behaviour* (The University of Birmingham, Centre for Urban and Regional Studies, Occasional Paper No. 15).

Townroe, P. M., 1972, 'Some behavioural considerations in the industrial location decision', *Regional Studies*, **6**, 261–72.

Traigle, J., 1975, 'Louisiana's financial future: oil and gas', *Louisiana Business Survey*, **6** (January), 2–4.

Ullman, E. L., 1958, 'Regional development and the geography of concentration', *The Regional Science Association Papers and Proceedings*, **4**, 179–98.

U.S. Bureau of the Census, 1961, *Census of Population*, Vol. 1, Part A (Washington: Government Printing Office).

U.S. Bureau of the Census, 1972, *1970 Census of Population*, Vol. 1, Part A(1) (Washington: Government Printing Office).

U.S. Congress, 1972, *Coastal Zone Management Act of 1972* [Public Law 92–583] (Washington: Government Printing Office).

U.S. Congress, 1974, *Housing and Community Development Act of 1974* [Public Law 93–383] (Washington: Government Printing Office).

U.S. Congress, 1976, *Coastal Zone Management Act Amendments of 1976* [Public Law 94–370] (Washington: Government Printing Office).

U.S. Congress, 1977, *Housing and Community Development Act of 1977* [Public Law 95–128] (Washington: Government Printing Office).

U.S. Geological Survey, 1976, *Outer Continental Shelf Statistics* (Washington: Department of the Interior).

Vance, J. E., 1960, 'Labor-shed, employment field, and dynamic analysis in urban geography', *Economic Geography*, **36**, 189–220.

VanLandingham, H. W., 1975, 'Energy impact analysis for Louisiana: an input–output study', unpublished M.A. thesis (University of New Orleans, Urban Studies Institute).

Verband Der Automobilindustrie E. V., Tatsachen und Zahlen (Frankfurt-am-Main, 1951–71).

Wadekin, K. E., 1977, 'Agro-industrielle Integration in Bulgarien', *Agrarwirtschaft* (Hannover), **2**, 51–6.

Wadley, D. A., 1974, 'Corporate decision-making during recession: product franchisors in the Australian agricultural machinery industry 1967–72', unpublished Ph.D. dissertation (Canberra: Australian National University).

Wagner, F. W. and Durabb, E. J., 1976, 'The sinking city: floating in concrete', *Environment*, **18**(4), 32–9.

Walmsley, D. J., 1972, *Systems Theory: A Framework for Human Geographical Enquiry* (Canberra:Australian National University, Department of Human Geography Publication HG/7).

Ward, J. M., 1963, 'Hierarchical grouping to optimize an objective function', *Journal of the American Statistical Association*, **58**, 236–44.

Warren, K., 1973, 'The location of British heavy industry: problems and policies', *The Geographical Journal*, **139**, 76–83.

Watts, H. D., 1974, 'Locational adjustment in the British beet sugar industry', *Geography*, **59**, 10–23.

Weaver, J. C., 1954, 'Crop-combination regions in the middle west', *The Geographical Review*, **44**, 175–200.

Webber, M. J., 1972, *Impact of Uncertainty on Location* (Cambridge, Mass.: M.I.T. Press).

Weber, A., 1909, *Uber den Standort der Industrien*, translated by C. J. Friedrich as *Theory of the Location of Industries* (1929), (University of Chicago Press).

Webster, F. E., 1965, 'Modeling the industrial buying process', *Journal of Marketing Research*, **2**, 370–6.

Weingardt, C. -A., 1971–72, 'Organization structure and communication in the Unilever company', *International Studies of Management and Organization*, **1**, 377–93.

Weiss, L. W., 1969, 'Advertising, profits, and corporate taxes', *The Review of Economics and Statistics*, **5**, 421–30.

Western, J. S. and Wilson, P. R. (Eds.), 1977, *Planning in Turbulent Environments* (Brisbane: University of Queensland Press).

Weston, J. F. and Brigham, E. F., 1975, *Managerial Finance* (Hinsdale, Ill.: Dryden Press).

White, R. L. and and Watts, H. D., 1977, 'The spatial evolution of an industry: the example of broiler production', *Institute of British Geographers Transactions*, **2** New Series, 175–91.

Wiederscheim-Paul, F., 1972, *Uncertainty and Economic Distance—Studies in International Business* (Uppsala: Almqvist & Wiksell).

Wilcock, R. C., 1957, 'Employment effects of a plant shutdown in a depressed area', *Monthly Labour Review*, **80**, 1047–52.

Williams, W. T. *et al.*, 1966, 'Multivariate methods in plant ecology: V. similarity analyses and information-analysis', *The Journal of Ecology*, **54**, 427–45.

Williamson, J., 1966, 'Profit, growth and sales maximization', *Economica*, **33** New Series, 1–16.

Wood, P. A., 1969, 'Industrial location and linkage', *Area*, No. 2, 32–9.

Yoshino, M. Y., 1968, *Japan's Managerial System: Tradition and Innovation* (Cambridge, Mass.: M.I.T. Press).

Yudin, E. G., 1973, 'Metodologicheskaya priroda sistemnogo podkhoda' [The methodological nature of the systems approach] in *Sistemn'ye Issledovaniya*, (Moscow; Nauka), 37–45.

Index

References to geographic names are given in italics (e.g. *Aachen*) while the names of economic organizations are presented in small capitals (e.g. AB CEMENTA).